Great Britain and Ireland
0
100
200
300 km
0
100
200 miles
ORKNEY ISLANDS
TER
BRIDES
Highlands
Inverness
Loch Ness
Ben Nevis
Aberdeen
SCOTLAND
Stirling
Glasgow
Edinburgh
Edinburgh Castle
Hadrian's Wall
Newcastle
Stapleton
Tyne
Giant's Causeway
Belfast
THERN IRELAND
Lake District
Pennines
ISLE OF MAN
York
Hull
Irish Sea
Liverpool
Manchester
Dublin
Nottingham
Snowdon
Trent
ENGLAND
Cambrian Mountains
Birmingham
Severn
Cambridge
St. George's Channel
WALES
Big Ben
The Cotswolds
Oxford
London
Greenwich
Thames
Heathrow
Margate
North Sea
THE NETHERLANDS
Swansea
Cardiff
Stonehenge
Dover
EURO TUNNEL
BELGIUM
Brighton
Devon
ISLE OF WIGHT
Newquay
Cornwall
Plymouth
Penzance
English Channel
ISLES OF SCILLY
FRANCE
CHANNEL ISLANDS

Blue Line 3

Ausgabe für Bayern (Mittelschulen) Klasse 7 M-Zug

Die Mediencodes (Beispiel: Find more online: 92m8cf) enthalten zusätzliche Unterrichtsmaterialien, die der Verlag in eigener Verantwortung zur Verfügung stellt.

Im Lernmittel wird in Form von Symbolen auf eine CD verwiesen. Diese enthält – bis auf die Hörverstehensübungen – ausschließlich optionale Unterrichtsmaterialien. Die CD unterliegt nicht dem staatlichen Zulassungsverfahren.

Zusatzmaterial für Schülerinnen und Schüler u. a.:
Blue Line 3 Bayern M-Zug Workbook mit Audio-CD (ISBN 978-3-12-548363-7)

1. Auflage 1 5 4 3 2 1 | 23 22 21 20 19

Herausgeber: Wolfgang Hamm, Marktredwitz
Autorinnen und Autoren: Daniel Shatwell, Hanau sowie
Gillian Bathmaker, Sachsenheim; David Brimage, Brighton; Chris Caridia, London; Andrew Cowle, Glasgow; Jo Cummins, London; Wolfgang Hamm, Marktredwitz; Melanie Ku, Köln; Jon Marks, Ventnor; Michael Meisenzahl, Karlstadt; Karen Seekings, London; Clare Treleaven, Castellón; Anna Weber, Taufkirchen; Alison Wooder, Ventnor
Beratung: Michaela Cavallucci, München; Gaby Fruhmann, Parsberg; Michael Meisenzahl, Karlstadt; Lisa Schubert, Altdorf; Anna Weber, Taufkirchen

Redaktion: Claudia Schwarz-Brownbill; William Sears; Daniel Shatwell, Hanau; Judith Pfeiffer-Ley, Mainz
Herstellung: Kathrin Schindler

Umschlaggestaltung und Gestaltungskonzept: know idea, Freiburg; Koma Amok, Stuttgart
Umschlagfotos: Alamy stock photo (Top-Pics TBK), Abingdon, Oxon; Getty Images (Photolibrary), München
Illustrationen: Kirill Chudinskiy, Köln; Christian Dekelver, Weinstadt; Marcus Wilder, Hamburg; Steffen Wolff, Herzogenrath sowie Friederike Ablang, Berlin; Verena Ballhaus, München; Lars Benecke, Hannover; Marek Blaha, Offenbach am Main; Gilles Bonotaux, Paris; Andrea Büdinger, München; Martina Burghart-Vollhardt, Kamenz; Francois Davot, Troyes; Axel Fahl, Reichelsheim; Anke Fröhlich, Leipzig; Rob Harvey, Cirencester Glos; Susann Hesselbarth, Leipzig; Carmen Hochmann, Bielefeld; Steffen Jähde, Sundhagen; Peer Kramer, Düsseldorf; Hendrik Kranenberg, Drolshagen; Helga Merkle, Albershausen; Lutz-Erich Müller, Leipzig; Axel Nicolai, Brauweiler; David Norman, Meerbusch; Liliane Oser, Hamburg; Sven Palmowski, Barcelona, El Prat de Llobrega; Katja Rau, Berglen; Anja Rieger, Berlin; Wolfgang Schaar, Grafing; Friederike Schumann, Berlin; Aurel Voigt, Waiblingen; Steffen Walentowitz, Jever; Sylvia Wolf, Wiesbaden; Dorothee Wolters, Köln
Satz: graphitecture book & edition; Fotosatz Kaufmann, Stuttgart
Reproduktion: Schwabenrepro GmbH, Stuttgart
Druck: Firmengruppe APPL, aprinta druck, Wemding

Printed in Germany
ISBN 978-3-12-548343-9

9 783125 483439

Blue Line 3

Ausgabe für Bayern (Mittelschulen) Klasse 7 M-Zug

Herausgeber: Wolfgang Hamm

Ernst Klett Verlag
Stuttgart • Leipzig

Inhalt

L = Listening M = Mediation R = Reading S = Speaking V = Viewing W = Writing

L = Listening M = Mediation R = Reading S = Speaking V = Viewing W = Writing

Inhalt

L = Listening M = Mediation R = Reading S = Speaking V = Viewing W = Writing

L = Listening M = Mediation R = Reading S = Speaking V = Viewing W = Writing

So lernst du mit Blue Line

So lernst du mit deinem Buch.
Das Buch hat vier Units (Kapitel).
Jede Unit ist gleich aufgebaut.

Intro

Hier steigst du in das neue Thema ein. Dazu gibt es auch einen kurzen Film.

Im gelben Kasten siehst du, was du in der *Unit* lernen wirst.

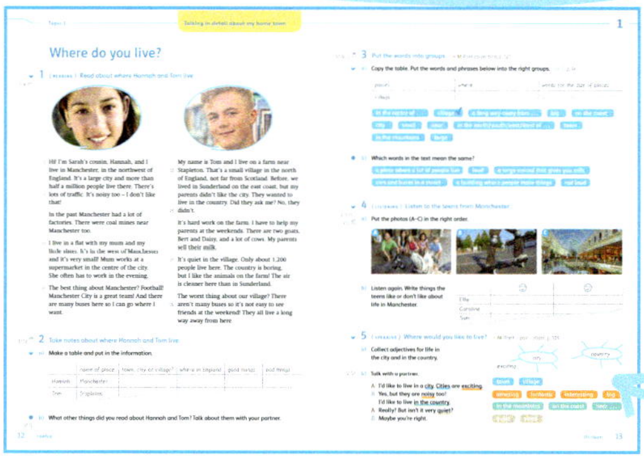

Topics

In jeder *Unit* gibt es zwei *Topics*, in denen du viele neue Dinge lernst. Hier kannst du erkennen, wie schwer eine Übung ist:

● schwer ◒ mittel ○ leicht

In der *Task* kannst du zeigen, dass du alles verstanden hast, und deine eigenen Ideen einbringen.

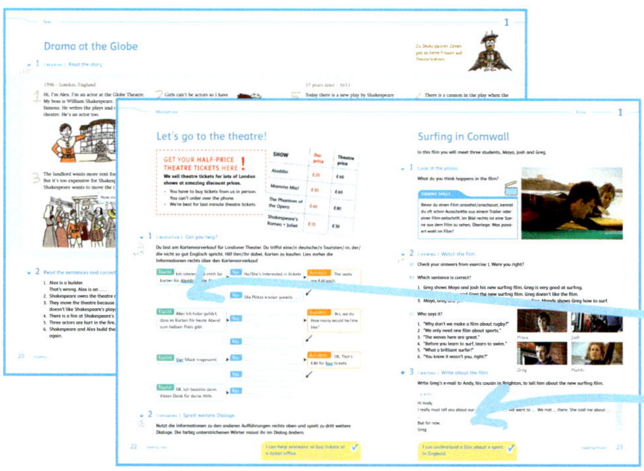

Text

Auf den *Text*-Seiten findest du spannende Geschichten und andere Texte.

Mediation/Film

Auf der linken Seite geht es darum, englische Informationen auf Deutsch weiterzugeben. Das nennt man *Mediation*.

Auf der *Film*-Seite geht es um einen englischen Film.

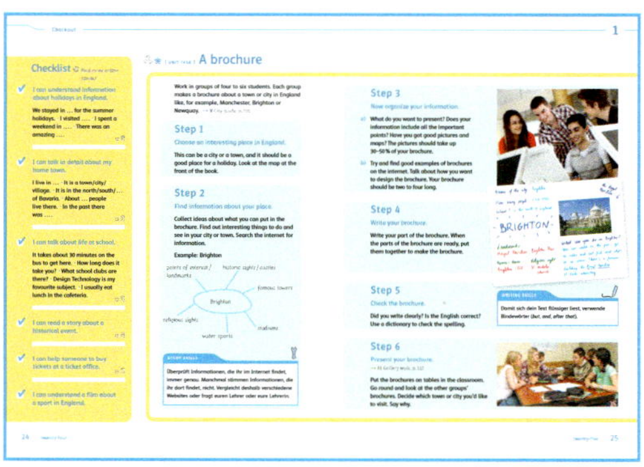

Checkout

Auf dieser Doppelseite kannst du zeigen, ob du in der *Unit* alles verstanden hast. In der *Checklist* sind alle Lernziele noch einmal aufgelistet.

Die Abschluss-Aufgabe (*Unit task*) sollt ihr zu zweit oder in der Gruppe lösen.

More about

Hier findest du interessante weiterführende Informationen zur Region der *Unit*.

Skills

Auf jede *Unit* folgt eine Doppelseite, auf der du eine bestimmte Fertigkeit (*Skill*) besonders trainieren kannst, also z. B. das Lesen, Schreiben oder Sprechen.

Revision

Hier kannst du das Wichtigste aus Klasse 6 wiederholen.

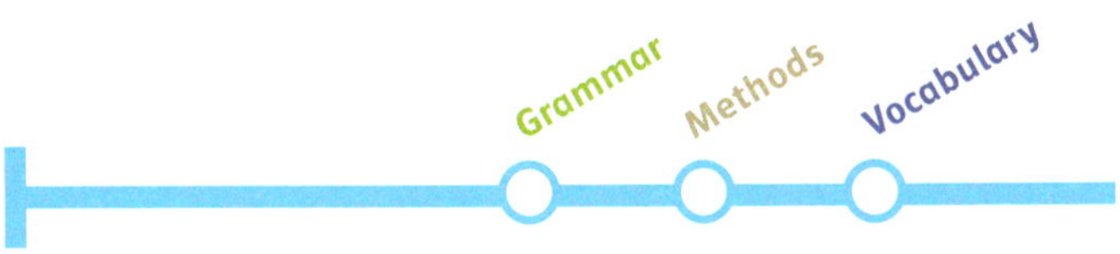

Im Anschluss an die vier *Units* gibt es noch weitere nützliche Seiten:

Grammar: Hier findest du alle Regeln und Erklärungen zur Grammatik, Übungen und eine Liste der unregelmäßigen Verben.

Methods: Manche Übungen könnt ihr auf eine bestimmte Art und Weise bearbeiten.
Das erkennst du an diesem Symbol: → M.
Wie es genau funktioniert, kannst du hier nachlesen.

Vocabulary: Im *Vocabulary* findest du alle neuen Wörter in der Reihenfolge, in der sie in der *Unit* auftauchen.
Im *Dictionary* sind die Wörter noch einmal alphabetisch aufgelistet: zuerst Englisch-Deutsch und dann Deutsch-Englisch.

Symbol	Erklärung
○ ◐ ●	leicht/mittel/schwer (Niveaudifferenzierung)
✿	individualisierende Aufgabe (natürliche Differenzierung)
→ ○ p. 131	Verweis auf leichtere Parallelübung auf der *Diff corner*-Seite
OR	Aufgabe zur Auswahl (Wahldifferenzierung)
P	Hier entsteht ein Produkt für das Portfolio.
4/1	Verweis auf eine Übung im *Workbook*
→ G6, p. 145	Verweis auf den Grammatikanhang (*Grammar*)
→ M	Verweis auf die Methodenseiten (*Methods*)
→ V	Verweis zum Wortfeld im Vokabular (*Vocabulary*)
	Partnerarbeit
	Gruppenarbeit
	Verweis auf die Lehrer-CD (Audio)
	Verweis auf die Lehrer-DVD (Film)
Find more online: 8gr8f2	Code auf www.klett.de eingeben und Zusatzinformationen erhalten

Zoom in – The British Isles

The British Isles

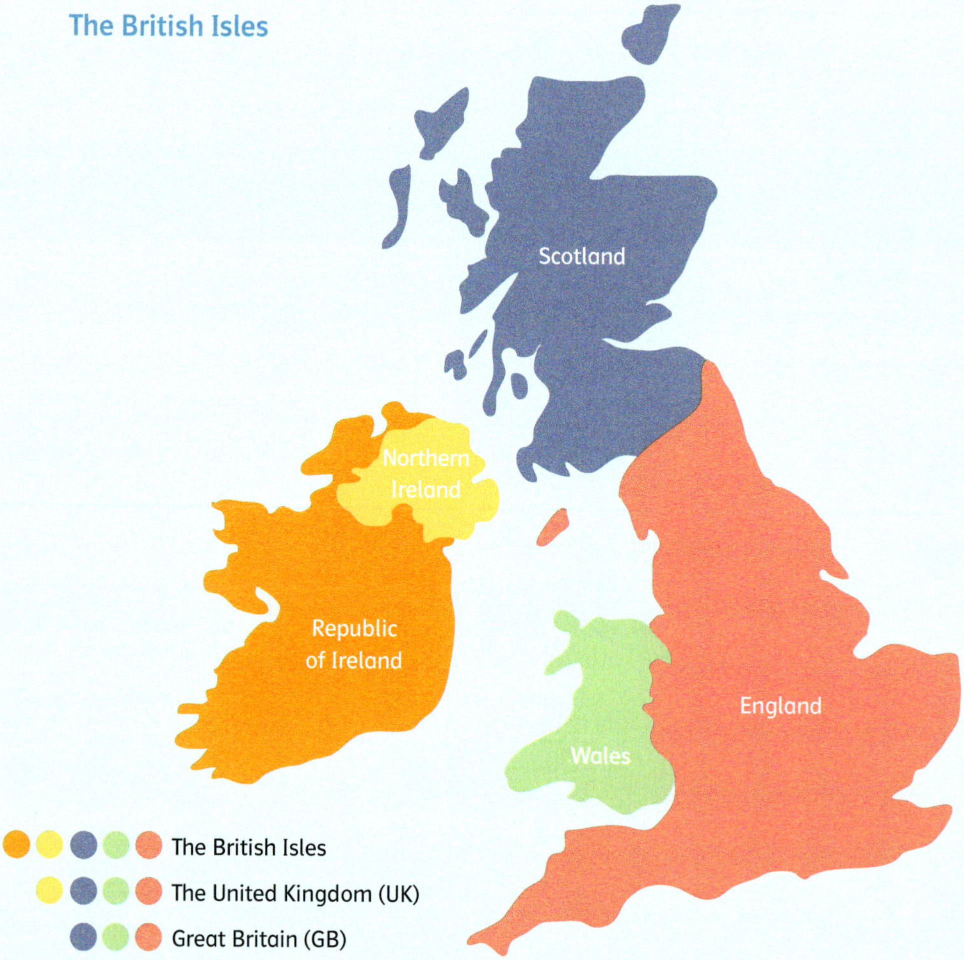

1 Do the British Isles quiz with a partner.

1. What are the names of the five countries of the British Isles?
2. Which is the biggest country in the United Kingdom (UK)?
3. Which is bigger, Northern Ireland or the Republic of Ireland?
4. Which is bigger, Scotland or Wales?
5. Which country is in the UK but not in Great Britain (GB)?
6. Which is the capital of the UK?
7. Which country is not in the UK?
8. The Channel Tunnel goes from France to which country?

Um die Fragen 6 und 8 zu beantworten, sieh dir auch die Karte auf der Vorderseite an. Du kannst deine Antworten auf Seite 199 überprüfen.

England

Wales

Scotland

Northern Ireland

Ireland

1,1 **2** (LISTENING) **Listen to five teenagers from the British Isles.**

Make a table. Then listen and take notes.

Name	From?	Age?	Hobbies?	Plans?
Emily				
Dylan				
Alison				
Sophie				
Patrick				

CULTURE

Die fünf Teenager kommen aus den verschiedenen Ländern der Britischen Inseln. Sie haben unterschiedliche Akzente. Welche Akzente findest du am einfachsten zu verstehen? Welche am schwierigsten?

Out and about in England

1 Look at the photos.

2/1 a) What can you see in the photos? Tell your partner. Can he or she find out which photo it is?

b) Now read the texts. Which activities would you / wouldn't you like to do?

I'd like to … because ….
I wouldn't like to … because I think ….

2 (READING) Name the place.

1. You can go and see plays here.
2. It's a good place for surfing.
3. Sarah saw an exhibition about robots here.
4. You can go canoeing here.

At the end of this unit, you can ...
- understand information about holidays in England.
- talk in detail about your home town.
- talk about life at school.
- read a story about a historical event.
- help someone to buy tickets at a ticket office.
- understand a film about a sport in England.

1

I spent a weekend in London with my mum and dad. We went to the Globe Theatre and saw *Romeo and Juliet*, a Shakespeare play. It was fantastic!

We also made a visit to the Science Museum when we were in London. There was an amazing exhibition about robots and rockets.

Last weekend we drove to Brighton on the south coast. We went canoeing there. It was great!

3 (LISTENING) Right or wrong?

1, 3
2/2

1. Sarah and Hannah talk about what they did at the weekend.
2. Sarah didn't have a great time in Newquay.
3. She only fell off once.
4. Sarah went to a theme park with her aunt and uncle.
5. Hannah went on a rollercoaster at a theme park.
6. Hannah's brother was sick when the rollercoaster stopped.

I can understand information about holidays in England. ✓

Where do you live?

1 (READING) Read about where Hannah and Tom live.

1, 4

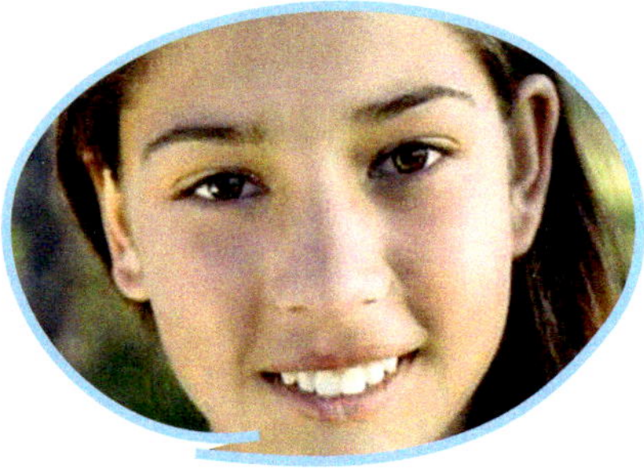

Hi! I'm Sarah's cousin, Hannah, and I live in Manchester, in the northwest of England. It's a large city and more than half a million people live there. There's lots of traffic. It's noisy too – I don't like that!

In the past Manchester had a lot of factories. There were coal mines near Manchester too.

I live in a flat with my mum and my little sister. It's in the west of Manchester and it's very small! Mum works at a supermarket in the centre of the city. She often has to work in the evening.

The best thing about Manchester? Football! Manchester City is a great team! And there are many buses here so I can go where I want.

My name is Tom and I live on a farm near Stapleton. That's a small village in the north of England, not far from Scotland. Before, we lived in Sunderland on the east coast, but my parents didn't like the city. They wanted to live in the country. Did they ask me? No, they didn't.

It's hard work on the farm. I have to help my parents at the weekends. There are two goats, Bert and Daisy, and a lot of cows. My parents sell their milk.

It's quiet in the village. Only about 1,200 people live here. The country is boring, but I like the animals on the farm! The air is cleaner here than in Sunderland.

The worst thing about our village? There aren't many buses so it's not easy to see friends at the weekend! They all live a long way away from here.

3/1a

2 Take notes about where Hannah and Tom live.

a) Make a table and put in the information.

	name of place	town, city or village?	where in England	good things	bad things
Hannah	Manchester				
Tom	Stapleton				

b) What other things did you read about Hannah and Tom? Talk about them with your partner.

3/1b–c

3 Put the words into groups. → M Peer correction, p. 123

a) Copy the table. Put the words and phrases below into the right groups. → ○ p. 94

places	where	words for the size of places
village		

in the centre of … | village ✓ | a long way away from … | big | on the coast | city | small | near | in the north/south/east/west of … | town | in the mountains | large

b) Which words in the text mean the same?

a place where a lot of people live | loud | a large animal that gives you milk | cars and buses in a street | a building where people make things | not loud

4 (LISTENING) Listen to the teens from Manchester.

1, 5
3/2

a) Put the photos (A–C) in the right order.

b) Listen again. Write things the teens like or don't like about life in Manchester.

	☺	☹
Ellie		
Caroline		
Sam		

5 (SPEAKING) Where would you like to live? → M Think – pair – share, p. 124

a) Collect adjectives for life in the city and in the country.

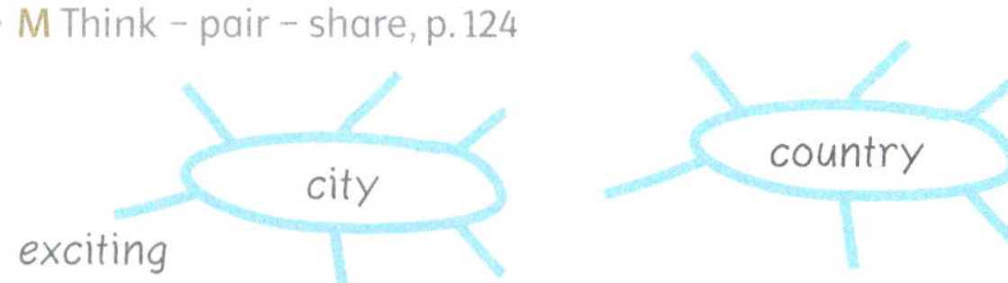

b) Talk with a partner.

A: I'd like to live in a city. Cities are exciting.
B: Yes, but they are noisy too!
I'd like to live in the country.
A: Really? But isn't it very quiet?
B: Maybe you're right.

town | village
amazing | fantastic | interesting | big
in the mountains | on the coast | near …
quiet | small

Language detectives → G1, p. 106

My parents wanted to live in the country.
They didn't like the city.
Did they ask me?

The play was fantastic!
There were many factories.

In welcher Zeitform sind die Sätze? Wie bildest du Frage und Verneinung?

4/3–4 **6** Complete Tom's story.

a) Complete the sentences. → ○ p. 94

1. Last Saturday morning a lot of things happened on our farm. (to happen)
2. I ___ a noise in the garden (to hear) and I ___. (to get up)
3. I ___ my dad in the garden. (to see)
4. He ___ to put Bert and Daisy, our goats, in the car. (to want)
5. Suddenly he ___ in the mud. (to fall)
6. It ___ so funny. (to be)
7. Dad ___ very happy. (to not be)

b) What happened next? Write two sentences. **shout** **be angry** **help** **...**

4/5 **7** (WRITING) What did Hannah and her dog, Kenny, do on Saturday?

a) Look at the pictures. Correct the sentences about Hannah and her dog, Kenny. → ○ p. 94

~~Hannah went to the supermarket in the morning.~~

~~Hannah was in the living room at two o'clock.~~

~~Hannah did her homework in the afternoon.~~

~~Hannah and her sister fed the dog at five o'clock.~~

~~Later she watched TV.~~

~~Hannah and her sister were at the cinema.~~

1. Hannah didn't go to the supermarket in the morning. She watched TV.

b) Look at the pictures again. What did Hannah's dog, Kenny, do?

Kenny didn't watch TV. He played with a ball.

8 (SPEAKING) Talk to a partner about the weekend.

5/6–7

a) Make questions.

1. have · you · a nice weekend? · Did
   Did you have a nice weekend?
2. at home all weekend? · Did · stay · you
3. you · to an interesting place with your family? · Did · go
4. What · you · do together? · did
5. the weather like on Sunday? · What · was
6. did · What time · get home? · you
7. Were · tired on Sunday evening? · your parents

b) Talk to a partner. Use the questions from a) and give answers.

visit my aunt and uncle ✓ | be at home | do my homework | read | watch TV | go swimming | on Saturday afternoon | on Sunday morning | ...

9 (TASK) Where I live

→ V Where I live, p. 128 → M 1-minute-presentation, p. 120

P

5/8

Give a short talk about where you live.

name of place: Bamberg / ...
size: small village / large town / city ...
where: the north / the east / the south / the west of ...
number of people living there: 2,000 / 20,000 / a million / ...
in the past: there was ... / there were ... / we didn't have ... / people worked in ... / ...
favourite place: the cinema / ...
what can I do there: watch films / play ...

CULTURE

Auf englischen Straßenschildern stehen die Angaben für Entfernungen in Meilen (miles) statt in Kilometern. Eine Meile sind 1,6 Kilometer. Wie viele Meilen sind es von deinem Zuhause zur Schule?

I can talk in detail about my home town. ✓

The new student

1 (READING) Read the dialogue.

1, 6

Today is Tom's first day at school.

George: Hi, look there's a calculator on that desk! Is it yours or hers? She doesn't have a calculator.
Tom: Oh hi. Yes, it's mine. I forgot it after the Maths lesson this morning. Thanks. I'm new here.
George: Are you? My name's George.
Tom: Yes, that's right. I'm Tom.
George: Where do you live, Tom?
Tom: On a farm near Stapleton. It takes about 30 minutes to get here by bus. How long does it take you in the morning?
George: Oh no, that's really far. I live here in Stapleton so I only take about ten minutes by bike.
Tom: Oh, you're so lucky. I have to get up at 7:15 a.m. to catch the bus at 8:05 a.m.
George: OK. I don't get up before a quarter to eight.

Tom: What school clubs are there?
George: Well, I'm in the drama club. It's really good. We want to show Shakespeare's *Romeo and Juliet* next summer.
Tom: Oh, wow! Do you have to act in the play?
George: You can act or you can do other things. I'm helping to make scenery for the stage, but you can also help with the costumes. Mr McCoy, the Art teacher, is helping us to design the scenery.
Tom: Cool. Design Technology is my favourite subject. When is the drama club?
George: It's on Wednesdays after school.
Tom: When does it finish?
George: About 5:30 p.m. usually.

Tom: That's quite late I'm afraid because I have to get home. And where do you have lunch?
George: I usually eat lunch in the cafeteria, but I occasionally bring sandwiches.
Tom: How much is the food there?
George: About £3.
Tom: And what's it like?
George: It's OK. I often order burger and chips. They sometimes have pizza.
Tom: That doesn't sound very healthy.

2 Match the sentence parts.

6/1

1. Tom comes to school
2. George doesn't get up
3. Tom would like to know
4. George is helping to make scenery
5. The drama club finishes
6. George occasionally
7. Tom doesn't think that the food

a. at the drama club.
b. brings sandwiches.
c. by bus.
d. in the cafeteria is very healthy.
e. more about school clubs.
f. at about 5:30 p.m.
g. before 7:45 a.m.

Denkt dran: Bei der Uhrzeit im Englischen sagt man vormittags a.m. und nachmittags p.m.

6/2

3 George's school day

a) Write the answers to the questions about George.

1

What time does he get up?
He gets up at ___ a.m.

2

How does he get to school in the morning?
He gets there by ___ .

3

How long does it take him to get to school?
It takes him ___ minutes.

4

What's his favourite subject at school?
His favourite subject is ___ .

5

What school club is he in?
He's in the ___ .

6

What time does school usually finish?
It finishes at ___ p.m.

b) Now ask and answer the questions for your school day.

1, 7
6/3

4 (LISTENING) Carol is in Hannah's class. Listen and choose the right answers.

1. Hannah is in the **basketball club / football club / computer club**.
2. Carol often helps **her parents / her brother / her sister** in the kitchen.
3. Carol was in the **school band / computer club / cooking club** at her old school.
4. The computer club is **after school / at lunchtime / at 12:30 p.m.** on Tuesday.
5. The school band is at lunchtime **on Tuesdays / Wednesdays / Thursdays**.

6/4

5 (SOUNDS) Which words rhyme?

a) Find the pairs.

design, late, quarter, write, play, new, drama, eat

great, farmer, away, blue, right, climb, meet, water

b) Listen and check your answers.

1, 8

c) Add one more rhyming word to each pair.

6 Complete the sentences with one of the verbs.

7/5

go | be | not do | get up ✓ | make | take | give | not get home

1. I always get up before 7 a.m.
2. My dad often ___ sandwiches for me.
3. He never ___ me sweets.
4. I ___ to school by bus in the morning.
5. I usually ___ about 20 minutes to get to school.
6. My favourite subject ___ PE.
7. I ___ my homework in the kitchen.
8. My dad ___ before 6 p.m.

He, she, it – das -s muss mit!

Language → G 2, p. 107

I usually eat lunch in the cafeteria.
It sounds great.

I don't get up before a quarter to eight.
It doesn't sound very healthy.

7 (SPEAKING) Interview your partner.

→ M Double circle, p. 121

7/6

a) Ask a partner. He or she answers. → ○ p. 95

A:

Do Does	you your friends they your mum/dad he	sometimes often usually	go to the cinema? do your homework? play football? watch TV? go shopping?

B: Yes, I do.
No, I don't.
Yes, she/he does.
No, she/he doesn't.
Yes, they do.
No, they don't.

b) Make more short dialogues. Use these words.

A: Do you come to school by bus?
B: No, I don't. I usually ride my bike to school.

come to school by bus | go to a school club on Thursdays | have to stay at school in the afternoon | ...

8 (WRITING) Make questions for the answers.

8/7

Language → G 3, p. 108

Where do you live?
What school clubs are there?

a) Complete the questions and find the answers. → ○ p. 95

1. Where ___ the Art Club (to be)?
   Where is the Art Club? → c.
2. When ___ it ___ (to finish)?
3. How ___ you ___ home after school (to get)?
4. How long ___ it ___ (to take)?
5. What subjects ___ new this year (to be)?
6. How many lessons ___ you ___ every day (to have)?
7. How often ___ you ___ PE (to have)?

a. Design Technology and Biology.
b. I have it once a week.
c. It's in Room 22.
d. I have six lessons every day.
e. It finishes at 5:30 p.m.
f. It takes about ten minutes.
g. I usually ride my bike.

b) Make three more questions and answers. Use the words to help.

Where do ...? / Do you like ...?

eat lunch | the food in the cafeteria | ...

Language detectives → G4, p. 109

Look, there's a calculator. Is it yours?
No, it's not mine.
It's hers.

Schau dir die Sätze an. Wofür stehen *mine* und *yours*? Was drücken die unterstrichenen Wörter aus?

8/8 9 Whose is it? → ◯ p. 96

a) Rewrite the sentences.

Language → G4, p. 109

my – mine	your – yours
his – his	her – hers
our – ours	their – theirs

1. It's your rubber. – It's yours.
2. It's George's exercise book. – It's ....
3. It's my sister's phone. – It's ....
4. It's my ruler. – It's ....
5. It's Mum and Dad's room. – It's ....
6. It's our dog. – It's ....
7. It's Tom's calculator. – It's ....

b) Match the pictures with the people and make sentences.

Sarah ✔ | George | Hannah | Tom | the girl

1. It's Sarah's ruler. → It's hers.

10 (TASK) A survey about life at school. → V School day, p. 129

8/9

a) Work in groups of four. Think of six questions about your partners' school day.

Where do you ...? | How often do you ...? | What is your favourite ...? | What don't you like about ...? | How long do you take to ...?

b) Ask your classmates your questions. What are their answers? You can make a table with your information. → M Milling around, p. 122

c) Make a poster with the answers and present it to your class.

I can talk about life at school. ✔

Drama at the Globe

1 (READING) Read the story.

1, 9

1596 – London, England

1 Hi, I'm Alex. I'm an actor at the Globe Theatre. My boss is William Shakespeare. He's very famous. He writes the plays and owns the theatre. He's an actor too.

2 Girls can't be actors so I have to play the parts of the girls and the women!

3 The landlord wants more rent for the land. But it's too expensive for Shakespeare. So Shakespeare wants to move the theatre.

4 Builders have to carry the theatre in pieces across the River Thames because land is cheaper there.

2 Read the sentences and correct them.

1. Alex is a builder.
   That's wrong. Alex is an ….
2. Shakespeare owns the theatre and the land.
3. They move the theatre because the landlord doesn't like Shakespeare's plays.
4. There is a fire at Shakespeare's house in 1617.
5. Three actors are hurt in the fire.
6. Shakespeare and Alex build the theatre again.

CULTURE

Der englische Schriftsteller William Shakespeare lebte vor über 400 Jahren, aber seine Theaterstücke sind heute immer noch beliebt. Eines davon heißt *Romeo und Julia*. Was weißt du darüber?

Zu Shakespeares Zeiten gab es keine Frauen auf Theaterbühnen.

17 years later – 1613

5 Today there is a new play by Shakespeare at the Globe.

I have a very big part as a man in the play. I am very excited!

6 There is a cannon in the play when the King arrives, but the cannon ball falls on the theatre and there's a fire!

7 But nobody gets hurt.

8 Now I don't have a job or any money. The builders have to build the Globe again.

3 Choose one of the tasks.

10 + 11

a) Write a caption for each picture.

1. Alex is an actor at Shakespeare's Globe Theatre.
2. Men play women.
3. …

OR

b) Work in groups of three. Choose one of the scenes from the story and make a freeze frame. The others have to find out what it is.

→ M Freeze frame, p. 121

I can read a story about a historical event. ✓

Let's go to the theatre!

GET YOUR HALF-PRICE THEATRE TICKETS HERE!

We sell theatre tickets for lots of London shows at amazing discount prices.

- You have to buy tickets from us in person. You can't order over the phone.
- We're best for last minute theatre tickets.

SHOW	Our price	Theatre price
Aladdin	£20	£40
Mamma Mia!	£30	£60
The Phantom of the Opera	£40	£80
Shakespeare's Romeo + Juliet	£15	£30

1 (MEDIATION) Can you help?

9/1

Du bist am Kartenvorverkauf für Londoner Theater. Du triffst eine/n deutsche/n Touristen/-in, der/die nicht so gut Englisch spricht. Hilf ihm/ihr dabei, Karten zu kaufen. Lies vorher die Informationen rechts über den Kartenvorverkauf.

Tourist Ich interessiere mich für Karten für *Aladdin* heute Abend. ▶ **You** He/She's interested in tickets for *Aladdin* for this evening. ▶ **Assistant** The seats are £40 each.

You Die Plätze kosten jeweils ….

Tourist Aber ich habe gehört, dass es Karten für heute Abend zum halben Preis gibt. ▶ **You** …. ▶ **Assistant** Yes, we do. How many would he/she like?

You ….

Tourist Vier Stück insgesamt. ▶ **You** …. ▶ **Assistant** OK. That's £80 for four tickets.

You ….

Tourist OK. Ich bezahle dann. Vielen Dank für deine Hilfe. ▶ **You** ….

2 (SPEAKING) Spielt weitere Dialoge.

Nutzt die Informationen zu den anderen Aufführungen rechts oben und spielt zu dritt weitere Dialoge. Die farbig unterstrichenen Wörter müsst ihr im Dialog ändern.

I can help someone to buy tickets at a ticket office. ✓

Surfing in Cornwall

In this film you will meet three students, Maya, Josh and Greg.

1 Look at the photo.

What do you think happens in the film?

VIEWING SKILLS

Bevor du einen Film ansiehst, kennst du oft schon Ausschnitte aus einem Trailer oder einer Filmzeitschrift. Im Bild rechts ist eine Szene aus dem Film zu sehen. Überlege: Was passiert wohl im Film?

2 (VIEWING) Watch the film.

2

a) Check your answers from exercise 1. Were you right?

b) Which sentence is correct?

1. Greg shows Maya and Josh his new surfing film. Greg is very good at surfing.
2. Josh shows Maya and Greg the new surfing film. Greg doesn't like the film.
3. Maya, Greg and Josh watch their new film about surfing. Mandy shows Greg how to surf.

c) Who says it?

1. "Why don't we make a film about rugby?"
2 "We only need one film about sports."
3. "The waves here are great."
4. "Before you learn to surf, learn to swim."
5. "What a brilliant surfer!"
6. "You know it wasn't you, right?"

Maya

Josh

Greg

Mandy

3 (WRITING) Write about the film.

Write Greg's e-mail to Andy, his cousin in Brighton, to tell him about the new surfing film.

E-MAIL

Hi Andy,
I really must tell you about our new surfing film. We went to .... We met ... there. She told me about ....
...
Bye for now,
Greg

I can understand a film about a sport in England. ✓

Checklist

Find more online: 92m8cf

I can understand information about holidays in England.

We stayed in … for the summer holidays. • I visited …. • I spent a weekend in …. • There was an amazing ….

12

I can talk in detail about my home town.

I live in … • It is a town/city/village. • It is in the north/south/… of Bavaria. • About … people live there. • In the past there was ….

12

I can talk about life at school.

It takes about 30 minutes on the bus to get here. • How long does it take you? • What school clubs are there? • Design Technology is my favourite subject. • I usually eat lunch in the cafeteria.

12

I can read a story about a historical event.

13

I can help someone to buy tickets at a ticket office.

13

I can understand a film about a sport in England.

(UNIT TASK) A brochure

Work in groups of four to six students. Each group makes a brochure about a town or city in England like, for example, Manchester, Brighton or Newquay. → V City guide, p. 130

Step 1

Choose an interesting place in England.

This can be a city or a town, and it should be a good place for a holiday. Look at the map at the front of the book.

Step 2

Find information about your place.

Collect ideas about what you can put in the brochure. Find out interesting things to do and see in your city or town. Search the internet for information.

Example: Brighton

STUDY SKILLS

Überprüft Informationen, die ihr im Internet findet, immer genau. Manchmal stimmen Informationen, die ihr dort findet, nicht. Vergleicht deshalb verschiedene Websites oder fragt euren Lehrer oder eure Lehrerin.

Step 3

Now organize your information.

a) What do you want to present? Does your information include all the important points? Have you got good pictures and maps? The pictures should take up 30–50 % of your brochure.

b) Try and find good examples of brochures on the internet. Talk about how you want to design the brochure. Your brochure should be two to four long.

Step 4

Write your brochure.

Write your part of the brochure. When the parts of the brochure are ready, put them together to make the brochure.

Step 5

Check the brochure.

Did you write clearly? Is the English correct? Use a dictionary to check the spelling.

WRITING SKILLS

Damit sich dein Text flüssiger liest, verwende Bindewörter (*but*, *and*, *after that*).

Step 6

Present your brochure.

→ M Gallery walk, p. 122

Put the brochures on tables in the classroom. Go round and look at the other groups' brochures. Decide which town or city you'd like to visit. Say why.

1, 10

Art and culture in England

1 Museums in London

London has amazing museums, lots of cinemas and theatres, great restaurants and street markets. Visit Kensington in London and you can go to three museums: the Natural History Museum, the Victoria and Albert Museum and the Science Museum.
At the Natural History Museum you can see a gallery of dinosaurs and many other exciting exhibitions. At the Victoria and Albert Museum you will find fantastic exhibitions for design and fashion.

2 Musicals

If you visit London, then you have to go and see a musical. There are so many shows like *The Lion King*, *The Phantom of the Opera* and *Mamma Mia!*. Musicals are shows with singing, dancing, dialogue and acting. Sometimes you can get very cheap tickets if you buy them online or in Leicester Square.

culture – *Kultur*
dinosaur – *Dinosaurier*
to start – *gründen*

3 Aardman Animations

Maybe you know *Wallace and Gromit* or *Shaun the Sheep* on TV. The animation films of Peter Lord, Nick Park and David Sproxton are famous. They started Aardman Animations in Bristol in 1976. They wanted to make animated films for children as well as adults. Their films like *Chicken Run* and *Wallace and Gromit* are famous all around the world. Aardman Animations do live shows, theme parks and exhibitions as well as animation films.

4 Pop Music

Music is a very important part of British culture. You can hear music everywhere in films, on TV and radio. A lot of people like listening to music. British pop music first became famous with the Beatles. They had their first hit songs in the early 1960s. Today there are many different popular cultures in Britain and you can see this in British pop music. Young people in Britain can listen to many kinds of pop music like Britpop, hip hop, techno and many others.

1 Choose one of the tasks.

a) Choose one example and write two to three sentences about an interesting place or event in Germany.

OR

b) Which picture do you like best and why? Give a summary of the text in German.

Schlüsselwörter, die du nicht kennst, kannst du im Wörterbuch nachschlagen.

An advert for a bike tour

A Come on a bike tour of Manchester with us!

How long? 3 hours
How much? £15 (adults) and £10 (children)
When? Every Friday and Saturday at 10 a.m.
Where? Piccadilly Gardens

We will meet at Piccadilly Gardens and rent a bike. First stop – the Museum of Science and Industry!

The Museum of Science and Industry has five buildings where you can see all kinds of amazing exhibitions about transport and technology. Learn about flying and rockets. You can also do some experiments.

B

Then we will ride to the Manchester Ship Canal. Our next stop is the Old Trafford Museum. Here you can learn about Manchester United Football Club. You can go on special tours of the Old Trafford Stadium and learn all about life as a football player.

C

After that we will ride to Salford to visit the Lowry Arts Centre. There is the largest collection of pictures by the famous Manchester artist L. S. Lowry. He painted people and factories in Manchester.

D

The last stop on the tour is Media City where the BBC makes a lot of its programmes like BBC Breakfast and BBC Sport. You can learn a lot here about TV and radio. You can also make your own news and weather programme! About 2,700 people work here. From here we ride back to Piccadilly Gardens.

Du kannst hier verschiedene Lesestrategien kennenlernen.

1 Skim the texts. → V City guide, p. 130

a) What type of text is it? Why?

a story — a song
a brochure — an e-mail
It's a … because there is / there are ….
It has …. / It doesn't have ….

> Um sagen zu können, um welche Textsorte es sich handelt, musst du dir den Aufbau des Textes ansehen. Jede Textsorte hat ganz bestimmte Merkmale.

b) What is part A of the text about?

It's about ….

c) Now skim part B of the text.

Write down the main words.
Compare with your partner.
→ M Think – pair – share, p. 124

> *Skimming a text* bedeutet: einen Text zu „überfliegen“. Die Überschrift und die Bilder geben Hinweise auf den Inhalt. Suche dann Schlüsselwörter. Im A-Teil sind die wichtigsten Schlüsselwörter bereits in blau unterstrichen.

16 + 17

2 Scan the texts.

a) Answer the questions about part C.

1. **Why** will they ride to Salford?
2. **Who** is a famous Manchester artist?
3. **What** is he famous for?

> *Scanning a text* bedeutet: einen Text so genau zu lesen, dass du bestimmte Einzelheiten herausfindest. Das ist z. B. wichtig, wenn du konkrete Fragen zum Text beantworten sollst.

Schlage unbekannte Wörter in einem zweisprachigen Wörterbuch nach.

b) Now answer the questions about part D.

1. **Where** can you see the BBC studios?
2. **Which** programmes does the BBC make there?
3. **What** can you learn there?
4. **How** many people work there?

> Nun versuche es einmal selbst. Lies dir die vier Fragen durch und suche im Text nach den Stellen, die Antworten auf die Fragen bieten.

A visit to the transport museum

1 (LISTENING) Listen to the four dialogues.

1, 11
20/1

Match the four dialogues with the people (A–D) in the picture.

2 (SPEAKING) Act the dialogue.

20/2

You and your English-speaking friend are at the transport museum. Talk about what you want to see there.

A: There's an animation film about skateboards. Let's go to that.
B: That sounds good. When does it start?
A: It's at 3:30 p.m. It's on the second floor.
B: OK. What about the tour of the rocket exhibition at 2:00 p.m.
A: We can go there first. I'd like to see the trains on the first floor.
B: Well, the museum closes at 5:30 p.m. Why don't we go there later?
A: OK. Let's do that.

trams | rockets | ships
bikes | cars | ...
3:00 | 3:15 | ...
first | third | fourth | fifth
tram | ship | bike | ...
2:15 | 2:30 | ...

Hier wiederholst du,
- wie du dich in einem Museum zurechtfindest.
- wie du etwas einkaufen kannst.

3 (LISTENING) Listen to the two customers in the museum souvenir shop.

1, 12
21/3

a) Look at the things and listen. Who buys which thing(s)?

Customer 1 buys ….

b) Listen again. How many things do the customers buy? How much do the customers pay?

Language → G 3, p. 108

When does the rocket film start?
Do you sell rubbers as souvenirs?
Where is the tram exhibition?

Do you remember?
So stellst du Fragen.

4 Work with shopping phrases.

21/4

a) Put the phrases for the shop assistant and the customer in the right order.

Shop assistant:

Yes, we do. | Can I help you? | These are £3. How many do you want? | Of course. That's £6. | Goodbye! | Thank you and here's £4 change.

Customer:

Here you are. | How much are those? | Yes, do you sell … as souvenirs? | Bye. | Thank you. | Can I have two …, please?

b) Practise the dialogue with your partner.

5 (SPEAKING) Act a shopping dialogue with your partner.

21/4

One of you is the assistant in the souvenir shop. The other one is the visitor to the museum. Make your own dialogue.

Assistant: Can I help you?
You: Yes. Do you have …?
Assistant: Yes. We have them in …
You: How much is/are …?
Assistant: They're / It's ….
You: OK. I'll take …. And how much is/are …?
Assistant: They're / It's ….
You: Can I have …, please?
Assistant: Of course.

Fun in Wales and Scotland

Wales

Ride down a mountain. Mount Snowdon is the highest mountain in Wales (1,085 metres). The longest zip line is near here. It's a mile long and it's open from 9:00 a.m. until 4:00 p.m. You can go skiing here in winter too.

The capital city of Wales is Cardiff. Visit Cardiff Castle in the city centre. It's nearly two thousand years old! People often make films here too.

1 What do you know?

a) Describe one picture to a partner.
- A man is ...ing ....
- On the right / On the left there are ....
- Behind ... I can see ....

b) Copy the table. Put in facts from the texts.

	music	capital	history	sport
Wales				
Scotland				

2 (READING) Match the headings with photos or texts.

22/1

a. Skirts for men?
b. A famous Scot
c. The highest mountain in Wales
d. Sport and culture in Scotland
e. A very old castle

At the end of this unit, you can …
- understand information about Wales and Scotland.
- present your favourite activity.
- arrange to meet somebody.
- read a comic strip about Scottish history.
- understand a programme of events for a music festival.
- understand a film about an adventure in Wales.

Scotland

Robert the Bruce lived from 1274 until 1329. He fought against the English. Today Scotland is part of the UK, but in the past it had its own king or queen.

Highland Games are sports events in Scotland. There are competitions in hammer throwing and Highland dancing.

Edinburgh is the capital city of Scotland. There are lots of Scottish traditions. People play the bagpipes and the men wear kilts (that's a skirt) on special days.

1, 14
22/2

3 (LISTENING) Choose the right answers.

1. Teens in Wales learn Welsh until they are **14** · **15** · **16**.
2. About one person in five is good at **singing songs** · **speaking Welsh** · **speaking English**.
3. A lot more people speak Welsh **in South Wales** · **in East Wales** · **in North and West Wales**.
4. There are **Welsh computer games** · **Welsh supermarkets** · **Welsh sports centres**.
5. 'Plant' is the Welsh word for **bananas** · **children** · **trees**.

I can understand information about Wales and Scotland. ✔

A trip to the adventure centre

1 (READING) Read the messages.

1, 15

Beth and Mark are 13 and go to the same school in Cardiff. They are chatting on the internet about their school trip to an adventure centre in the Black Mountains in Wales.

INTERNET

Bethy13: Hi Mark. I really can't wait for our trip to the adventure centre.
Macca2004: Yes, it was great last year. The people were so nice. I've already packed my bag.
Bethy13: I've looked at the new activities on their website. I'd like to play rugby this time. I've never done that before.
Macca2004: Really? I've played rugby before and I've seen it on TV. You need to be big and strong. The last time I played rugby I hurt myself.
Bethy13: I'm small but I'm fit and strong. What are you going to do?
Macca2004: My sister and I are going to go rock climbing, but we haven't booked it yet.
Bethy13: Rock climbing in the Black Mountains? Isn't that difficult and dangerous? Have you got helmets?
Macca2004: Of course! We've already been to the Amazing Walls Centre and we've always wanted to climb a mountain. It's really exciting and it's safe if you're careful.
Bethy13: Tell your sister I've already booked the zip line.
Macca2004: OK. I'll tell her. I know she hasn't decided yet. I've thought about it too, but I haven't booked it.
Bethy13: Oh, Mark. Please book it. You two can go rock climbing and I'll play rugby. We can all go on the zip line together. Then we can go to the snack bar and talk about our adventures.

2 Complete the sentences.

23/1

1. Beth and Mark can't wait for ….
2. Mark has already packed ….
3. Mark has played ….
4. Mark has always wanted to ….
5. He says climbing isn't dangerous if you ….
6. Beth wants to talk about their … at the snack bar.

Language → G 5, p. 110

What are you going to do?
I'm going to play rugby.

CULTURE

Rugby ist ein beliebter Mannschaftssport in englischsprachigen Ländern. Der ovale Ball wird mit der Hand oder mit dem Fuß gespielt. Es gibt mehrere Wege, Punkte zu bekommen, um das Spiel zu gewinnen.

23/2 ## 3 Find the right adjectives. → M Bus stop, p. 120

a) Find the opposites. → ○ p. 96

1. easy ✓	a. dangerous
2. dry	b. difficult ✓
3. exciting	c. loud
4. small	d. wet
5. safe	e. big
6. quiet	f. boring

WRITING SKILLS

Adjektive machen einen Text interessanter. Wenn du einen Text schreibst, überlege: Wo kannst du Adjektive ergänzen, um Personen oder Gegenstände zu beschreiben?

b) Complete the sentences.

serious | lucky | tired | careful

1. It can be dangerous to climb if you don't wear a helmet. You have to be very ___ .
2. He has played rugby all afternoon. Now he feels really ___ .
3. He thought it was funny when she fell off her bike but it was a ___ accident.
4. She was ___ that she only hurt her leg a little.

4 (WRITING) Write a text about canoeing. Use the adjectives in the box.

23/3

great | dry | interesting ✓ | nice | exciting | easy

Canoeing is an interesting (1) sport for people from 12 to 99.
Spend a ___ (2) day on the river.
Meet lots of ___ (3) people.
Canoeing is ___ (4) to learn but you won't stay ___ (5).
You'll love our ___ (6) trips.

5 (SOUNDS) Read, say and listen.

24/4

a) Make a chart. Say each word aloud. Which part of the word is stressed? Put the words into the right group.

together ✓ | interesting | dangerous ✓ | adventure
canoeing | horse riding | rock climbing | amazing

Ooo	oOo
dangerous	together

1, 16 b) Listen to the words and check the chart.

Im Wörterbuch und in den Wortlisten ab S. 139 kannst du die Aussprache eines Wortes nachschlagen. Bei mehrsilbigen Wörtern steht vor der betonten Silbe eines Wortes das Zeichen ['].

Language detectives → G 6, p. 111

Wann verwendest du „have ('ve)", und wann „has"?

Mark: I've already packed my bag.
Mark has seen rugby on TV.
We've already been to the Amazing Walls Centre.

Beth hasn't done it before. We haven't booked the rock climbing yet.
Mark: My sister hasn't decided yet.

Du lernst hier eine weitere Zeitform kennen: das *present perfect*. Wie wird es gebildet? Welche Signalwörter zeigen dir, dass im Satz das *present perfect* stehen muss?

6 Complete the sentences. Use have or has and the right form of the verb.

24/5

1. Beth: I ___ never ___ rugby before. (play)
   I have never played rugby before.
2. Mark ___ already ___ to the Amazing Walls Centre. (be)
3. Mark: We ___ always ___ to climb a mountain. (want)
4. Mark's sister ___ not ___ yet what she wants to do. (decide)
5. Beth ___ already ___ at the adventure centre website. (look)
6. Mark and his sister ___ not ___ the zip line yet. (book)

7 (SPEAKING) Make sentences.

24/6

a) Mark has a list of jobs to do. What has he already done? What hasn't he done yet? → ◯ p. 96
→ M Walking sentences, p. 125

1. book zip line
2. pack bag ✓
3. do homework
4. check the time for the bus ✓
5. phone Beth
6. take out the rubbish
7. make the bed ✓

be – has/have been
do – has/have done
have – has/have had
make – has/have made
see – has/have seen
take – has/have taken

1. Mark hasn't booked the zip line yet.

b) What about you? Make sentences about what you have done today.

I've	+	clean have take out tidy	+	an English lesson. breakfast. the rubbish. my teeth. my bedroom.

„Already" und „never" kommen im Satz normalerweise direkt nach „have". „Yet" und „before" kommen meistens am Satzende.

25/7-8 8 (WRITING) What have you done before?

a) Write sentences about yourself. → ○ p. 97

be on

play

do

visit

wash

climb

1. I have/haven't been on a night walk.

b) Tell a partner three more things you have or haven't done.
→ M Milling around, p. 122

I have ....

9 (TASK) A poster about your favourite activity

→ V Sports and activities, p. 131 → M Gallery walk, p. 122

25/9

a) Make a poster about your favourite sport or activity. Make notes. Find more information. Add pictures.

- What's the sport like?
- What do you do?
- What must you be like?
- What clothes have you got for it?
- Where have you done your sport?
- How often have you done it?
- What do you want to do but haven't done yet?

Skiing is an exciting sport. It's easy. You can ski fast. You must be fit and careful. You can borrow helmets and special clothes. I have often gone skiing near my village. I have watched skiing races on TV but I haven't been to a race yet.

b) Present your poster.

STUDY SKILLS

Schreibe deine Notizen auf Karten. Übe, was du sagen willst, bevor du dein Poster präsentierst.
Sprich langsam und deutlich. Frage bei deinen Zuhörern nach, ob sie alles verstanden oder noch Fragen haben.

I can present my favourite activity. ✓

When can we meet?

1 (READING) Read the dialogue.

1, 17

Fiona and her friend, Kirsty, are 13 and live near Stirling in Scotland. There are Highland Games in Stirling this weekend. Fiona wants to go to the games with Kirsty. They are talking on the phone.

Fiona: Hello Kirsty.
Kirsty: Hi Fiona.
Fiona: I've got tickets for the Highland Games in Stirling for today. Would you like to come?
Kirsty: Yes, please. Have you ever been there before?
Fiona: No, I haven't. But it sounds fun. The Highland dancing is on today.
Kirsty: Great. Have your parents already bought the tickets?
Fiona: Yes, they have. My dad bought them on the internet. We've got one left because Stuart has just decided that he doesn't want to come.
Kirsty: Has Stuart been to the Highland Games before?
Fiona: Yes, he has. So, do you want to come over to my house?
Kirsty: Now? I haven't helped Dad yet. Can we meet later?
Fiona: OK. I haven't tidied my bedroom yet. So let's say half past five at my house.
Kirsty: OK. See you later then!
Fiona: Great. Bye, Kirsty.

2 Find the information in the dialogue and write down the lines.

26/1

Find out …

1. where Fiona wants to go.
   Fiona wants to go to the Highland Games.
   That's in line 3.
2. what event is on today.
3. where Fiona's dad bought the tickets.
4. why Fiona has got one ticket left.
5. why Kirsty can't go and see Fiona now.
6. what time they decide to meet.

CULTURE

Highland Dancing ist ein schneller Tanzstil mit kraftvollen Sprüngen. Die Tänzer und Tänzerinnen werden von einem Dudelsack begleitet. Welche Arten von Tanz kennst du?

1, 18 26/2

3 (LISTENING) Stuart wants to meet Jim. Listen to the phone call.

Find out:
- Why?
- What?
- Who?
- When?
- Where?

Take notes.

LISTENING SKILLS

- Höre dir das Gespräch einmal komplett an. Versuche zunächst herauszufinden, worum es geht. Mache Notizen zu den *wh*-Fragen.
- Höre dir das Gespräch ein zweites Mal an. Ergänze deine Notizen.
- Überprüfe die Ergebnisse mit einem/einer Partner/in. Wenn ihr euch nicht einig seid, dann sprecht darüber, was ihr herausgefunden habt.

26/3

4 Find the right verbs for the phrases.

to clean	to tidy	to help	to feed
to finish ✓	to take	to do	to make

to finish lunch	___ breakfast	___ my bike
___ the dog for a walk	___ my homework	___ the cat
___ Mum and Dad	___ your bedroom	

26/3

5 (SPEAKING) Jobs around the house

a) Tell your partner about what you do at home. → ○ p. 97

I	always usually often sometimes occasionally never	tidy feed clean make take do help	Mum and Dad. my bike. my pet. my bedroom. my homework. breakfast. the dog for a walk.

I sometimes listen to music.

b) Write the sentences about your partner and report to the class.

Benedikt often takes his dog for a walk.
He occasionally cleans his bedroom.

Language detectives → G 7, p. 112

Have you been to the Highland Games before? – No, I haven't.
Have your parents already bought the tickets? – Yes, they have.
Has Stuart been to the Highland Games before? – Yes, he has.

Wie fragst du, ob jemand bereits oder jemals etwas gemacht hat?

Bei folgenden Signalwörtern wird das present perfect verwendet: yet, already, ever, never, just, before.

6 Ask questions. Use have/has and the correct form of the verb.

27/4

1. ___ you ___ to the Highland Games before? (be)
2. ___ she already ___ the tickets? (buy)
3. ___ you ___ your dad in the garden yet? (help)
4. ___ Fiona ___ her bedroom yet? (tidy)
5. ___ Kirsty ___ her German words? (learn)
6. ___ you ___ your homework? (do)

7 (SPEAKING) Interview your partner.

27/5–6

a) Think about questions for these pictures and interview your partner. Take turns. → ○ p. 98

1

2

3

4

5

6

to dance | to visit | to see | to help | to make | to play

a film | cricket | another person | in the snow | a stadium | a dinosaur

A: Have you ever played cricket?
B: Yes, I have. / No, I haven't.

B: Have you ever …?
A: Yes, … .

b) Ask another partner and find out three more things that you have both done. Tell the class what you found out.

We have … .

28/7–8

8 Present perfect or simple past?

a) Choose the right form for these sentences. → p. 98

1. Fiona	already watched has already watched	a film.
2. She	has watched watched	the film last week.
3. Stuart	has phoned phoned	Jim on Saturday.
4. Dad	has already bought already bought	the tickets.
5. I	didn't clean haven't cleaned	my bike yesterday.
6. Have you ever been Did you ever go		to Sterling?
7. Have you helped Did you help		Mum in the garden yesterday?

Wenn man sagen will, wann etwas passiert ist, dann braucht man das simple past.

Language → G1, p. 106

Kirsty went home ten minutes ago.
I did my homework last night.
I took my dog for a walk yesterday.

b) Use the words in the box to write sentences.

I didn't do my homework last night.
I've never seen a famous star.

on Sunday • never • last night • yet • two days ago

28/9

9 (TASK) Let's meet! → V What time is it?, p. 132

Make a role play with a partner.

A: Do you want to go to …? We can … at 2:00. Have you done your jobs yet?
B: Sorry, I can't come. I haven't … yet. Have you done your German homework already?
A: No, I haven't. What about 5:30 then? Is that OK for you?
B: That's fine. Let's meet at the bus stop at 5:00.
A: Great! See you at the bus stop at 5:00.
B: Cool! See you later!

at 3:45 | …
helped my … in the …
had lunch | cleaned my bike | …
the school | the cinema
my house | …

Remember: 'Place before time!'

I can arrange to meet somebody. ✔

Robert the Bruce

Robert the Bruce was a popular king of Scotland. The Scots liked him. He lived until 1329.

1 Look at the pictures and tell your partner what you think the story is about.

2 (READING) Read the text.

1, 19

1 Welcome to the 14th century! At this time there are lots of battles between Scotland and England.

2 In 1306 …

3 Edward I, the king of England, has a strong army …

4 After the sixth battle, Robert the Bruce sees a spider.

3 Talk about the story.

Did you like the story? Talk about it with a partner and say why (or why not).

4 Answer the questions.

1. Say why Robert the Bruce decided to never give up.
2. Who fought at Bannockburn?
3. Who won at Bannockburn and why did they win?

Kannst du die englische und die schottische Flagge entdecken?

5 A week later …

6 In 1314, at Bannockburn, near Stirling …

7 It rains at Bannockburn …

8 After two days …

Robert the Bruce made peace in Scotland and it was a free country. He was a brave man.

5 Choose one of the tasks.

30/1
31/2–4

a) Search the internet about the life of Robert the Bruce. Then write a short biography. Add pictures. → M Peer correction, p. 123

OR

b) Make a poster about the battle of Bannockburn. Search the internet. Find pictures. Add some information.

STUDY SKILLS

Wenn du im Internet Informationen zu einer Person suchst, suche nur nach den wichtigsten Daten und Fakten. Schreibe dir diese als Stichpunkte auf. Benutze sie dann, um die Biografie zu schreiben.

I can read a comic strip about Scottish history. ✓

Come to the festival!

THE BRECON BEACONS MUSIC FESTIVAL

SATURDAY 31ST JULY starting 6:00 p.m.

COME TO THE FANTASTIC MUSIC FESTIVAL FOR THE BEST NEW SOUNDS.

BLACK STAGE

LAYLA Enjoy the beautiful voice of this singer from Swansea. She sings lovely soul and pop songs.

RHYME Don't miss the energy from this alternative rock band with hip-hop influences from Stirling.

SPIRIT A rock band all the way from Manchester. You'll love their songs.

WHITE STAGE

TASTE OF STYLE An amazing electronic duo from Cardiff. Enjoy their unique blend of house music with funk and techno.

STREET BROTHERS Get dancing to the energy of this band and their latest songs.

BRAVE MEN You'll enjoy this exciting duo from New York with their alternative hip-hop and electropop sounds.

1 Lies das Veranstaltungsprogramm für ein Musikfest. Fasse den Text in 3–4 Sätzen auf Deutsch zusammen.

2 (MEDIATION) Vervollständige die Sätze.

29/1

1. Die Band ___ kommt aus Cardiff.
2. Die Band ___ kommt aus Nordengland.
3. Die Sängerin mit der wunderschönen Stimme heißt ___.
4. Auf der ___ Stage wird Soul und Rock gesungen.
5. Spirit tritt als letzte Band auf der ___ Stage auf.
6. Das Duo Brave Men stammt aus ___.
7. ___ ist die erste Band auf der White Stage.
8. Die Band ___ kommt aus England.

3 (SPEAKING) Which band would you like to go to? → M Round robin, p. 124

Say which band or bands you find interesting and why.
Have you ever been to a music festival or concert? Talk about it.

I can understand a programme of events for a music festival. ✔

The briefcase

This is a film about Laura from Greenwich and her friend Alicia.

1 Look at the photo and guess.

Where are Laura and Alicia?
What time of year is it?
What's in the briefcase?

2 (VIEWING) Watch the film. Right or wrong?

4

a) Check your answers from exercise 1. Were you right?

b) Right or wrong?

1. Laura and Alicia are in Scotland.
2. The girls go shopping after lunch.
3. Then they see a man. He has got a phone and a briefcase.
4. A man runs after the girls.
5. The briefcase is a prop for a film.

CULTURE

Es gibt unterschiedliche Strände in Wales – wenn du Surfer bist, findest du im Westen perfekte Bedingungen. Aber es gibt auch Strände, wo du Seehunde und sogar Delfine beobachten kannst! Würdest du gerne an einen dieser Strände fahren?

3 (SPEAKING) Talk about the film.

Watch the last part of the film again (from 2:56).
Did you like it? Give reasons.

I liked the last part of the film because .... I thought .... I was worried/surprised when	I didn't like the last part of the film because .... I thought .... It was boring/exciting when ....

VIEWING SKILLS

In jedem guten Film gibt es einen Wendepunkt. Das ist der Moment, in dem sich die Handlung plötzlich ändert. Was ist der Wendepunkt in diesem Film?

I can understand a film about an adventure in Wales.

Checklist

Find more online: 92m8cf

✓ **I can understand information about Wales and Scotland.**

The capital city of … is … . • It's nearly … years old. • You can go … here too.

32

✓ **I can present my favourite activity.**

I'd like to play rugby this time. • Isn't that difficult and dangerous? • We've already been to the Amazing Walls Centre. • Have you got helmets? • Of course!

32

✓ **I can arrange to meet somebody.**

Have your parents bought the tickets? • Yes, they have. • Have you been there before? • No, I haven't. • I haven't helped Dad yet. • Can we meet later?

32

✓ **I can read a comic strip about Scottish history.**

33

✓ **I can understand a programme of events for a music festival.**

33

✓ **I can understand a film about an adventure in Wales.**

(UNIT TASK) A game of bingo

Make a game of 'Have-you-ever?-bingo'. Play the game in class.

Step 1

Collect ideas. → V Have you ever …?, p. 133

Write six questions. Your questions must all start like this: Have you ever …?

a) Think of ideas for questions with 'been'.

to London • to another country • to the new shopping centre • …

Have you ever been to London?

b) Think of ideas for questions with other verbs.

buy a festival ticket • play tennis • …

Have you ever bought a festival ticket?

Step 2

Find a partner and choose ten questions.

Read your partner's questions. He/She reads your questions. Then choose the ten best ideas together.

Step 3

Make a table.

Make a table for your ten questions.
Then write your questions in the table.

Have you ever …?	✓	✗
1. Have you ever been to London?		
2. …		
…		

Du kannst die Verbformen in der Liste auf S. 118 überprüfen.

STUDY SKILLS

Überprüfe immer deinen Text:
- Ist die Rechtschreibung korrekt?
- Hast du die richtigen Verbformen benutzt?

Step 4

Play in class. → M Milling around, p. 122

Walk around in class with your partner.
Ask your questions.
Write names in your table.
Find a different name for each answer (✓ and ✗).

Have you ever …?	✓	✗
1. Have you ever been to London?		Leah
2. …	Tim	
…		

Have you found two names (one for ✓ and one for ✗) for every question?
Shout "BINGO!" You are the winner!

1, 20

The Highland Games

A History

A long time ago in the 11th century, the Scottish king Malcolm III wanted to find some very fast men. He wanted the men to work for him and carry his messages from one place to another. He decided to have a competition for the job. The men had to run up mountains, throw and lift different things.

B Today

Today you can see the same sports at the Highland Games. There are games everywhere in Scotland and they are very popular. There are also games in other countries now. The 'heavy' events for very strong people are very popular, but there's also lots of music and dancing. There are also children's Highland Games for young people from 5 to 18.

C Caber toss

The best heavy event is the caber toss. The caber is five metres long and very heavy (about 45 kg). People hold it at one end and throw it so that it falls on the other end. It can be dangerous, but there are rarely any accidents.

D Hammer throwing

The 'hammer' is a heavy ball (about 8 kg) at the end of a long chain. People swing it above their heads very fast. Then they throw it as far as they can.

E Stone put

People use a heavy stone (about 8 kg), for example from a river, and throw it as far as they can. There are two ways to throw a stone. You can stand (then you use a heavier stone) or you can run with the stone (then it's not so heavy.)

F Music and dancing

It's always great at the Highland Games. In the past, people played music, danced and had a lot of fun. Bagpipes and Highland dancing are a big part of the modern Highland Games too.

1 Talk with a partner about the Highland Games. → M Round robin, p. 124

A Malcolm needed fast men. Why? How did he find the men?
B Say three things about the *caber toss*.
C People swing the hammer above their heads. How is that possible?
D How do you do the *stone put*?
E Why is Scottish music special?
F Are there *Highland Games* only in Scotland today? Who can take part?

to lift – *heben*
caber toss – *Baumstammwerfen*
chain – *Kette*
to swing – *schwingen; schwenken*
stone – *Stein*
way – *Art und Weise*

A presentation about a city

GLASGOW

The biggest city in Scotland

Many people from other countries visit Glasgow for holidays and weekend trips. A lot of tourists come from Europe and the United States.

PEOPLE:
- about 600,000 people live there

WEATHER:
- the same as in England; it rains a lot and is often cold!

CULTURE:
- a lot of museums and theatres
- a lot of the museums are free
- famous for its street art

OTHER FACTS:
- has the third-oldest underground in the world
- has one of the oldest universities in the UK
- has a lot of modern buildings; for example: the famous bridge: Clyde Arc
- twin town: Nuremberg

SPORT:
- people love football
- two famous football teams: Celtic and Rangers

Hier lernst du, wie du eine Präsentation vorbereitest und hältst.

36/1 37/2 **1**

The introduction

First say what you are going to talk about.
Choose a town in Scotland or Wales.
It can be a city like Edinburgh, Cardiff, ...
Then give some basic information. Don't use lots of numbers and dates – they can be boring.

Example:

> Hello, today I'm going to talk about Glasgow. It is the biggest city in Scotland. Many people from other countries visit Glasgow for holidays and weekend trips. A lot of tourists come from ....

→ Always look at your class and be friendly. Speak slowly and clearly.

37/3 **2**

More details

Now you can say what interesting things people can see and do in Glasgow.

Example:

> In Glasgow you can visit interesting museums like the new Riverside Museum, the Scottish Football Museum etc. Don't forget – most museums in Glasgow are free. In the evening you can go to ....

→ Add photos to your presentation. Repeat facts to show that they are important. Find a video on the internet where people say difficult place names so that you can hear how to say them.

37/4 **3**

More facts

Now you can inform the class about more interesting facts:

Example:

> More interesting facts about Glasgow:
> It has got the third-oldest underground in the world.
> Do you like watching football? Then you can go and see a match at Celtic Park Stadium. It's really fantastic. ...
> And did you know that Glasgow is the twin town of Nuremberg?

→ Ask questions to get your people's attention.
Always practise your presentation in front of a mirror, your family or a friend.

Welcome to Ireland

Welcome to Ireland! The Republic of Ireland is in the European Union and it uses the euro. But it isn't part of the United Kingdom.

Irish people like singing and telling old stories. There are lots of famous Irish bands, and people often make music at home and in the streets. Many cities have a youth orchestra too.

1 What is happening in the photos?

→ M Think – pair – share, p. 124

I can see ....
There is .... There are ....
A man/woman is ....
The people are ....

2 (READING) Correct the wrong sentences.

40/1

1. The Irish use the pound.
2. The Irish often make music in the streets.
3. About half of people living in Dublin are older than 65.
4. The Irish celebrate St Patrick's Day on 17th March.
5. Hurling is a game with two teams of 11 players.

At the end of this unit, you can ...
- understand information about Ireland.
- plan a journey on public transport.
- give somebody advice.
- read a story about moving to another country.
- understand information about a star.
- understand a film about an argument.

3

Dublin is the capital of Ireland. It is by the sea and a lot of young people live there. About half of people living in Dublin are younger than 25.

Every year on 17th March the Irish celebrate St Patrick's Day. People wear shamrocks and green clothes. Green is the colour of the shamrock. There are many parties.

Hurling and Gaelic football are Irish sports. The games are very fast and a lot of fun! In hurling there are two teams of 15 players.

3 (LISTENING) **Listen to the dialogue and complete the sentences.**

2, 2
40/2

1. Tom is in Dublin for the ____ time.
2. Irish people love Gaelic ____ like Gaelic football and hurling.
3. People play Gaelic ____ and hurling at Croke Park.
4. You can go on a ____ of the stadium.
5. The stadium is on the Western Commuter ____ .

I can understand information about Ireland. ✓

How do we get there?

1 (READING) Read the flyer and the dialogue.

2, 3
41/1

Jamie and Lisa are 14 years old and live just outside Dublin. They want to go to an acting workshop in Dublin and talk about how they can get there.

Jamie: I can't wait to go to the Visions acting workshop tomorrow. I'm sure it'll be amazing.
Lisa: Yes, I'm sure it will. But we need to get there by public transport. My parents can't drive us.
Jamie: Where is the workshop?
Lisa: It's in Abbey Street. It's not far from The Spire on O'Connell Street.
Jamie: How do we get there?
Lisa: Here, I've got the timetables. So, we can take the number 9 bus to Goldenbridge. We have to get off there and change to the tram. Then it's ten stops on the Red Line to Abbey Street.
Jamie: How long does the journey take?
Lisa: About an hour. The bus is usually late.
Jamie: Well, the workshop starts at ten. Why don't we meet at the bus stop near my house? You can help me with the wheelchair.
Lisa: OK, there's a bus at twenty to nine.
Jamie: So let's meet at the bus stop at twenty-five to nine. How much are the tickets?

Lisa: We can buy all-day tickets for three fifty each. But a single ticket costs one forty and a return ticket costs two fifty.
Jamie: OK, let's buy a return ticket then. Where are my keys? Oh no. They're in the snack bar.
Lisa: Let's go back and check. You'll have to leave a notice if we can't find them.
Jamie: Oh, no!

2 Getting around in Dublin

a) Put the statements in the correct order.

a. Jamie can't find his keys.
b. Lisa tells Jamie how to get to the workshop on public transport.
c. Lisa says Jamie will have to leave a notice.
d. Lisa and Jamie decide where and what time to meet.
e. They talk about how much the journey will cost.

b) Answer the questions.

1. Who wants to go to the workshop?
2. Where is the workshop?
3. What time does it start?
4. What public transport can they use?
5. Why do they buy a return ticket?

41/2

3 Words, words, words

a) Which word doesn't fit? → ○ p. 99

1. train · bus · ticket · tram
2. stop · line · ticket · museum
3. at 5:00 p.m. · sure · late · early
4. ticket · timetable · map · diary

b) Find words in the text on page 54 for A–D. Can you find the line?

A a ticket for one journey
B where you find the times of buses or trains
C the place where you wait for a bus
D when you travel to a place and back

4 Find out what the words mean.

a) Find the words in the vocabulary on pages 149–150. Choose the right German meaning.

1. You can buy the ticket on the bus.
2. He left his keys at the snack bar.
3. My school is near the hospital.
4. The tram takes ten minutes.

b) Gib die Sätze auf Deutsch wieder.

Achte auf den Zusammenhang, in dem das Wort steht.

2, 4
41/3

5 (LISTENING) Listen and say where Jamie goes.

Look at the Dublin tram map at the back of the book.

42/4

6 (SPEAKING) Find the way.

→ M Milling around, p. 122

a) Look at the map at the back of the book and find the best way to get from Goldenbridge to ….
→ ○ p. 99

- George's Dock
- Trinity
- Blackhorse

Example:
To get from Goldenbridge to George's Dock, take the Red Line. It's eight stops. Get off the tram and you're there.

b) Make a list with four places. Partner A's list are the starting points and partner B's list is where you want to go. Give each other directions.

7 (READING) Read the notices. Find the sentences with information about a place and a time.

Lost

I left my house keys in the computer room on 14th February at 3:35 p.m. Please phone Shay on 658-7743 if you find them.

We can't find Hector, our black and white cat. We lost him near Bridge Street on 10th February.
Contact: 648-5460
Thank you!

HELP!

I lost my skateboard at the D10 skate park in Dublin on 17th February at 3:45 p.m. The skateboard is blue and has red wheels. Please call Jackie on 706-5767. Thanks.

Language detectives → G 8, p. 113

Let's meet at the bus stop at twenty to nine.
I left my house keys in the computer room on 14th February at 3:35 p.m.
We lost Hector near Bridge Street on 10th February.

Schau dir die Sätze an. Es gibt Angaben des Ortes und der Zeit. Was kommt im Satz zuerst: Ort oder Zeit?

42/5 ## 8 (WRITING) Find the right order.

a) Make sentences. → ○ p. 100

1. Jamie lost his	15 JANUARY		
2. Lisa left her			10 DECEMBER
3. We lost our		12 NOVEMBER	
4. I left my	2 JANUARY		
5. My sister lost her			27 DECEMBER
6. My friend left his		5 JANUARY	

1. Jamie lost his keys at the snack bar on 15th January.

b) Choose three of the situations in a) and write notices. → M Writers' conference, p. 125

We can't find .... • We lost .... • I left my ....

9 (SPEAKING) Act a phone call with your partner.

43/6

A: Hello?
B: Hi, it's … here. There's a pop band at the stadium on Sunday evening. Do you want to come?
A: On Sunday? What time?
B: At 8:00 p.m.

A: Yes, I can.
B: Great!

A: No, sorry. I can't. I have to help my parents.
B: Oh no!

funny play • rocket exhibition • science fiction film • …

at the theatre • at the science museum • at the cinema • …

Saturday evening • Tuesday afternoon • Thursday afternoon • …

7:30 • 3:30 • 4:30 • …

do my homework • visit Grandma • go shopping • …

10 (TASK) A journey by public transport → V Public transport, p. 134

43/7

a) Find out how to get from the train station to your house on public transport.

b) Phone or write to a friend.
Give him or her advice how to get to your house from the train station.

Make notes about the journey first.

- take the train from … at … p.m.
- change at ….
…
…

Take ....
Then ....
It's … stops.
You have to change at ....
The journey takes ....
The bus/train leaves … at ....
You'll arrive at … at ....
It costs ....
I'll meet you at ....

I can plan a journey on public transport.

I'm really fed up

1 (READING) Read the e-mails. → ○ p. 100

2, 5
44/1

E-MAIL

Hi Julie,
Can you give me any advice? I'm really fed up. Mum and Dad don't have any time for me any more. They're busy with their new bed & breakfast. They work hard all day and in the evenings they're tired. We all had so much fun together back in Dublin. But now?
At the weekends Mum always tells me to tidy the house. But Ashley helps me a lot! Little brothers aren't always so bad. ☹
I know that I shouldn't say this, but I can't stand living in the B&B. There are new people every day and they always ask the same questions. Someone last week had a really strong American accent and I didn't understand anything.
It's not easy to make friends here. There's nobody who I can talk to. I miss you!
I have to go now. I think somebody rang the doorbell.

See you,
Linda ☺

E-MAIL

Hi Linda,
I miss you too. It's so boring here without you. There's nothing to do now.
Can't you talk to your parents? You can tell them how you feel and maybe they'll understand. Try and be positive. Speak to your dad first. I'm sure he will listen.
I don't think I'd like to live in a B&B. But think positive. New guests aren't always boring. Maybe they can tell you some interesting stories! Is there anybody at school that you can talk to? Make a list of the good things that happen.
I'd like to visit you in our next holidays, but I have to go to Cork with my family, so there's no chance.
Why don't you come to Dublin soon? I'm sure we can think of something amazing to do. There's a cool new snack bar in town where we can go.

I'll call you tomorrow.
Julie XOX

2 Find the answers.

1. Does Linda like the new place?
2. What are Linda's problems?
3. What advice does Julie give Linda?

There are .... | She feels .... | Her parents .... | She can .... | She should ....

3 (SPEAKING) What do you think? → M Double circle, p. 121

a) Talk about these questions. → ○ p. 101

1. Can you understand how Linda feels? Why? Why not?
2. Is Julie's advice OK? Why? Why not?

I'm not sure because ....
I think it's OK / a problem / not so easy because ....
That's a good idea / not a good idea because ....

b) Make questions.

What questions do the guests at the B&B have?

Is there a …?

Are there any …?

Can you tell me where …?

Do you know …?

sights · places to visit · restaurants · shopping centre · museums · doctor

4 (LISTENING) Listen to the phone call.

2, 6 44/2 a) Choose the right answer.

1. Who called Linda?
   Ashley · Julie · Linda's dad
2. When was Linda fed up?
   yesterday · two days ago · last week
3. Who will Linda talk to later that week?
   her dad · her mum · Ashley
4. When will the girls talk again?
   tomorrow morning · tomorrow afternoon · tomorrow evening

b) What about you? Can you always talk to your parents? Tell your partner.

44/3 5 Work with adjectives.

a) Make a table. Sort the adjectives. → p. 101 → M Bus stop, p. 120

sad ✓ · angry · funny · worried · happy · positive · unhappy

☺	☹
…	*sad*

b) Find more adjectives and add them to the table.

6 (WRITING) Describe an important person in your life.

→ M Peer correction, p. 123

a) Choose a person (family or friend). Think about what is good about him/her. Take notes.

b) Write a short text about the person.
Use some of the adjectives in exercise 5.

My best friend always listens to me. He's funny and knows a lot of things. He also …. But he's often late. Then I get really angry. Sometimes he ….

7 (SOUNDS) Listen, read and say.

2, 7

bad, had, sad, and
The big cat was on the old black hat.

[æ]

bed, head, said, end
Ten friends said they helped their pets.

[e]

Language detectives → G 9, p. 114

Maybe they can tell you some interesting stories!
Mum and Dad don't have any time for me.
Can you give me any advice?
There's no chance.

I'm sure we can think of something amazing to do.
There's nothing to do now.

Is there anybody at school that you can talk to?
There's nobody who I can talk to.

In welchen Satzarten benutzen wir *some* und in welchen *any*? Wann wird *no* benutzt?
Welche Wörter benutzt man für Sachen und welche für Personen?

45/4

8 Some, any or no?

a) Put in some, any or no. → ○ p. 101

1. I'd like to buy — comics.
   I'd like to buy some comics.
2. Did we get — homework yesterday?
3. Oh no! I don't have — money!
4. Can you help me? I have — idea what to do.
5. I need — help with my project.
6. Sorry, there's — ice cream left.

b) Make the second sentence.

1. I can't go to the cinema today. (have to • do • homework)
   I have to do some homework.
2. "Can I help you?" "Yes, …" (have • blue T-shirts in my size?)
3. Can I come back tomorrow? … (have • time today)
4. I'm very hungry. … (there • be • sandwiches in the kitchen?)

9 Match a sentence from box A with one from box B.

45/5

A:
1. I've got something in my eye.
   I can look at it.
2. Have you got anything cheaper?
3. Has anybody seen my phone?
4. Would you like a bottle of orange juice?
5. Who helped you with your homework?
6. I need somebody to help me.

B:
a. Nothing to drink, thank you.
b. I'm sure you left it in this room.
c. Nobody helped me.
d. That's OK. I'm not doing anything at the moment.
e. I can look at it. ✓
f. Well, this costs only € 2.

10 (WRITING) Write the e-mail.

46/6

You have a problem with your sister because she never helps at home. You write an e-mail to a friend about it. Put the sentences in your friend's e-mail in the right order.

E-MAIL

a. Thank you for your e-mail.
b. Why don't you make a list with jobs that are for you and jobs for your sister?
c. See you soon,
d. You should talk to your mum and dad about your sister.
e. Make the list with your mum and dad first. Then they can talk to your sister when she doesn't do her jobs.
f. Hi!
g. I know it's not easy for you at the moment.

Terry

11 (TASK) An e-mail with advice → V Giving advice, p. 135

46/7

a) Read the e-mail. What is Jamie's problem?

E-MAIL

Hi Julie,
I've got a big problem. 'Tigerboy III' is in cinemas now. My mum hates these films. But I really wanted to see it. Yesterday I told her: "I have to do some homework with Lisa." But Lisa and I went to watch the film. I hoped not to see anybody that knows my mum. Then something really bad happened. We walked into the building and my mum's best friend was there. Of course she saw me.
What should I do now? Mum will be really angry ...
Do you have any ideas? Please help me! Thanks!
See you,
Jamie

P b) Write an e-mail to Jamie and give him some advice. These phrases can help.
→ M Writers' conference, p. 125

That sounds awful. / That's bad news.
Think positive. / I have a good idea.
Why don't you ...?
Can't you ...?
You should tell ....
What about talking to your mum's friend ...?
Call me later. / Let's talk soon.

WRITING SKILLS

Folge diesen Schritten:
- Denke an eine Anrede und einen Schluss.
- Zeige, dass du das Problem verstanden hast.
- Gib zwei Tipps.

I can give somebody advice. ✔

A different kind of gold

1 Have you ever moved to another place or to another school?

How did you feel? Why?

2 (READING) Read the story.

2, 8

1 It was St Patrick's Day yesterday. And I wasn't back home in Ireland. My dad and I moved here two months ago and I still miss my Irish friends and our nice little home in Donegal.

2 Oh, I should introduce myself to you. My name is Niamh. That's an old Irish girl's name. You say it 'neve', like 'leave'. I always have to tell people that here in Northampton in England. That's where we moved. Dad worked in a factory in Donegal until it closed last year. He tried to find a new job in Donegal, but lots of other factories had to close too. He finally found a job but that meant that we had to move to England.

3 So yesterday it was my favourite day. St Patrick's Day. Back home there are lots of parties. Everyone wears green clothes. The whole city is green. We send cards with shamrocks and rainbows on and give each other sweets in gold paper. The rainbows and sweets are from an old Irish story. It says there's a pot of gold at the end of the rainbow.

4 There were parties here in Northampton too. It nearly felt like being back in Donegal, but I still don't know a lot of people and places. So I stayed at home. That's why the day just made me very sad. I got even sadder because the netball girls Sonya, Billy and Nisha, who I really like, didn't answer any of my phone calls.

3 Match the headlines (A–G) to the parts of the story.

A St Patrick's Day
B An old Irish poem
C I miss my life in Ireland
D At the end of the rainbow
E New friends
F Sad in Northampton
G Moving to England

Example: 1. Part 1 is headline ....

Be careful! There are more headlines than parts of the story!

4 Talk about feelings.

a) Make a list of adjectives and verbs that describe how Niamh feels. Compare with a partner.

b) How do Niamh's feelings change in the last paragraph? Give reasons.

First Niamh feels/is ... because .... | **Then she feels ... because ....** | **She is ....**

READING SKILLS

Nicht immer sprechen Menschen in Geschichten ihre Gefühle direkt an. Wenn du aber genau liest und dir die Situation vorstellst, kannst du sicher erahnen, wie sich die Personen fühlen oder was passiert, aber nicht beschrieben ist. Man nennt das „zwischen den Zeilen" lesen.

5 When Dad came home from work that afternoon, I was just standing by the window. "Are you OK, Niamh?" he asked me.
"Yes," I said.
But Dad didn't believe me. So he showed me this old poem (don't ask me where he got that one from):

At the end of the rainbow is a pot of gold,
That is what my dad said to me.
We packed our bags, our house was cold,
We went across the Irish Sea.
But until the stories he has told,
Are clear for me to see,
The fun of friends and family old,
Is gold enough for me.

It didn't help much. I still felt sad. Do you know what I mean?

6 Later that day in the late afternoon, our doorbell rang. Dad said, "You can go to the door." When I opened it I couldn't believe it. The netball girls. All three wearing green clothes and big green party hats.

I just had to laugh. "Surprise!" they said. "Your dad says it's OK to take you to a St Patrick's Day party at our youth centre. Do you want to come with us?" I ran into my room and came back with my St Patrick's Day costume.

So I went to my first St Patrick's Day party in England. And I went there together with the girls. Maybe this was the beginning of something great.

5 Choose one of the tasks.

48/1
49/2–4

a) Imagine there's a new boy or girl in your class who often feels lonely. How can you help? Collect ideas and present them to the class.

I'd like to .... We can ....

OR

b) Imagine you are Niamh and went to the St Patrick's Day party. Write a diary entry about what happened there.

WRITING SKILLS

Einleitung: Schreibe rechts oben das Datum und fange an mit *Dear Diary*, ...
Hauptteil: Beschreibe was passiert ist und wie du dich dabei gefühlt hast. Erwähne vielleicht deine Hoffnungen oder Träume: *I (really) hope that ....*
Schluss: Beschreibe, wie du darüber denkst. Setze deinen Namen ans Ende des Eintrags.

I can read a story about moving to another country.

Meet a German star

2, 9

1 (LISTENING) Listen to the radio announcement.

1. What kind of announcement is it?
   a. traffic news b. advertisement for the start of a film c. casting for a talent show
2. Who can take part?

2 (MEDIATION) Talk about Emilia Schüle.

47/1

INTERNET

EMILIA SCHÜLE

Die Schauspielerin Emilia Schüle kam als Einjährige 1993 aus Russland nach Deutschland. Bereits mit acht Jahren begann sie, Balletstunden und Unterricht in Hip-Hop und Street Dance zu nehmen. Mit 13 Jahren nahm sie am Theaterworkshop „Talents Getting Started" teil und beeindruckte die Jury mit ihrem Können. Danach erhielt sie erste Rollen als Schauspielerin und spielte auch in einigen Werbefilmen mit.

Ihre erste Hauptrolle hatte sie 2007 in dem Film „Manatu – Nur die Wahrheit rettet dich", in dem es um ein magisches Brettspiel geht. Auch in der bekannten Serie „Tatort" spielte sie schon mit. Bekannt wurde sie schließlich durch die beiden Filme „Freche Mädchen" und „Freche Mädchen 2", in denen sich alles um Teenagerfreundschaften und erste Liebesprobleme dreht.

Emilia Schüle

Emilia hat in dieser kurzen Zeit ihrer Schauspielerkarriere schon einige Preise verliehen bekommen: Im Jahr 2014 erhielt sie die „Goldene Kamera" und den „Deutschen Schauspielerpreis" in der Kategorie „Beste Schauspielerin Nachwuchs". Trotz dieser frühen Erfolge war es ihr sehr wichtig, die Schule abzuschließen. Während des letzten Schuljahres arbeitete sie sogar nebenher als Schauspielerin.

You are on an exchange visit in Ireland. Your exchange partner sees the article and is interested in acting. Tell him or her about Emilia Schüle. Say:

1. who she is
2. how she became an actor
3. what TV and film work she has done. Use these ideas:
   to act in … • TV series • to win prizes • best young actor

3 (SPEAKING) And you? → M Round robin, p. 124

Would you like to be an actor or a star? Say why or why not.

I understand information about a star. ✓

The cousin from Northern Ireland

In this film you will meet Sean. Sean is Laura and Nathan's cousin.

1 Talk about the photos.

Look at the photos from the film. What do you think is happening?

2 (VIEWING) Watch the film.

6

a) Check your answers from exercise 1. Were you right?

b) Choose the right answer.

1. Sean is **good** · **not very good** at basketball.
2. During the break Nathan talks to **Marley** · **Laura**.
3. **Marley** · **Laura** understands Sean's problem.
4. Nathan sees something awful **in a magazine** · **on his computer**.
5. **Sean** · **Marley** can help Nathan with the problem.
6. The boys want to **go to the cinema** · **cook a meal** together.

CULTURE

Viele (Nord-)Iren sind in der Vergangenheit nach Großbritannien gezogen. Heute haben etwa sechs Millionen Menschen in Großbritannien zumindest einen (nord-)irischen Vorfahren. Hast du Familienmitglieder, die in anderen Ländern wohnen?

3 (SPEAKING) Talk about the film.

Watch the film again from the start to 1:00.
How do the kids feel? Match the feelings with the names and tell your partner.

Sean · Nathan · Laura · Marley · angry · happy · unhappy · sorry · …

VIEWING SKILLS

An einem Filmdreh sind viele Personen beteiligt, z. B. ein Drehbuchautor, ein Regisseur, ein Kameramann oder Make-up artists. Würdest du gerne bei einer Filmproduktion mitmachen?

I can understand a film about an argument. ✓

Checklist

Find more online: 92m8cf

✔ **I can understand information about Ireland.**

Irish people like .... • Many cities have ....

50

✔ **I can plan a journey on public transport.**

We can take the number 9 bus to .... • We have to get off there and change to the tram. • The journey takes about an hour. • A single ticket costs one forty.

50

✔ **I can give somebody advice.**

Can't you talk to your parents? • Try and be positive. • You should speak to your dad first. • Is there anybody at school you can talk to? • Why don't you come to Dublin soon?

50

✔ **I can read a story about moving to another country.**

51

✔ **I can understand information about a star.**

51

✔ **I can understand a film about an argument.**

(UNIT TASK) A photo story

Work in groups of three or four students. Each group makes a photo story, presents it and gets feedback from the other groups.

Step 1

Find a good story.

→ M Placemat, p. 123

Collect ideas and pictures. Your story can be about:

- a sporting event
- public transport
- losing something
- meeting a star
- ...

Don't mix comics with photos. You can also take your own photos.

STUDY SKILLS

Wenn du mit einem Computer arbeitest, speichere deine Dateien in einen Ordner. Benenne die Dateien und den Ordner sinnvoll.

Step 2

Make a plan.

Put the pictures in a good order.
Remember:
Your story must have a beginning, a middle and an ending.

OUR PHOTO STORY
1. Our story is about ....
2. Plan your story

STUDY SKILLS

Es gibt spezielle Computerprogramme, die dir helfen können, deine Fotos zu einer Geschichte zusammenzusetzen. Frage deine/n Informatiklehrer/in, wenn du Hilfe brauchst.

	The beginning	The middle	The ending
Where?			
Who?			
What?			
How many photos?			

Step 3

Add texts to your pictures.

You can have speech bubbles and/or captions.

Hey! That's so cool!

Step 4

Check your draft. → M Peer correction, p. 123

Does it have all the important information? Check the spelling. Ask a friend to read the story. What advice can he or she give you?

WRITING SKILLS

Du kannst Adverbien der Zeit benutzen, um zu sagen, wann etwas geschieht, z. B.: *the next day*, *later*, *after that*, *then*.

Step 5

Write the clean copy of your draft.

The clean copy should have no mistakes. Write or type as carefully as you can!

Step 6

Present your story to the other groups and get feedback. → M Tip top, p. 125

Which story was the best and why?

The Troubles and after

2, 10

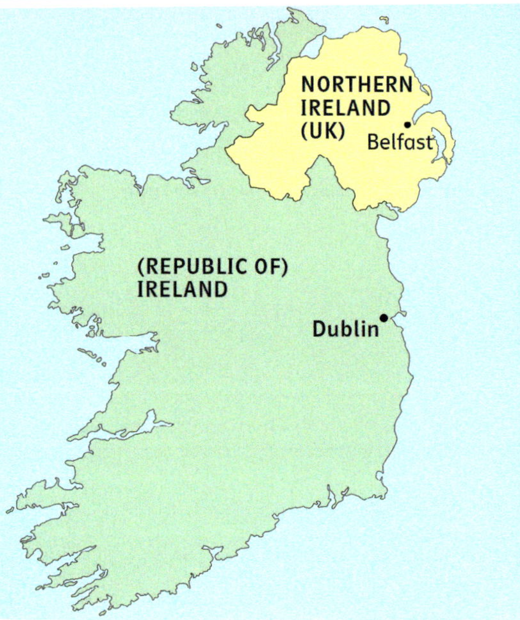

A Two countries

There are two countries on the island of Ireland: the Republic of Ireland and Northern Ireland. The capital of the Republic of Ireland is Dublin. The capital of Northern Ireland is Belfast. Here you can see a lot of large pictures on buildings. They show events and people from the past. A lot of the pictures are from the time that we call 'The Troubles'.

B Different schools

In Northern Ireland, most people are Protestant, but a lot of Catholics live there too. Some people (usually Protestants) want Northern Ireland to stay in the UK. Others (usually Catholics) want it to be part of the Republic of Ireland.
Catholic and Protestant children in Northern Ireland often go to different schools. Even in small towns there are often two schools – one for the children of each religion.

Northern Ireland – *Nordirland*
trouble – *Schwierigkeiten; Ärger*
Catholic – *katholisch*
Protestant – *protestantisch*
religion – *Religion*
a Catholic – *Katholik; Katholikin*
a Protestant – *Protestant; Protestantin*
terrorism – *Terrorismus*

C The Troubles

'The Troubles' (late 1960s–1998) were a very bad time in Northern Ireland's history. There was a lot of terrorism and more than 3,500 people died. When the British Army came to help in 1969, people wanted them to help, but many Catholics soon felt the army was not on their side.

D Belfast – then and now

During 'The Troubles', there were high walls between Protestants and Catholics. People called these walls 'peace walls'. A lot has changed since then. Now everyone is working for a better life. Many of the walls are still there, but now you can walk from one side to the other. More schools for Protestant and Catholic children open every year too.

1 Talk about the text.

A Which part of Ireland is still part of the United Kingdom?
B What are the two types of schools in Northern Ireland?
C Why were 'The Troubles' a bad time for Northern Ireland?
D What positive signs are there in Belfast now? (One fact)

Picture-based interview: The campsite

A

Schaut euch das Bild ungefähr 30 Sekunden lang genau an. Dann beginnt das Interview.

B

Hier kannst du lernen, wie du über ein Bild sprichst.

1 Look at picture A. Then answer the questions.

→ V Picture description, p. 136

a) What can you see in the picture?
– I can see a campsite.

b) Who can you see?
– I can see some people/men/women, some children, a cat ….

> Sage ganz generell, was und wen du siehst.
> Denke auch an Tiere.

54/1

2 Describe the picture in detail.

a) What can you see in the foreground/middle/background of the photo?
– In the foreground there is/are ….

b) Who is on the left/right/next to …?
– On the right is …./There is a boy with ….

> Sprich nun darüber, wo die einzelnen Personen oder Gegenstände sich befinden. Verwende die Ortsangaben im Bild. Achte auf die Einteilung des Bildes!

Überlege dir, in welcher Reihenfolge du vorgehen möchtest.
Tipp: im Uhrzeigersinn

54/1a

3 Talk about the activities in the picture.

a) What are the people doing?
– Three people are playing cards.
– The woman is writing postcards.

b) What are the people wearing?
– The man is wearing a pink shirt and blue jeans.

> Verwende bei Bildbeschreibungen das present progressive:
> *A man is …-ing, he is …-ing.*

55/4

4 What about you?

a) Do you like this campsite?
– I think this campsite is …./looks ….

b) Do you go camping?
– I (often/sometimes/never/…) go camping.

c) What do you do at the weekend?
– I buy …, meet …, visit …, play …, watch ….

> Nenne Gründe: z. B. *nice*, *cool*, *old*, *large*, *interesting*, *boring* etc.

55/2–3

5 Describe picture B.

Now look at picture B and interview your partner.
Use the questions from 1–4.

A day at the theme park

map in English

1 (LISTENING) Look at the plan of the theme park and listen to the directions.

2, 11
58/1
59/2

A group of students from Britain are visiting a theme park in Germany. They ask for directions to different places. Where do the children want to go?

The people are at **X** on the map.
The first person wants to go to the ....

Language

Go across the river.
It's next to you.
Take the first road on the right.
It's in front of you.
It's opposite the ....

Do you remember? Solche Sätze benutzt du, wenn du jemandem den Weg erklärst.

Hier wiederholst du,
– wie du einen Weg beschreiben kannst.
– wie du Essen und Getränke bestellst.

2 (SPEAKING) Give directions.

59/3

a) Look at the map on page 72. Work with your partner and ask for directions.
One of you is a visitor to the theme park and the other one works there and gives you directions.
You are at the big wheel. How do you get to the snack bar? Start like this:

> Excuse me. Can you tell me the way to …?

b) Act more dialogues. Change roles and ask about different places on the map.

3 (LISTENING) Listen to the two students at the snack bar.

2,12

What do the students buy? Choose the right answer.

A	B	C	D
cheese sandwich burger + chips 1 orange juice	pizza cheese sandwich 1 orange juice	cheese sandwich pizza 2 orange juices	salad + chips cheese sandwich 2 orange juices

4 (LISTENING) Listen again and complete the sentences.

2,12

1. I'd ___ a salad and chips.
2. I'd like something to ___ .
3. Are you ___ to order?
4. There are no salads ___ , I'm afraid.
5. Would you like ___ to drink?
6. Two ___ of orange juice, please.

5 A scene at a snack bar

59/4

You (A) are at a snack bar with an English-speaking friend (B). C works at the snack bar.
Act the scene in groups of three.

A: Frage B, was er oder sie essen möchte. What would you like to eat?
→ B: Sage, was du möchtest.
A: Frage B, ob er oder sie etwas trinken möchte.
→ B: Sage ja und bestelle dein Essen und Trinken.
A: Sage C, was B und du essen und trinken möchten.
→ C: Sage A, wie viel es kostet.
A: Gib C das Geld.
→ C: Gib A das Wechselgeld.
A: Sage danke und verabschiede dich.
→ C: Verabschiede dich.

USA – here we come!

The Grand Canyon is a river valley in the state of Arizona. It is in Grand Canyon National Park, one of the huge national parks where you can see some of America's most fantastic plants and animals. You can take part in great rafting trips here.

New York is the biggest city in the United States. The Statue of Liberty was a present from France more than 100 years ago.

1 Talk about the pictures.

→ M Round robin, p. 124

a) Choose your favourite photo.

Why do you like it best? Tell a partner.
I like photo X best because ....
In the photo I can see ..../ there's ....

b) What other places do you know in the USA? Think about cities, national parks or things to do. You can look on the internet if you like.

2 (READING) Find the right words.

60/1

1. France gave it as a present to the USA. That's the —— .
2. It is a river valley in Arizona.
3. The LA Chargers play this sport.
4. You can learn a lot about space here.
5. They lived in North America before the first Europeans arrived.
6. You can see plants and animals there.

At the end of this unit, you can ...
- understand information about the USA.
- write about how you use social media.
- talk about a summer camp.
- learn something about sports.
- pass on information about a summer camp.
- understand a film about a trip to the USA.

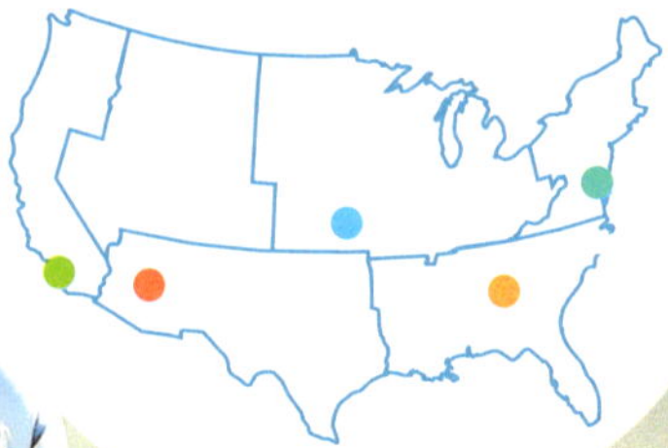

3

The US Space and Rocket Center in Huntsville, Alabama has a great collection of rockets and other things from space. Some people call it "the Earth's largest space museum".

4

Native Americans are people who lived in North America before the first Europeans arrived and settled there. Native Americans still live in some parts of the USA.

5

My favorite sport is American football. I like soccer too, but football is more popular in the USA. I play on my school football team! I'm a big fan of the LA Chargers.

3 (LISTENING) Listen to the interview with Wayne. What does he say about his trip?

2, 14
60/2

1. Wayne is first going to visit ___.
   Huntsville • New York • the Grand Canyon
2. When Wayne is older, he wants to become ___.
   a teacher • an engineer • a police officer
3. Wayne wants to go ___ on the Colorado River.
   rafting • canoeing • skating
4. Wayne hopes to visit the Navajo people near ___ Valley.
   Napa • Monument • Silicon
5. Wayne's mum comes from ___.
   Boston • New York • Los Angeles

I can understand information about the USA. ✔

Keep in touch

2, 15

1 (READING) Read the blog about Wayne's trip around the USA.

INTERNET

Hi everyone!

I'm still on vacation, my favorite time of the year! I met the Navajo people in Monument Valley on the weekend. It's a beautiful place. There are 500 tribes of Native Americans in the USA. The Navajo is one of the largest tribes in the USA.

I was really surprised when I heard that not all Navajo people have internet at home or at school. ☹ A lot of them live in reservations a long way from towns and cities so the internet is important to them. My Navajo friend, Atsa, told me that they are very interested in news from other Native people. Young people use social media for: sharing stories, information and funny videos, keeping in touch with each other, getting news from other reservations and also for posting photos of themselves. I often use social media for the same things. Usually I use my dad's old laptop, but I bought my own tablet for this trip.

Of course, the Navajo use different websites than me and my friends. I can't remember the names, but there is one that is the most important website for Native Americans. This website is more interesting than other famous US websites. It's the best to get the latest information about the Navajo and it's the least difficult one to use. Newspapers and TV are less popular than the internet for younger Navajo. American newspapers aren't interested in Native Americans and don't have many stories about them.

It's nearly 8:00 p.m. here now, 10:00 p.m. at home in Washington, and we're going to watch a movie in half an hour. Tomorrow it's the Grand Canyon! I'll write about my trip there on Thursday. And next week I'm going to go to the summer camp at Crystal Falls in Michigan.

This is the most exciting summer vacation I've ever had! ☺

Bye!

CULTURE

Die Vereinigten Staaten von Amerika sind ein sehr großes Land mit mehreren Zeitzonen. Washington D.C. liegt nicht weit von der Ostküste der USA. Wayne befindet sich 5660 km entfernt in Monument Valley. Dort ist es zwei Stunden früher als in Washington D.C. Wenn es 12.00 Uhr mittags an der Ostküste der USA ist, wie spät ist es dann in Deutschland?

CULTURE

Ein paar Wörter unterscheiden sich im britischen und amerikanischen Englisch. Schreibweise und Aussprache sind manchmal auch anders.

British	American
holidays	vacation
film	movie
favourite	favorite

Wie lauten die Wörter Herbst, Keks und Fußball in britischen bzw. amerikanischen Englisch? Schlage in einem Wörterbuch nach.

2 Find the information.

a) Correct the sentences. → ○ p. 102

61/1

1. Wayne went to the Grand Canyon on the weekend.
2. A lot of Navajo people live in towns and cities.
3. Atsa said that they are very interested in news from other countries.
4. Many younger Navajo use the internet only for sharing stories and videos.
5. They often read newspapers and watch TV.
6. American newspapers think stories about native people are exciting.

b) Find out more details.

1. Why is the internet important for a reservation?
2. Why do the Navajo people use social media?
3. Why is this website the best one for them?
4. Why are American newspapers less good for them?

61/2

3 (SPEAKING) Talk to a partner about social media. → V Social media and technology, p. 137

a) Make five statements about social media. Use these words and find the right combinations.

to send · to talk · to write · to play · to go · to post · to read · to share · to chat · to find · to watch

online · e-mails · with a friend · photos · messages · a game · a video · information · stories

Example:
A: I send about ten messages every day. What about you?
B: I send about fifteen messages every day, but I also post a lot of ….

b) What do you or your family do with social media?
Make a table.

who?	what?
mum	send messages, post photos
…	…

4 (LISTENING) Listen to a radio report about the use of media.

2, 16
61/3

Answer the questions.

1. Where did the man talk to the teens?
2. How many teens said that they are always online?
3. What was the second question?
4. How many messages does a teen write every day?
5. What kinds of online activity are more popular with girls?
6. What is the boys' favourite online activity?

LISTENING SKILLS

Lies dir vor dem ersten Anhören zunächst die sechs Fragen genau durch. Achte beim Anhören genau auf diese Teile im Text.

Language detective → G10, p. 115

This website is more interesting than other famous US websites.
That is the most important website for Native Americans.
Newspapers and TV are less popular than the internet.
It's the least difficult one to use.

Was wird mit more und most ausgedrückt?
Wie heißt das Gegenteil von more?
Und von most?

Vergiss das Wort „the" nicht!

62/4–5

5 What do you think?

a) Compare the things. Use more or less.

1. I think tablets are (**more** / **less**) useful than laptops.
2. I think this tablet in the shop is (**more** / **less**) expensive than my tablet.
3. I think online shopping is (**more** / **less**) interesting than video games.
4. I think German is (**more** / **less**) difficult than Music.
5. I think friends are (**more** / **less**) important than hobbies.
6. I think basketball is (**more** / **less**) boring than football.

b) Compare these things. Use the words on the right.

1. canoeing • rock climbing
2. campsite • bed & breakfast
3. newspapers • TV
4. rugby • football

dangerous | useful | exciting | interesting | expensive | boring

62/6a

6 Put in the most or the least.

1. The USA is one of the most beautiful countries in the world. (beautiful)
2. Newspapers are ___ way to read the news. (interesting)
3. Writing messages is one of ___ online activities. (expensive)
4. Computers are ___ things of all. (useful)

62/6b

7 (SPEAKING) Ask your partner.

A: What do you think about computer games?
B: I think they're the most exciting thing ever.
A: Really? I think they're very boring.

social media | cats | museums | ... | least

boring | interesting | useful | ...

Die Lösungen findet ihr im Buch auf S. 199.

63/7 **8** (WRITING) **Make a quiz.** → M Bus stop, p. 120

a) Complete the questions about the USA. → ○ p. 103

1. Which state in the USA has the ___ weather? (cold)
   Which state in the USA has the coldest weather?
2. Which is the ___ sport in the USA? (popular)
3. Which is the ___ state in the USA? (small)
4. Which is the ___ city in the USA? (big)
5. Who is the ___ Native American woman? (famous)

b) Answer the questions with a partner.
Use the internet if you need help.

1. Florida · Alaska · Maine
2. basketball · soccer · American football
3. Rhode Island · Arizona · Delaware
4. Chicago · New York · Dallas
5. Pocahontas · Squanto · Geronimo

63/8 **9** (TASK) **Your statement about keeping in touch** → V Social media and technology, p. 137

a) Work with a partner. Make lists of what is good and what isn't so good about social media and the internet.

good	not so good
It's easy to keep in touch with people.	… is the least useful thing because ….
… is the most useful/important thing for me because ….	… is less useful than ….
… is better than ….	… is worse than ….

b) Write a short statement about how you use the internet and social networks.
Say which computing devices you use.
Present your statement to the class. → M 1-minute presentation, p. 120

I can write about how I use social media. ✓

A rafting adventure

1 Look at the photo.

Where are the people? What are they doing? Would you like to be with them? Say why or why not.

2 (READING) Read the story.

2, 17

"Mrs Price, please can we go rafting on the river?"
"No! For the 200th time, you can't."
"But why not?"
"No. I told you. You can't go. It's too dangerous."
"Yes, I know, but we're not little children. We'll be very careful!"
Wayne and his three friends Rick, Emma and Tony were at a summer camp which was OK, but didn't organize very many exciting activities. Stella Price, the camp leader said they had to stay together with the others. After the 43rd song around the fire Wayne and his friends decided to take a raft and paddle down the Colorado River to the Grand Canyon.
Suddenly a helicopter flew behind them. Stella Price was in the helicopter. She had a megaphone and shouted at them to stop, but they just wanted to have fun. What was wrong with that? How many teens were brave enough to go on a rafting trip? Not many, Wayne thought.
The friends arrived at the Crystal Falls. There was so much water. The huge waves were scary. The raft went into the dangerous rapids. Wayne's heart went crazy. The raft went very fast into the rapids. There were huge waves between the rocks in the middle of the river. The river then fell into a deep hole.
Wayne paddled and tried to fight against the current. He paddled … and paddled … but he couldn't do it. A huge wave pushed the raft up and over the hole. The raft fell, and then it turned over. Wayne shouted as they all fell out of the raft. He tried to swim but the current pulled him down – deeper and deeper …
"Wake up! Wayne." Stella Price stood next to him. "Come on. It's time for breakfast. We don't have much time. We want to go rafting today."
Oh no! Wayne thought.

CULTURE

In *Summer camps* können Jugendliche einige Wochen im Sommer verbringen. Dort können sie Neues lernen und erleben. Die *camps* bieten manchmal spezielle Aktivitäten, wie z. B. Wassersportarten oder Musik.

3 Right or wrong?

64/1

1. The summer camp was interesting.
2. They stopped when Stella shouted.
3. Wayne was excited.
4. It was only a dream.

4 Who or what is it?

1. It didn't organize many exciting activities. – That's the summer camp.
2. They went on a raft down the Colorado River.
3. She told the friends to stop.
4. There was so much water there.
5. He tried to paddle against the current.
6. It turned over on the rapids and everyone fell out of it.

5 Find the words.

a) Find the words in the story for the things (1–6) in the picture. → p. 103

1. ___ 2. ___ 3. ___

4. ___ 5. ___ 6. ___

b) Find the words for the things (A–E) in the picture.

6 Find the answers. Use the internet to help.

64/2

1. The 40th president of the USA was also an actor.
2. The 41st president of the USA was the father of the 43rd president.
3. The 42nd president of the USA played the saxophone.
4. The 44th president of the USA was the first black president.
5. The 45th president of the USA became president in January 2017.

a. George H. W. Bush
b. Barack Obama
c. Ronald Reagan
d. Donald Trump
e. Bill Clinton

32nd	thirty-second
33rd	thirty-third
40th	fortieth
41st	forty-first
50th	fiftieth
60th	sixtieth
100th	hundredth
101st	hundred and first

2, 18 7 (SOUNDS) Same sound, different word

a) Choose the right words.

1. **There** · **Their** are many different activities at the summer camp.
2. The **four** · **for** young camp leaders are really nice.
3. The children can always go **to** · **two** the camp leaders and ask for advice.
4. Rick and Tony's team **won** · **one** the football match yesterday.
5. Emma went to bed at **eight** · **ate** last night.
6. Last weekend Wayne **read** · **red** a great blog about the Navajo.

b) Make sentences with the words you didn't use in a).

1. The children never clean their bikes.

Language detective → G11, p. 116

The camp didn't organize many exciting activities.
How many teens were brave enough to go on a rafting trip?

There was so much water.
We don't have much time.

Wann benutzt man much?
Wann benutzt man many?

65/3 8 Complete the sentences.

a) Fill in much or many. → ○ p. 103

1. Wayne hasn't got ___ time today.
2. He has got so ___ things to do.
3. Did Wayne take ___ photos of the Grand Canyon?
4. I'm feeling hungry. I haven't had ___ to eat today.
5. The summer camp is great! There are so ___ fantastic activities.
6. How ___ money did the summer camp cost?
7. How ___ children are in the camp?
8. We didn't have ___ lunch yesterday.

b) Complete the sentences with much or many and one of the words on the right.

1. (**Much / Many**) ___ play football at the weekend.
2. Do you have (**much / many**) ___ for hobbies after school?
3. Are there (**much / many**) old ___ in your town?
4. I didn't buy my friend a big birthday present because I haven't got (**much / many**) ___ .

buildings
time
money
people

9 Choose the right words. → M Peer correction, p. 123

65/4

Look at the pictures and choose the right words for each one.

much | many | water | books | snow | clothes ✓ | money | people

1 There are too —— clothes.

2 That's too —— ....

3 There are too —— ....

4 There is too ....

5 There are ... in the queue.

6 There is ....

10 (TASK) Going to a summer camp → V Summer camp activities and places, p. 138

66/5–6

You have found out about a summer camp on the internet and would like to go with your best friend. Tell your parents why.

a) Collect ideas. → M Think – pair – share, p. 124

- Where you want to go: to the mountains, to the sea, ...?
- What you like: (water) sports, art, music, dancing, computers, ...?
- Do you want to learn a new activity or get better at an activity that you can already do?
- Do you want to try a lot of different activities or just one or two?

b) Write your ideas. Here is some help:

I'd like to go to .... You know that I love ....
You can do many ... at this camp. ... I can make
many new friends / learn .... Can I go, please?

c) Act your ideas in class. → M Tip top, p. 125

Ask your friends for feedback.

I can talk about a summer camp. ✓

Popular American sports

1 (READING) Read the information about American sports.

2, 19

INTERNET

American football

... is the most popular sport in the USA. Do you know Super Bowl? It's the most important football match and the most popular sports event of the year in the USA. American football isn't the same as football in Germany. In the USA, people call German football soccer. In American football the ball is oval like a rugby ball. Players must be fast and strong. They wear helmets and special clothes. A team can have eleven players on the playing field at the same time.

Baseball

... is a very popular game for everyone. In baseball there are two teams, each with nine players: one team throws a small hard ball (called a baseball) and the other team tries to hit it with a bat. There are baseball teams and competitions in nearly every school in the USA. You don't need to be tall or strong to play. But the bat is long and the ball is small and hard, so you must have good eyes.

2 Match the parts of the sentences.

1. An American football player has to
2. In basketball games, the teams have
3. In cheerleading, you have to
4. In baseball, there are two teams
5. American football teams can have
6. Cheerleaders try

a. five players each.
b. eleven players on the playing field.
c. to motivate the players and fans.
d. be fast and strong.
e. with nine players.
f. be good at dancing.

INTERNET

Basketball

... is the number 3 sport in the USA. A lot of basketball players in the USA are famous like pop stars!
There are two teams with five players each. They try to throw a ball in a basket, and make points against the other team.
Players can bounce the ball and run with it or throw it to other players on the team. Basketball players are often very tall. But everyone can play basketball. You'll see tall people and small people playing basketball in parks and playgrounds all over America.

Cheerleading

... is a sport that you'll see at nearly all big sports events in the USA. Cheerleaders dance and jump. It can be dangerous and you have to be fit!
The first cheerleaders were men, but today 95% of cheerleaders are girls. Their job at matches is to motivate the players and the fans. But there are also cheerleading competitions – cheerleading is a sport. Cheerleading started in the USA, but is now popular in many countries. There are now about 100,000 cheerleaders all around the world.

3 Find sports words. → M Peer correction, p. 123

68/1
69/2–4

Sort these words into one of the groups.

American football **baseball**
basketball **cheerleading**

to dance • long bat • tall players • hard ball • to jump • oval ball • to bounce a ball

4 Choose one of the tasks. → V Sports and activities, p. 131

69/5

a) Work with a partner. Interview your partner about his/her favourite sport and write what he/she says. Some ideas:

- What do you need to play the sport?
- Where do you play the sport?
- How often do you practise?

Tell the class about your partner's sport.

OR

b) Work with a partner. Write about a sport that you are both interested in.

How do you play it? Explain the rules. What do you need to have for the sport? Name people who are famous in the sport.

Record the text and play it to the class.

I learned something about sports. ✓

Let's go to a summer camp

INTERNET

< 1 > Home < 2 > About < 3 > News < 4 > Info

MOUNTAIN CAMP WOODSIDE, CA

Have the best summer of your life!

- Play tennis, soccer and basketball, try drama or make art!
- Live in small wooden cabins with seven other campers – all boys or all girls about the same age.
- Stay for one week or more. Lots of children stay for six!
- Pay less if you stay for three weeks or more. Bring your brothers and sisters for half price!
- You are vegetarian or you have allergies? No problem – our cooks cook good, healthy food for everybody.
- The camp is run by fun, young adult camp leaders. (Dear parents, don't worry: They are all trained in first aid – and a hospital and doctors are only two miles away.)

1 (MEDIATION) Beantworte die Fragen deiner Eltern auf Deutsch.

67/1

Du hast im Internet eine Webseite über summer camps gesehen und zeigst sie deinen Eltern.

1. Wie lange dauert so ein Feriencamp?
2. Was kann man alles unternehmen?
3. Wie wird man untergebracht?
4. Das ist bestimmt teuer. Gibt es Sonderangebote?
5. Wer kümmert sich um euch?

MEDIATION SKILLS

Du brauchst nicht alle Informationen. Überfliege den Text zuerst. Lies dann die Fragen und suche gezielt die benötigten Informationen im Text. Mache dir stichpunktartige Notizen.

2 (READING) Read the form for registration to a summer camp.

Find the English words in the form for:

- Postleitzahl
- männlich
- Unterschrift
- Anmeldeformular
- Alter
- Nachname
- Geburtsdatum

REGISTRATION FORM SUMMER CAMP

First name: *Wayne*
Date of birth: *23rd February*
Address: *1200 Park Rd NW*
City: *Washington*
Zip code: *DC 20010*
Name of school: *Bell High School*
Preferred type of camp: *water sports*
Favorite hobby: *surfing*
Favorite food: *fish and rice*

Family name: *Thompson*
Age: *13*
MALE ☒ FEMALE ☐
Telephone number: *617 XXX XXXX*
E-mail: *xxx@xxx*

Signature:
CHILD *Wayne Thompson* PARENT *Susan Thompson*

I can pass on information about a summer camp. ✔

Go, Greg, go!

This is a film with the students Greg, Maya and Josh. They are in the USA for the first time.

1 What sport can you see in the picture?

Make a list or mind map with things you know about this sport.

2 (VIEWING) Watch the film.

8

a) Watch from the beginning to 01:53. Choose the right answers.

1. The students are in **LA** • **Washington, D.C.**
2. They travel by car and arrive **at a café** • **at a hotel**.
3. Carmen is **a student** • **a teacher**.
4. Maybe Greg can **eat cake** • **play football**.

b) Watch from 01:54 to the end. Right or wrong: Does the coach say this to Greg?

1. "England? That surprises me, pal." – That's ....
2. "Of course I know Arsenal, Chelsea and Liverpool!"
3. "You can join our practice today."
4. "You really want to show us that English football is better than what we play here?"
5. "Let's give him another chance."

3 What is Greg thinking?

Match the sentences with the right picture.

1. This is fantastic!
2. I'm scared!
3. I've never played American football.
4. I'm the greatest!
5. What can I do?

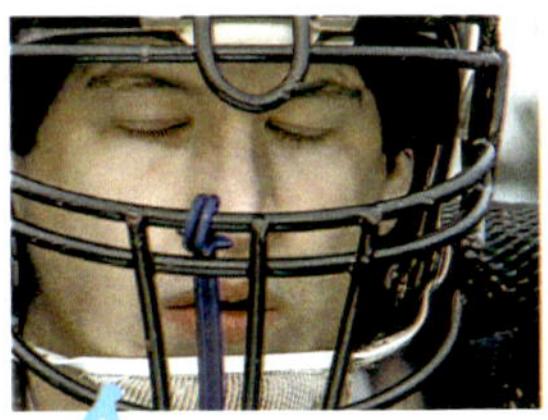

A

B

4 (SPEAKING) Talk about the film.

A: Did you like the film?
B: Yes, I did. I thought it was .... • No, ...
A: Which scene did you like most?
B: I liked the scene with ... because ....

VIEWING SKILLS

Das Gespräch ist in einem Film wichtig, aber du sollst auch die Gesichter und Körpersprache der Menschen beobachten. Sie können dir verraten, was gerade passiert, und dir Auskunft darüber geben, wie die Leute sich fühlen.

I can understand a film about a trip to the USA. ✓

Checklist

Find more online: 92m8cf

- I can understand information about the USA. 70

- I can write about how I use social media.

  This website is more interesting than other famous US websites. • It's the least difficult one to use • Newspapers and TV are less popular than the internet. 70

- I can talk about a summer camp.

  Please can we go …? • For the 200th time, you can't. • How many teenagers were brave enough to go …? 70

- I learned something about sports. 71

- I can pass on information about a summer camp. 71

- I can understand a film about a trip to the USA.

(UNIT TASK) The USA quiz

Work in groups and write questions for a quiz about the USA. Each group writes eight questions. The groups are the teams when you do the quiz.

Step 1

Collect ideas and think of your questions.

→ M Think – pair – share, p. 124

a) Collect ideas for questions about the USA.

Here are some ideas for questions:
- people?
- sport?
- cities?
- famous person?
- flag?
- national parks?
- …

b) Make a long list with everyone's ideas. Then look at all the ideas together and make a short list.

→ M Placemat, p. 123

STUDY SKILLS

Hört euch zunächst alle Ideen an. Gebt jedem die Chance, zu erklären, was er oder sie gemeint hat. Einigt euch auf die Fragen, die ihr stellen wollt. Sie sollten mit W-Wörtern beginnen, also *where? what? who?*. Ihr sollt keine Fragen stellen, die mit *ja* oder *nein* beantwortet werden können.

Step 2

Write your questions and check the answers.

a) Each student writes a card with one question and the answer on the back.
b) Another student checks the English. A third student checks that the answer is correct.
c) Each student in the team has to read one or more questions. Think of the order of the questions and practise before you do the quiz.

Step 3

Get ready for the quiz.

1. When can you do the quiz?
2. Who can start/finish the quiz?
3. Which team reads its questions first?

Jedes Team kann eine Flagge vorbereiten. Ihr könnt auch ein Maskottchen mitbringen. Viel Glück!

Step 4

Do the quiz.

Each team reads its questions.
The other teams write the answers.

Can you say that again, please?

Sorry, I didn't understand that!

Can you speak louder, please?

One student from each team checks the answers at the end and gives the results to the umpire. The umpire says who the winner is.

SPEAKING SKILLS

Lest die Fragen laut und deutlich vor. Seht die anderen Teams an, wenn ihr eure Fragen vorlest. Wenn ihr eine Frage nicht versteht, fragt höflich nach. (Wenn ihr die Antwort wisst, behaltet sie zunächst für euch.)

Step 5

Talk about the quiz. → M Think – pair – share, p. 124

Did you enjoy the quiz? What was good / not so good about it?

Special days in the USA

2, 20

JANUARY Martin Luther King Day

1 I have a dream

This day is around the birthday of the civil rights activist, Martin Luther King. He lived at a time when African Americans didn't have the same rights as white Americans. He used peaceful ways to protest against this. American children often learn about Martin Luther King and civil rights at school.

JULY Independence Day

2

4th July celebrates the USA's independence from Great Britain in 1776. People wear red, white and blue clothes – like the American flag. They have picnics or barbecues and there are fantastic fireworks everywhere.

civil rights – *Bürgerrechte*
activist – *Aktivist; Aktivistin*
to protest – *protestieren*
flag – *Flagge; Fahne*
fireworks – *Feuerwerk*
Thanksgiving – *Erntedankfest*

OCTOBER Columbus Day

Columbus first saw America in 1492. Today people still celebrate the event. Some people don't like this holiday because Columbus didn't really discover America. Columbus Day celebrates a man of ideas and dreams. Many countries in South America celebrate Columbus Day too.

NOVEMBER Thanksgiving

The history of Thanksgiving began in 1621 when the Europeans settled and celebrated their first year in their new country. Some local Native Americans invited them to their meal. Thanksgiving is a family day – often with the tradition of a Thanksgiving dinner. Football games are usually a big part of the day too.

1 Which picture belongs to which text?

A

B

C

D

2 Choose one text and find more about the topic on the internet (2 or 3 interesting facts).

a) What celebration would you like to take part in? Say why.

OR

b) Choose one text and say in German what it tells you about the topic.

WRITING SKILLS

An e-mail from a new friend

→ M Writers' conference, p. 125

E-MAIL

A SUBJECT: First contact

Hi Bastian,

B I saw your photo and your profile in Penfriends Worldwide.
I have always wanted to have contact with a boy or girl in Germany because my grandfather came to the USA from Fürth in Bavaria more than 50 years ago. He died when I was five.

C My name is Hannah and I'm 14. I live in Orlando, Florida with my parents, my younger brother, Ryan and our cat, Larry. We live in a small house; it has got a kitchen with a small breakfast room, a living room, a bathroom, three bedrooms and a small garden. I like it here.
Can you tell me something about yourself, your family, the place where you live?

D I go to the Baker Middle School in Orlando. My school is some miles away from our home so I have to take the bus every day. My favorite subjects are Math and Biology. What subjects do you like best? I'm in the school drama club. Next month we will take part in the Orlando theater festival. I'm acting "Juliet" in Shakespeare's "Romeo and Juliet". Have you got school clubs in Bavaria too?

E My best friends are Leah and Joshua. They are in the same class. After school we often go to the school café. We can chat online there. At the weekends we sometimes go shopping. Occasionally, if it's warm and sunny, we also go canoeing or rafting on Lake Apopka. That's always a lot of fun and quite exciting. And what do you do in your free time?

F That's all for today. Please write soon!

Best wishes

Hannah

Hier lernst du, wie man eine E-Mail schreibt.

1 Read Hannah's e-mail.

Then match the parts of the e-mail with the sentences in the boxes.
Write A, B, C etc.

> Eine E-Mail hat immer einen ähnlichen Aufbau. Sieh dir dazu das Beispiel genau an.

1. At the end of the e-mail Hannah writes that she hopes her partner will answer soon.
2. Hannah says who she is and where she lives with her family.
3. She writes about her favourite activities and hobbies.
4. Here she writes about her school (subjects, clubs, projects).
5. The subject line says what she wants to write about.
6. At the beginning she says why she is writing.

74+75

2 Write an e-mail to Hannah.

a) Look at Hannah's e-mail again. Which questions did she ask? Make notes.

> Überlege dir, was du antworten willst. Kannst du einzelne Wörter oder Redewendungen für deine E-Mail verwenden?

b) Write a draft of an e-mail. Don't forget to write who you are.

> Wenn du den ersten Entwurf schreibst, achte auf die richtige Reihenfolge.

c) Read your draft and think of words like always, often, sometimes, occasionally.

> Überprüfe die Rechtschreibung mit einem Wörterbuch/Rechtschreibprogramm.

d) Now write a clean copy of the e-mail.

> Schreibe nun deine E-Mail sauber auf, wenn möglich mit dem Computer.

e) Read a partner's e-mail and give feedback.

> Sage, ob der Aufbau in Ordnung war. Hat er/sie etwas Wichtiges vergessen?

Unit 1, p.13

3 Put the words into groups. → M Peer correction, p.123

a) Copy the table. Put the words and phrases below into the right groups.

places	where	words for the size of places
village	near	big

in the centre of ... | village ✓ | a long way away from ... | big ✓ | on the coast | city | small | near ✓ | in the north/south/east/west of ... | town | in the mountains | large

Unit 1, p.14

6 Complete Tom's story.

a) Complete the sentences.

happened ✓ | fell | wanted | wasn't | heard | saw | got up | was

1. Last Saturday morning a lot of things happened on our farm. (to happen)
2. I ___ a noise in the garden (to hear) and I ___. (to get up)
3. I ___ my dad in the garden. (to see)
4. He ___ to put Bert and Daisy, our goats, in the car. (to want)
5. Suddenly he ___ in the mud. (to fall)
6. It ___ so funny. (to be)
7. Dad ___ very happy. (to not be)

Unit 1, p.14

7 (WRITING) What didn't Hannah and her dog, Kenny, do on Saturday?

a) Make sentences with didn't, wasn't or weren't.

1 Hannah didn't go to the supermarket in the morning.

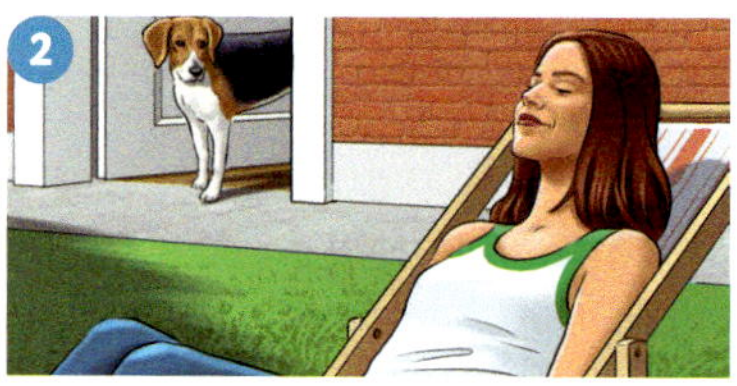

2 Hannah ___ (not be) in the living room at two o'clock.

3 Hannah ___ (not do) her homework in the afternoon.

Hannah and her sister ___ (not feed) their dog at five o'clock.

Later she ___ (not watch) TV.

Hannah and her sister ___ (not be) at the cinema.

Unit 1, p. 18

7 (SPEAKING) Interview your partner. → M Double circle, p. 121

a) Ask a partner. He or she answers.

A: Do you		go to the cinema?	B: Yes, I do.
Do your friends	sometimes	do your homework?	No, I don't.
Do they	often	play football?	Yes, she/he does.
Does your mum/dad	usually	watch TV?	No, she/he doesn't.
Does he		go shopping?	Yes, they do.
			No, they don't.

Do you often go shopping? – Yes, I do. / No, I don't.

Unit 1, p. 18

8 (WRITING) Make questions for the answers.

a) Complete the questions. → M Walking sentences, p 125

Language → G 3, p. 108
Where do you live?
What school clubs are there?

1. Where ___ the Art Club (to be)?
   Where is the Art Club? – It's in Room 22.
2. When ___ it ___ (to finish)? – It finishes at 5:30 p.m.
3. How ___ you ___ home after school (to get)? – I usually ride my bike.
4. How long ___ it ___ (to take)? – It takes about ten minutes.
5. What subjects ___ new this year (to be)? – Design Technology and Biology.
6. How many lessons ___ you ___ every day (to have)? – I have six lessons every day.
7. How often ___ you ___ PE (to have)? – I have it once a week.

Unit 1, p. 19

○ 9 Whose is it?

a) Rewrite the sentences. Use possessive pronouns.

1. It's **your** rubber. – It's yours.
2. It's **George's** exercise book. – It's ....
3. It's **my sister's** phone. – It's ....
4. It's **my** ruler. – It's ....
5. It's **Mum and Dad's** room. – It's ....
6. It's **our** dog. – It's ....
7. It's **Tom's** calculator. – It's ....

Language → G 4, p. 109

my – mine	your – yours
his – his	her – hers
our – ours	their – theirs

Unit 2, p. 35

○ 3 Find the right adjectives. → M Bus stop, p. 120

a) Find the opposites.

dangerous | difficult ✓ | loud | wet | big | boring

1. easy – difficult
2. dry – w
3. exciting – b
4. small – b
5. safe – d
6. quiet – l

Unit 2, p. 36

○ 7 (SPEAKING) Make sentences.

a) Mark has a list of jobs to do. What has he already done? What hasn't he done yet?
→ M Walking sentences, p 125

1. book zip line
2. pack bag ✓
3. do homework
4. check the time for the bus ✓
5. phone Beth
6. take out the rubbish
7. make the bed ✓

1. Mark hasn't booked the zip line yet.
2. He has already ....
3. He hasn't ... yet.
4. He has already ....
5. He hasn't ... yet.
6. He hasn't ... yet.
7. He has already ....

do – has/have done
make – has/have made
take – has/have taken

Unit 2, p. 37

8 (WRITING) What have you done before?

a) Write sentences about yourself.

tennis | magic tricks | a car | a mountain | a night walk ✓ | a theme park

be on

play

do

visit

wash

climb

1. I have/haven't been on a night walk.

Unit 2, p. 39

5 (SPEAKING) Jobs around the house.

a) Tell your partner about what you do at home.

I +	always usually often sometimes occasionally never	+ tidy my bedroom. feed my pet. clean my bike. make breakfast. take the dog for a walk. do my homework. help Mum and Dad.

Unit 2, p. 40

7 (SPEAKING) Interview your partner.

a) Think about questions for these pictures and interview your partner. Take turns.

1

to play

2

to help

3

to visit

4

to make

5

to dance

6

to see

a film | cricket | a dinosaur | in the snow | another person | a stadium

A: Have you ever played cricket?
B: Yes, I have. / No, I haven't.

B: Have you ever …?
A: Yes, … .

Unit 2, p. 41

8 Present perfect or simple past?

a) Choose the right form for these sentences.

1. Fiona	already watched has already watched	a film.
2. She	has watched watched	the film last week.
3. Stuart	has phoned phoned	Jim on Saturday.
4. Dad	has already bought already bought	the tickets.
5. I	didn't clean haven't cleaned	my bike yesterday.
6. Have you ever been Did you ever go		to Stirling?
7. Have you helped Did you help		Mum in the garden yesterday?

Fiona has already watched a film.

Language → G 6, p. 111

present perfect	simple past
already	last night
ever	on Saturday
yet	yesterday

Unit 3, p. 55

3 Words, words, words

a) Which word doesn't fit? Think of times, transportation, travelling.

1. train · bus · ticket · tram
2. stop · line · ticket · museum
3. at 5 p.m. · sure · late · early
4. ticket · timetable · map · diary

A: Ticket doesn't go with the other words. The other words are transportation words.
B: ___ doesn't go with the other words. The other words are ___ words.

Unit 3, p. 55

6 (SPEAKING) Find the way. → M Milling around, p. 122

a) Look at the map at the back of the book and find the best way to get from Goldenbridge to …

- George's Dock
- Trinity
- Blackhorse

Example: To get from Goldenbridge to George's Dock, take the Red Line.
It's eight stops. Get off the tram and you're there.

Stay on the tram for … stops.

Take the Green Line.

Take the Red Line for … .

Change at … and walk to … .

…

Unit 3, p. 56

○ 8 (WRITING) Find the right order.

a) Make sentences.

1. Jamie lost his … on 15th January • keys • at the snack bar
   Jamie lost his keys at the snack bar on 15th January.
2. Lisa left her … at the farm • bike • on 10th December
3. We lost our … dog • on 12th November • in the park
4. I left my … on 2nd January • at the supermarket • phone
5. My sister lost her … at the museum • laptop • on 27th December
6. My friend left his … saxophone • on the 5th January • at the shopping centre

Unit 3, p. 58

○ 1 (READING) Read the e-mails.

Alle neuen Wörter sind unterstrichen. Schlage sie in der Liste ab Seite 139 nach.

E-MAIL

Hi Julie,
Can you give me any advice? I'm really fed up. Mum and Dad don't have any time for me any more. They're busy with their new bed & breakfast. They work hard all day and in the evenings they're tired. We all had so much fun together back in Dublin. But now?
At the weekends Mum always tells me to tidy the house. But Ashley helps me a lot! Little brothers aren't always so bad. ☹
I know that I shouldn't say this, but I can't stand living in the B & B. There are new people every day and they always ask the same questions. Someone last week had a really strong American accent and I didn't understand anything.
It's not easy to make friends here. There's nobody who I can talk to. I miss you!
I have to go now. I think somebody rang the doorbell.

See you,
Linda ☺

E-MAIL

Hi Linda,
I miss you too. It's so boring here without you. There's nothing to do now.
Can't you talk to your parents? You can tell them how you feel and maybe they'll understand. Try and be positive. Speak to your dad first. I'm sure he will listen.
I don't think I'd like to live in a B & B. But think positive. New guests aren't always boring. Maybe they can tell you some interesting stories! Is there anybody at school that you can talk to? Make a list of good things that happen.
I'd like to visit you in our next holidays but I have to go to Cork with my family, so there's no chance.
Why don't you come to Dublin soon? I'm sure we can think of something amazing to do. There's a cool new snack bar in town where we can go.

I'll call you tomorrow.
Julie XOX

Unit 3, p. 58

3 (SPEAKING) What do you think? → M Double circle, p. 121

a) Talk about these questions.

1. Can you understand how Linda feels? Why? Why not?

I can understand how she feels I can't understand how she feels	because	her parents don't have time for her. she's new. she doesn't know a lot of people. she moved to an interesting place. she will meet new people. ....

2. Is Julie's advice OK? Why? Why not?

I think it's OK I think it's a problem / not so easy	because	Linda's dad is OK. Linda will learn a lot from the guests. .... her parents are very busy. there are new guests every day. ....

Unit 3, p. 59

5 Work with adjectives.

a) Make a table. Sort the adjectives. → M Bus stop, p. 120

sad ✓ angry funny worried happy positive unhappy

☺	☹
f ...	sad
h ...	a ...
p ...	w ...
	u ...

Unit 3, p. 60

8 Some, any or no?

a) Put in some, any or no.

In verneinten Aussagen und Fragen steht „any"!

1. I'd like to buy (**any**/**some**) comics.
   I'd like to buy some comics.
2. Did we get (**no**/**any**) homework yesterday?
3. Oh, no! I don't have (**any**/**no**) money!
4. Can you help me?
   I have (**some**/**no**) idea what to do.
5. I need (**no**/**some**) help with my project.
6. Sorry, there's (**any**/**no**) ice cream left.

Unit 4, p.77

2, 15

2 (READING) Read the blog about Wayne's trip around the USA.

INTERNET

Hi, everyone!

I'm still on vacation, my favorite time of the year! 👍 I met the Navajo people in Monument Valley on the weekend. It's a beautiful place. There are 500 tribes of Native Americans in the USA. The Navajo is one of the largest tribes in the USA.

I was really surprised when I heard that not all Navajo people have internet at home or at school. ☹ A lot of them live in reservations a long way from towns and cities so the internet is important to them. My Navajo friend, Atsa, told me that they are very interested in news from other Native people. Young people use social media for: sharing stories, information and funny videos, keeping in touch with each other, getting news from other reservations and also for posting photos of themselves. I often use social media for the same things. Usually I use my dad's old laptop but I bought my own tablet for this trip. Of course, the Navajo use different websites than me and my friends. I can't remember the names, but there is one that is the most important website for Native Americans. This website is more interesting than other famous US websites. It's the best to get the latest information about the Navajo and it's the least difficult one to use. Newspapers and TV are less popular than the internet for younger Navajo. American newspapers aren't interested in Native Americans and don't have many stories about them.

It's nearly 8:00 p.m. here now, 10:00 p.m. at home in Washington, and we're going to watch a movie in half an hour. Tomorrow it's the Grand Canyon! I'll write about my trip there on Thursday. And next week I'm going to go to the summer camp at Crystal Falls in Michigan.

This is the most exciting summer vacation I've ever had! ☺

Bye!

61/1

a) Correct the sentences.

1. Wayne went to the Grand Canyon on the weekend.
2. A lot of Navajo people live in towns and cities.
3. Atsa said that they are very interested in news from other countries.
4. Many younger Navajos use the internet only for sharing stories and videos.
5. They often read newspapers and watch TV.
6. American newspapers think stories about other Native people are exciting.

Unit 4, p. 79

8 (WRITING) Make a quiz. → M Bus stop, p. 120

a) Complete the questions about the USA.

1. Which state in the USA has ___ weather? (cold)
   Which state in the USA has the coldest weather?
2. Which is ___ sport in the USA? (popular)
3. Which is ___ state in the USA? (small)
4. Which is ___ city in the USA? (big)
5. Who is ___ Native American woman? (famous)

Grammar → G10, p. 115

-est	most
big	beautiful
cold	famous
small	popular

Die Lösungen findet ihr im Buch auf S. 199.

Unit 4, p. 81

5 Find the words.

a) Find the words in the story for the things (1–6) in the picture.

wa · pad · riv · heli · ro · ra · copter · cks · er · dle · ft · ve

1. ___   2. ___   3. ___

4. ___   5. ___   6. ___

Unit 4, p. 82

8 Complete the sentences.

a) Fill in much or many.

1. Wayne hasn't got ___ time today.
2. He has got so ___ things to do.
3. Did Wayne take ___ photos of the Grand Canyon?
4. I'm feeling hungry. I haven't had ___ to eat today.
5. The summer camp is great! There are so ___ fantastic activities.
6. How ___ money did the summer camp cost?
7. How ___ children are in the camp?
8. We didn't have ___ lunch yesterday.

Grammar → G11, p. 116

much	many
food	activities
homework	children
money	photos
time	things
lunch	

G1

Mit G sind die Grammatikkapitel gekennzeichnet und der Reihe nach durchnummeriert. Eine Übersicht über alle Themen findest du auf der nächsten Seite.

Beim Lupen-Symbol findest du Besonderheiten und Tipps.

(TEST YOURSELF)

Am Ende jedes Grammatikkapitels kannst du ausprobieren, ob du alles verstanden hast. Die Lösungen dazu findest du auf S. 117.

R = Revision (Wiederholung)

	Englisch	Deutsch	Beispiel	Seite
G1	**R:** simple past	einfache Vergangenheit	I helped my dad. She was in Stapleton. They didn't like the city. We weren't happy.	106
G2	**R:** simple present – statements – negatives	einfache Gegenwart – Aussagen – Verneinung	I like drama. I don't take the bus to school. He often rides his bike.	107
G3	**R:** simple present – questions – short answers	einfache Gegenwart – Fragen – Kurzantworten	Does she act in the play? Yes, she does. No, she doesn't.	108
G4	possessive pronouns	Possessivpronomen	Is this my hat? No, it's hers.	109
G5	going to-future	Zukunft mit going to	I'm going to play football tomorrow.	110
G6	present perfect – statements – negatives	Perfekt – Aussagen – Verneinung	I have already fed our dog. I haven't finished my homework yet.	111
G7	present perfect – questions – short answers	Perfekt – Fragen – Kurzantworten	Have you already made breakfast? No, I haven't. Has she ever been there? Yes, she has.	112
G8	words of place and time – word order	Orts- und Zeitangaben – Satzstellung	They watched a play at the theatre on Wednesday.	113
G9	indefinite pronouns – some, any, no	Indefinitpronomen – some, any, no	We have some water, but there's no milk. Do we have any cheese?	114
G10	comparative forms of adjectives – more, the most – less, the least	Steigerung der Adjektive – more, the most – less, the least	This is the most important website for Native Americans. It is more interesting than other websites. Newspapers are less popular than the internet. This is the least interesting game.	115
G11	expressions of quantity – much and many	Mengenangaben – much und many	There are many things to see. But we don't have much time.	116

Unit 1

G1 R: Die einfache Vergangenheit

Revision: The simple past

Um über Dinge zu sprechen, die in der Vergangenheit passiert und vorbei sind, verwendest du die einfache Vergangenheit (**simple past**).

Signalwörter	
yesterday	gestern
last month	letzten Monat
a week ago	vor einer Woche

Das **simple past** bildest du so:
Hänge die Endung **-ed** an das Verb.
Achte auf unregelmäßige Verben, z. B.
do → **did**; get → **got**; go → **went**

Eine Liste der unregelmäßigen Verben findest du auf den Seiten 118–119.

Tom **helped** his parents last week.	Letzte Woche half Tom seinen Eltern.
He **took** the bus to school yesterday.	Er nahm gestern den Bus zur Schule.

Um zu sagen, was nicht passiert ist, setzt du **didn't** (= did not) vor das Verb.

I **didn't watch** the match yesterday.	Ich schaute das Spiel gestern nicht an.
Tom's parents **didn't like** Sunderland.	Toms Eltern gefiel Sunderland nicht.

Aussagen und Verneinungen mit **be** bildest du so:

I **was** in London. I **wasn't** at home.	Ich war in London. Ich war nicht zu Hause.
Tom **wasn't** here. He **was** on the farm.	Tom war nicht hier. Er war auf der Farm.
The students **were** at the theatre. They **weren't** at the cinema.	Die Schüler waren im Theater. Sie waren nicht im Kino.

Und so kannst du im **simple past** Fragen stellen und beantworten:

Did you **have** a nice weekend?	Yes, I **did**.	No, I **didn't**.
When **did** you **visit** your aunt?	I **visited** her last month.	
Were you at home?	Yes, I **was**.	No, I **wasn't**.

(TEST YOURSELF) Put in the verbs in the simple past.

1. Hannah — (talk) to her cousin a week ago.
2. I — (not visit) a museum last month.
3. — you — (have) a nice day?
4. What — you — (do) yesterday?
5. Tom — (not be) at home last Friday.
6. — (be) you in Brighton last summer?

G2 R: Die einfache Gegenwart: Aussagen, Verneinung

Revision: The simple present: statements, negatives

Wenn du einen Zustand beschreiben möchtest oder sagen willst, dass jemand etwas gewohnheitsmäßig tut oder dass etwas häufig oder regelmäßig geschieht, verwendest du das **simple present**.

Signalwörter	
every Monday	jeden Montag
always	immer
usually	normalerweise
often	oft
sometimes	manchmal
never	nie

He, she, it, das s muss mit!

I sometimes	**ride** my bike.	Ich fahre manchmal Fahrrad.
You	**live** on a farm.	Du lebst / Ihr lebt auf einem Bauernhof.
He	**likes** Maths.	Er mag Mathe.
She	**feeds** her dog every day.	Sie füttert jeden Tag ihren Hund.
The computer	**works**.	Der Computer funktioniert.
We always	**eat** in the cafeteria.	Wir essen immer in der Mensa.
They often	**eat** pizza at break.	Sie essen in der Pause oft Pizza.

Mit **don't** oder **doesn't** (bei he, she, it) kannst du sagen, was man nicht macht.

I **don't live** in a village.	Ich wohne nicht in einem Dorf.
She **doesn't get** home before 6:00 p.m.	Sie kommt nicht vor 18 Uhr nach Hause.
They **don't bring** sandwiches every day.	Sie bringen nicht jeden Tag Brote mit.

So bildest du im **simple present** Aussagen und Verneinung mit **be**:

I	am	I	'm
he / she / it	is	he / she / it	's
we / you / they	are	we / you / they	're

(TEST YOURSELF) **Put in the verbs in the simple present.**

1. George usually —— (eat) in the cafeteria.
2. George's dad often —— (make) sandwiches.
3. I —— (not eat) pizza.
4. Tom —— (not like) the village.
5. There —— (be) many different school clubs.
6. George —— (be) from Stapleton.

G3 R: Die einfache Gegenwart: Fragen, Kurzantworten

Revision: The simple present: questions, short answers

Do you remember?

Um Fragen im **simple present** zu stellen, brauchst du bei Vollverben (z. B. eat, drink, play etc.) **do** oder **does**.

Du kannst solche Fragen mit Kurzantworten beantworten. Das ist besonders höflich!

Do you **like** Oxford?	Magst du Oxford?	Yes, I **do**.	No, I **don't**.
Does he **miss** London?	Vermisst er London?	Yes, he **does**.	No, he **doesn't**.
Does she **work** every day?	Arbeitet sie jeden Tag?	Yes, she **does**.	No, she **doesn't**.
Do you **get up** early?	Steht ihr früh auf?	Yes, we **do**.	No, we **don't**.
Do they **meet** after school?	Treffen sie sich nach der Schule?	Yes, they **do**.	No, they **don't**.

Bei Fragen mit Fragewörtern stellst du das Fragewort immer an die erste Stelle:

What do you **like**?	Was magst du?
When does Tom **have** breakfast?	Wann frühstückt Tom?

Where? = Wo?
Which? = Welche?
Who? = Wer?
Why? = Warum?

Fragen und Kurzantworten mit **be** bildest du so:

Are you often late?	Kommst du oft zu spät?	Yes, I **am**.	No, I'**m not**.
Is he from England?	Ist er aus England?	Yes, he **is**.	No, he **isn't**.
Are we in your team?	Sind wir in eurem Team?	Yes, you **are**.	No, you **aren't**.
Are they in our class?	Sind sie in unserer Klasse?	Yes, they **are**.	No, they **aren't**.

Vergleiche die beiden Fragen. Im Deutschen werden Fragen genauso gebildet.

George and Tom are in the classroom. → Are George and Tom in the classroom?

George and Tom are in the classroom. → Where are George and Tom?

(TEST YOURSELF) Make questions. Write short answers for 1–5.

1. you • to the park • often go • do (☺)
2. Tom • 13 years old • is (☹)
3. the boys • lunch • do • at school • have (☺)
4. like • football • Tom • does (☺)
5. Hannah • in a house • live • does (☹)
6. get home • when • you • after school • do
7. you • live • where • do
8. live • how many • in Stapleton • people

G4 Possessivpronomen

Possessive pronouns

This isn't his ball.
It's mine.

Das ist nicht sein Ball.
Das ist meiner.

Du kennst schon Possessivbegleiter (my, your, his, …). Sie stehen vor einem Nomen.
Mit den Possessivpronomen kannst du sagen, wem etwas gehört, wenn kein Nomen folgt.

Possessive determiner	**Possessive pronoun**	**Possessivbegleiter**	**Possessivpronomen**
That's **my** book.	It's **mine**.	Das ist mein Buch.	Es ist meins.
Is that **your** scarf?	Is it **yours**?	Ist das dein Schal?	Ist das deiner?
This is **his** bag.	It's **his**.	Das ist seine Tasche.	Das ist seine.
It isn't **her** pen.	It isn't **hers**.	Es ist nicht ihr Füller.	Es ist nicht ihrer.
They are **our** bikes.	They are **ours**.	Es sind unsere Fahrräder.	Es sind unsere.
Is this **your** room?	Is it **yours**?	Ist das euer Zimmer?	Ist das eures?
This is **their** ball.	It's **theirs**.	Das ist ihr Ball.	Das ist ihrer.

Vergleiche die beiden Formen:
my → mine
your → yours
her → hers
our → ours
your → yours
their → theirs

(TEST YOURSELF) **Choose the right word.**

1. Is this your exercise book?
   – No, it's **your** • **yours**.
2. That's a cool car. Is it really **their** • **theirs**?
3. Our T-shirts are green. **Your** • **Yours** are blue.
4. Your bag looks just like **my** • **mine**.
5. Did you put **her** • **hers** pen in your bag?
6. Is that Tom's goat?
   – Yes, it's **its** • **his**.

Unit 2

G5 Die Zukunft mit going to

The going to-future

I'm going to visit my friends in Cornwall tomorrow.

Ich werde morgen meine Freunde in Cornwall besuchen.

Wenn du sagen willst, was du vorhast oder planst, benutzt du das **going to-future**.

Im Deutschen gibt es mehrere Möglichkeiten, das **going to-future** zu übersetzen:
Du wirst etwas tun oder du planst, hast etwas vor oder beabsichtigst, etwas zu tun.

Signalwörter	
tomorrow	morgen
next week	nächste Woche
soon	bald

Aussagen im **going to-future** bildest du so: **am/is/are + going to + Verb.**

I **am** (I'm) **going to buy** a present.	Ich werde ein Geschenk kaufen.
You **are** (You're) **going to buy** a present.	Du planst / Ihr plant, ein Geschenk zu kaufen.
He **is** (He's) **going to buy** a present.	Er hat vor, ein Geschenk zu kaufen.
She **is** (She's) **going to buy** a present.	Sie wird ein Geschenk kaufen.
We **are** (We're) **going to buy** a present.	Wir werden ein Geschenk kaufen.
They **are** (They're) **going to buy** a present.	Sie planen, ein Geschenk zu kaufen.

So bildest du die Verneinung im **going to-future**:

I **am** (I'm) **not going to play** rugby.	Ich habe nicht vor, Rugby zu spielen.
He **is** (He's) **not going to play** rugby.	Er wird nicht Rugby spielen.
They **are** (They're) **not going to play** rugby.	Sie werden nicht Rugby spielen.

(TEST YOURSELF) Put in the verbs in the going to-future.

1. I — (feed) my cat later.
2. Mark's sister — (ride) on the zip line.
3. We — (make) a pizza this evening.
4. Mark and his friends — (take) photos.
5. Beth — (not try) rock climbing.
6. Mark — (not play) rugby.

G6 Das Perfekt: Aussagen, Verneinung

The present perfect: statements, negatives

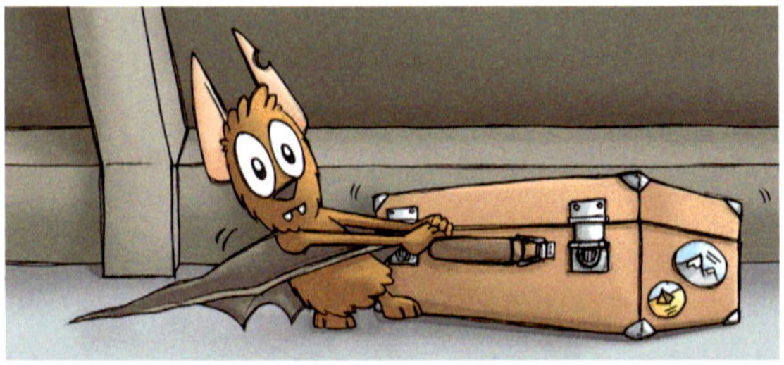

I've packed a lot of clothes.

Ich habe viele Kleider eingepackt.

Wenn eine Handlung in der Vergangenheit beginnt und in der Gegenwart zu einem Ergebnis führt, verwendest du das **present perfect**:
have/has + 3. Form des Verbs (past participle).
Bei den meisten Verben hängst du für die dritte Form ein **-ed** an das Verb: talk → **talked**

Signalwörter	
ever	jemals
yet	schon
already	schon
just	gerade

Einige Verben haben unregelmäßige dritte Formen:
go → went → **gone**, be → was/were → **been**

Eine Liste der unregelmäßigen Verben findest du auf den Seiten 118–119.

Es gibt Langformen und Kurzformen. Für I, you, we, they verwendest du **have** oder **'ve**.
Für he, she, it verwendest du **has** oder **'s**.

Langform	**Kurzform**	
I **have** just **started**.	I**'ve** just **started**.	Ich habe gerade angefangen.
He **has** just **left**.	He**'s** just **left**.	Er ist gerade gegangen.

Um Sätze zu verneinen, setzt du **haven't** (= **have not**) oder **hasn't** (= **has not**) vor die dritte Form.

I **haven't done** it yet.	Ich habe es noch nicht gemacht.
He **hasn't talked** to her yet.	Er hat noch nicht mit ihr gesprochen.

(TEST YOURSELF) Put in the verbs in the present perfect.

1. I — just — (clean) my bike.
2. She — already — (do) her homework.
3. They — (have) a picnic in the park.
4. I — already — (check) the prices.
5. He — (not ask) his sister yet.
6. We — (not go) on the zip line yet.

G7 Das Perfekt: Fragen, Kurzantworten

The present perfect: questions, short answers

Have you ever won a prize?

Hast du schon einmal einen Preis gewonnen?

Bei Fragen im **present perfect**, auf die man mit Ja oder Nein antwortet, steht **have** oder **has** am Satzanfang.
Auf diese Fragen kannst du höflich mit einer Kurzantwort antworten.

Signalwörter	
ever	jemals
yet	schon
already	schon

Have you ever **been** to Stirling?	Bist du / Seid ihr jemals in Stirling gewesen?	Yes, I/we **have**. No, I/we **haven't**.
Has Kirsty **had** breakfast yet?	Hat Kirsty schon gefrühstückt?	Yes, she **has**. No, she **hasn't**.
Have the Highland Games start**ed** already?	Haben die Highland Games schon angefangen?	Yes, they **have**. No, they **haven't**.

Bei Fragen mit Fragewörtern stellst du das Fragewort immer an die erste Stelle.

What **have** you **done** today, Fiona?	Was hast du heute gemacht, Fiona?
Which competitions **has** Fiona already watch**ed**?	Welche Wettkämpfe hat Fiona schon angeschaut?

Vergleiche die beiden Formen:

I / you / we / they → *have*

he / she / it → *has*

(TEST YOURSELF) Put in Has (2x), Have (2x) What has and Where have. Write short answers for 1–4.

1. ___ you seen hammer throwing before? (☺)
2. ___ Fiona called Kirsty yet? (☹)
3. ___ they ever done Highland dancing? (☹)
4. ___ Kirsty tidied her room yet? (☺)
5. ___ you been? – In the park.
6. ___ Kirsty bought? – Sandwiches.

Unit 3

G8 Orts- und Zeitangaben: Satzstellung

Words of place and time: word order

We had a picnic in the tree yesterday.

Gestern haben wir ein Picknick im Baum gemacht.

Wenn du sagen möchtest, wo und wann etwas passiert, verwendest du Orts- und Zeitangaben wie **in the park** und **today**.

Ortsangaben	Zeitangaben
at the bus stop	yesterday
at school	tomorrow
in the park	at 2:00 p.m.
near the supermarket	last weekend
in Dublin	in 2017

In Sätzen mit Orts- und Zeitangaben stellst du die Ortsangabe vor die Zeitangabe.

Jamie left his phone at home this morning. — Jamie vergaß heute morgen sein Telefon zu Hause.
Lisa will meet her sister in the park at 3:00 p.m. — Lisa trifft um 15 Uhr ihre Schwester im Park.

Ryan lost his laptop in the cafeteria at 12:30 p.m.

Ortsangabe (in the cafeteria) — Zeitangabe (at 12:30 p.m.)

(TEST YOURSELF) **Complete the sentences.**

1. Lisa met her friend —
   (at the cinema • on Saturday).
2. They are going to go shopping —
   (tomorrow • at the supermarket).
3. Lisa got off the bus —
   (near O'Connell Street • at 2:00 p.m.).
4. We will take the tram —
   (in the afternoon • from Goldenbridge).
5. Did you see my exercise book —
   (in the classroom • last Friday)?
6. Will you go —
   (in the summer • to Ireland)?

G9 Indefinitpronomen: Some, any und no

Indefinite pronouns: Some, any and no

I've just bought some balloons for my party. But now I don't have any money for a cake.

Ich habe gerade Luftballons für meine Party gekauft. Aber jetzt habe ich kein Geld mehr für einen Kuchen.

In positiven Aussagesätzen benutzt du **some**. Es muss nicht immer übersetzt werden.

The guests have **some** questions.	Die Gäste haben (ein paar) Fragen.
Julie spends **some** time in Cork.	Julie verbringt (etwas) Zeit in Cork.

In verneinten Aussagen und in den meisten Fragen steht **any**. Es muss auch nicht immer übersetzt werden.

I didn't find **any** maps.	Ich habe keine Karten gefunden.
Do you need **any** milk?	Braucht ihr (etwas) Milch?

Vor Nomen benutzt man in verneinten Aussagesätzen oft **no**. Es verstärkt die Verneinung. **No** steht nie zusammen mit **not**.

We have **no** guests in February.	Wir haben im Februar keine Gäste.

Die gleichen Regeln gelten für Zusammensetzungen (compounds) mit **some** und **any**:
Something (etwas), **(not) anything** und **nothing** (nichts) benutzt du für Dinge.
Somebody (jemand), **(not) anybody** und **nobody** (niemand) benutzt du für Personen.

He told me **something**.	Er hat mir etwas erzählt.
I don't want to buy **anything** expensive.	Ich möchte nichts Teures kaufen.
Would **anybody** like to come with me?	Möchte jemand mit mir mitkommen?
There's **nothing** to do here.	Es gibt hier nichts zu tun.

(TEST YOURSELF) Put in some or any.

1. Let's buy ___ food for Friday.
2. Is there ___ food in your bag?
3. There isn't ___ chocolate here.
4. I didn't buy ___ bananas at the market.
5. We have ___ fruit at home.
6. We don't have ___ ice cream. Sorry!

Unit 4

G10 Steigerung der Adjektive mit more, the most und less, the least

Comparative forms of adjectives with more, the most and less, the least

This is the most beautiful beach in the USA.

Das ist der schönste Strand der Vereinigten Staaten.

Du kennst schon die 1. und 2. Steigerung von Adjektiven zum Vergleich von Personen, Tieren oder Dingen mit **-er** und **-est.**
Für die 1. Steigerung bei längeren Adjektiven bildest du Vergleiche mit **more ... than** und **less ... than.**

This website is **more interesting than** other websites. — Diese Website ist interessanter als andere Websites.
TV is **less popular than** the internet. — Fernsehen ist weniger beliebt als das Internet.

Für die 2. Steigerung verwendest du bei längeren Adjektiven **the most** und **the least.**

Längere Adjektive haben zwei Silben oder mehr.

It is **the most important** website for Native Americans. — Es ist die wichtigste Website für die amerikanischen Ureinwohner.
Which is **the least expensive** tablet? — Welches Tablet kostet am wenigsten?

Vergleiche die verschiedenen Steigerungsformen:

small	→ small*er*	→ the small*est*
expensive	→ *more* expensive	→ the *most* expensive
boring	→ *less* boring	→ the *least* boring

(TEST YOURSELF) Put in more/most (☺) or less/least (☹).

1. American football is —— popular than soccer in the USA. (☺)
2. I think that Tower Bridge in London is —— famous than the Statue of Liberty. (☹)
3. What do you think is the —— amazing sight in New York? (☺)
4. The Space and Rocket Center is —— interesting than any other museum. (☺)
5. A trip to Huntsville is —— expensive than a trip to Chicago. (☹)
6. Those smartphones are the —— expensive phones in this shop. (☹)

G11 Mengenangaben: much und many

Expressions of quantity: much and many

We have many eggs, but we don't have much butter.

Wir haben viele Eier, aber wir haben nicht viel Butter.

Much und **many** sind Mengenangaben.

Did you see **many** animals?	Hast du / Habt ihr viele Tiere gesehen?
We didn't have **much** time.	Wir hatten nicht viel Zeit.

Many (viele) verwendest du mit zählbaren Nomen (countable nouns) in der Mehrzahl, z. B. people, friends, things, animals.

You can do **many** exciting things at the summer camp.	Man kann im Feriencamp viele spannende Dinge machen.
How **many** times did you go rafting?	Wie oft seid ihr raften gegangen?
Many teens were there.	Viele Jugendliche waren dort.

Much (viel) verwendest du mit nicht zählbaren Nomen (uncountable nouns) in der Einzahl, z. B. water, rain, time, money.

We didn't have **much** rain.	Wir hatten nicht viel Regen.
How **much** money did you spend?	Wie viel Geld hast du / habt ihr ausgegeben?

many – people, friends, animals, trees

much – water, rain, time, money

(TEST YOURSELF) Put in much or many.

1. We don't have — time for lunch today.
2. Are there — tourists at the Grand Canyon?
3. Wayne wanted to do — exciting activities.
4. Did you have — snow this winter?
5. They didn't take — money with them.
6. Did you take — photos?

Lösungen

TEST YOURSELF

G1
1. talked
2. didn't visit
3. Did … have
4. did … do
5. wasn't
6. Were

G2
1. eats
2. makes
3. don't eat
4. doesn't like
5. are
6. is

G3
1. Do you often go to the park?
   – Yes, I/we do.
2. Is Tom 13 years old?
   – No, he isn't.
3. Do the boys have lunch at school?
   – Yes, they do.
4. Does Tom like football?
   – Yes, he does.
5. Does Hannah live in a house?
   – No, she doesn't.
6. When do you get home after school?
7. Where do you live?
8. How many people live in Stapleton?

G4
1. yours
2. theirs
3. Yours
4. mine
5. her
6. his

G5
1. am going to feed
2. is going to ride
3. are going to make
4. are going to take
5. is not going to try
6. is not going to play

G6
1. have … cleaned
2. has … done
3. have had
4. have … checked
5. hasn't asked (has not asked)
6. haven't gone (have not gone)

G7
1. Have; Yes, I have.
2. Has; No, she hasn't.
3. Have; No, they haven't.
4. Has; Yes, she has.
5. Where have
6. What has

G8
1. Lisa met her friend at the cinema on Saturday.
2. They are going to go shopping at the supermarket tomorrow.
3. Lisa got off the bus near O'Connell Street at 2:00 p.m.
4. We will take the tram from Goldenbridge in the afternoon.
5. Did you see my exercise book in the classroom last Friday?
6. Will you go to Ireland in the summer?

G9
1. some
2. any
3. any
4. any
5. some
6. any

G10
1. more
2. less
3. most
4. more
5. less
6. least

G11
1. much
2. many
3. many
4. much
5. much
6. many

List of irregular verbs

Hier findest du alle unregelmäßigen Verben, die im Buch vorkommen. Die Liste enthält jeweils alle drei Formen, auch wenn sie noch nicht alle in den Units vorgekommen sind.

infinitive	simple past	past participle	German
to be [biː]	was, were [wɒz, wɜː]	been [biːn]	sein
to become [bɪˈkʌm]	became [bɪˈkeɪm]	become [bɪˈkʌm]	werden
to begin [bɪˈgɪn]	began [bɪˈgæn]	begun [bɪˈgʌn]	beginnen; anfangen
to bring [brɪŋ]	brought [brɔːt]	brought [brɔːt]	(mit)bringen
to build [bɪld]	built [bɪlt]	built [bɪlt]	bauen
to buy [baɪ]	bought [bɔːt]	bought [bɔːt]	kaufen
to catch [kætʃ]	caught [kɔːt]	caught [kɔːt]	(ein)fangen; nehmen
to cost [kɒst]	cost [kɒst]	cost [kɒst]	kosten
to choose [tʃuːz]	chose [tʃəʊz]	chosen [ˈtʃəʊzn]	(aus)wählen
to do [duː]	did [dɪd]	done [dʌn]	machen; tun
to drink [drɪŋk]	drank [dræŋk]	drunk [drʌŋk]	trinken
to drive [draɪv]	drove [drəʊv]	driven [ˈdrɪvn]	fahren; treiben
to eat [iːt]	ate [eɪt]	eaten [ˈiːtn]	essen
to fall [fɔːl]	fell [fel]	fallen [ˈfɔːln]	fallen
to feel [fiːl]	felt [felt]	felt [felt]	(sich) (an)fühlen; empfinden; glauben
to fight [faɪt]	fought [fɔːt]	fought [fɔːt]	kämpfen; (sich) streiten
to find [faɪnd]	found [faʊnd]	found [faʊnd]	finden
to fly [flaɪ]	flew [fluː]	flown [fləʊn]	fliegen
to forget [fəˈget]	forgot [fəˈgɒt]	forgotten [fəˈgɒtn]	vergessen
to get [get]	got [gɒt]	got [gɒt]	bekommen; werden; kommen
to give [gɪv]	gave [geiv]	given [ˈgɪvn]	geben; schenken; halten
to go [gəʊ]	went [went]	gone [gɒn]	gehen; fahren
to have [hæv]	had [hæd]	had [hæd]	haben; besitzen
to hear [hɪə]	heard [hɜːd]	heard [hɜːd]	hören
to hit [hɪt]	hit [hɪt]	hit [hɪt]	schlagen; treffen
to hold [həʊld]	held [held]	held [held]	(fest)halten
to hurt [hɜːt]	hurt [hɜːt]	hurt [hɜːt]	verletzen; wehtun
to keep [kiːp]	kept [kept]	kept [kept]	(be)halten; aufbewahren; belassen
to leave [liːv]	left [left]	left [left]	(ver)lassen; abfahren; weggehen; vergessen; hinterlassen
to lose [luːz]	lost [lɒst]	lost [lɒst]	verlieren
to make [meɪk]	made [meɪd]	made [meɪd]	machen; tun; bilden
to mean [miːn]	meant [ment]	meant [ment]	bedeuten; meinen
to meet [miːt]	met [met]	met [met]	(sich) treffen
to put [pʊt]	put [pʊt]	put [pʊt]	setzen; legen; stellen

infinitive	simple past	past participle	German
to read [riːd]	read [red]	read [red]	(vor)lesen
to ride [raɪd]	rode [rəʊd]	ridden ['rɪdn]	fahren; reiten
to ring [rɪŋ]	rang [ræŋ]	rung [rʌŋ]	klingeln
to run [rʌn]	ran [ræn]	run [rʌn]	laufen; rennen
to say [seɪ]	said [sed]	said [sed]	sagen; sprechen; nennen; nachsprechen
to see [siː]	saw [sɔː]	seen [siːn]	sehen
to sell [sel]	sold [səʊld]	sold [səʊld]	verkaufen
to sing [sɪŋ]	sang [sæŋ]	sung [sʌŋ]	singen
to sit [sɪt]	sat [sæt]	sat [sæt]	(sich) (hin)setzen; sitzen
to sleep [sliːp]	slept [slept]	slept [slept]	schlafen
to spend [spend]	spent [spent]	spent [spent]	verbringen; ausgeben
to stand [stænd]	stood [stʊd]	stood [stʊd]	stehen; ertragen; ausstehen
to swing [swɪŋ]	swung [swʌŋ]	swung [swʌŋ]	schwingen
to take [teɪk]	took [tʊk]	taken ['teɪkn]	nehmen; (hin)bringen; dauern; brauchen
to tell [tel]	told [təʊld]	told [təʊld]	erzählen; sagen
to think [θɪŋk]	thought [θɔːt]	thought [θɔːt]	denken; glauben
to throw [θrəʊ]	threw [θruː]	thrown [θrəʊn]	werfen
to understand [ˌʌndə'stænd]	understood [ˌʌndə'stʊd]	understood [ˌʌndə'stʊd]	verstehen
to wake up [ˌweɪk‿'ʌp]	woke up [ˌwəʊk‿'ʌp]	woken up [ˌwəʊkn‿'ʌp]	aufwachen; erwachen; aufwecken
to wear [weə]	wore [wɔː]	worn [wɔːn]	anhaben; tragen
to win [wɪn]	won [wʌn]	won [wʌn]	gewinnen
to write [raɪt]	wrote [rəʊt]	written ['rɪtn]	schreiben

1-minute-presentation

(Kurzpräsentation)

Step 1

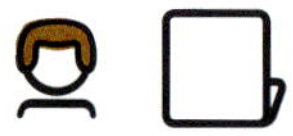

Nimm ein Blatt Papier im DIN A4-Format quer und falte es so, dass das untere Drittel nach hinten wegknickt.

Step 2

Schreibe den Vortragstext auf die oberen zwei Drittel.

Step 3

Streiche nun die wichtigsten Stichpunkte im Text an.
Notiere sie noch einmal auf dem unteren Drittel.
Das ist dein Spickzettel.

Step 4

In deiner Präsentation verwendest du nur den Spickzettel. Wenn du steckenbleibst, darfst du ihn umknicken und kurz auf den Text oben schauen.

Bus stop

(Lerntempoduett)

Step 1

Bearbeite die Aufgabe zunächst allein.
Schreibe deine Lösungen auf.

Step 2

Wenn du fertig bist, gehe zum „bus stop". Entweder wartet dort schon jemand oder du wartest dort auf die nächste Person. Vergleicht und korrigiert eure Ergebnisse zu zweit.

Step 3

Gehe danach wieder zu deinem Platz zurück.
Bearbeite die nächste Aufgabe.

Double circle

(Kugellager)

Step 1

Teilt euch in zwei Gruppen A und B auf.
Gruppe A bildet den inneren Kreis. Gruppe B bildet den äußeren Kreis. Steht dabei so, dass ihr euch anseht.

Step 2

Wenn ein Signal ertönt, sprecht ihr mit der Person, die euch gegenübersteht.

Step 3

Beim nächsten Signal rückt der innere Kreis zwei Plätze weiter nach rechts. Wiederholt den Vorgang.

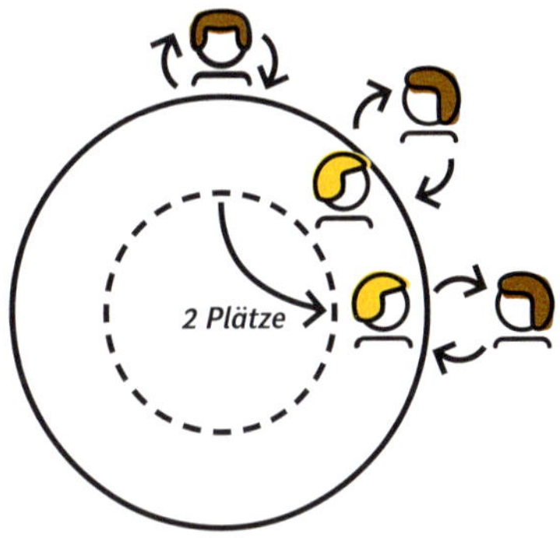

Freeze frame

(Standbild)

Step 1

Entscheidet euch in der Gruppe, welche Szene oder Personen ihr darstellen wollt. Verteilt die Rollen.

Step 2

Probiert verschiedene Standbilder aus und entscheidet euch dann für eines. Denkt daran: Ihr müsst euer Standbild eine Minute lang durchhalten. Keiner darf sich bewegen oder etwas sagen.

Step 3

Präsentiert der Klasse euer Standbild. Die anderen beschreiben, was sie sehen.

Gallery walk

(Galerierundgang)

Step 1

Hängt nach eurer Gruppenarbeit eure Produkte gut sichtbar im Klassenzimmer auf.

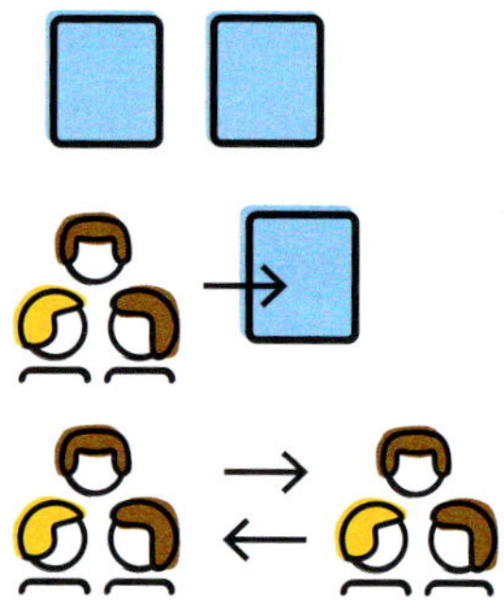

Step 2

Ein „Experte“ aus jeder Gruppe bleibt bei dem Produkt stehen und erklärt es den anderen. Der Rest der Gruppe geht im Klassenzimmer herum. Nach jedem Durchgang wechselt der Experte.

Step 3

Seht euch die Produkte der anderen an und bewertet sie.

Step 4

Wertet im Anschluss eure Ergebnisse in der Klasse aus.

Milling around

(Marktplatz)

Step 1

Bearbeite die Aufgabe zunächst allein.

Step 2

Auf ein Zeichen von eurem Lehrer oder eurer Lehrerin steht ihr auf und geht durch den Raum.
Vergesst nicht, die Aufgabe und einen Stift mitzunehmen.

Step 3

Wenn ein Signal ertönt, bleibt ihr stehen. Besprecht die Aufgabe mit der Person, die euch am nächsten steht.

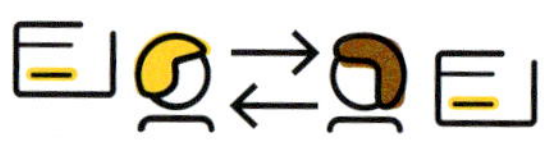

Step 4

Beim nächsten Signal trennt ihr euch und geht weiter durch den Raum. Wiederholt den Vorgang.

Peer correction
(Partnerkontrolle)

Step 1
Bearbeite die Aufgabe zunächst selbstständig.

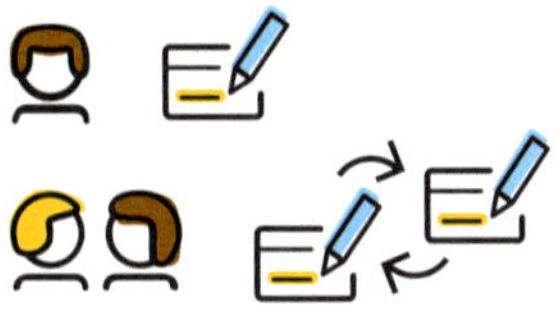

Step 2
Tausche deine Lösungen mit einem Partner oder einer Partnerin. Kontrolliere seine oder ihre Lösungen.

Step 3
Vergleicht eure Lösungen und korrigiert sie dann gemeinsam.

Placemat
(Platzdeckchen)

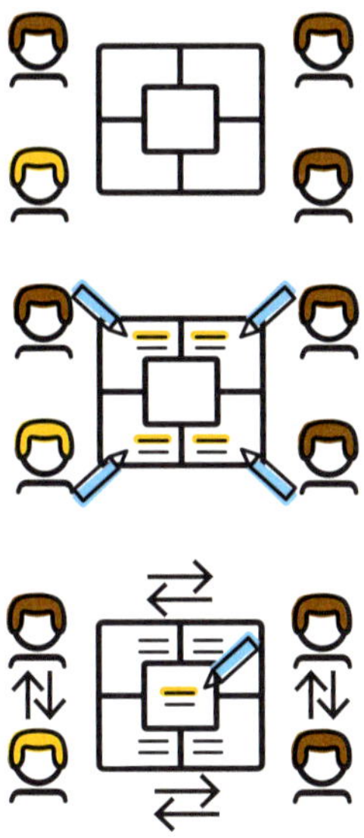

Step 1
Bildet Vierergruppen.

Step 2
Teilt ein großes Blatt Papier in fünf Bereiche ein.

Step 3
Setzt euch so hin, dass alle jeweils in eine Ecke des Blattes schreiben können.

Step 4
Jedes Gruppenmitglied denkt allein über das Thema nach und schreibt Ideen auf seinen Teil des Blattes.

Step 5
Tauscht euch über die Ideen aus. Einigt euch auf die besten Ideen und schreibt diese in die Mitte des Blattes.

Round robin

(Blitzlicht)

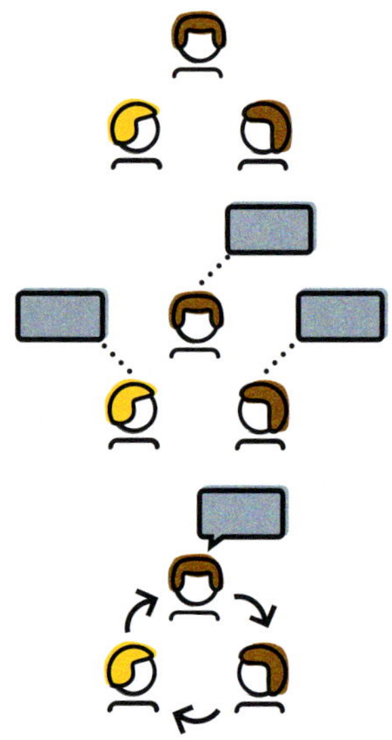

Step 1
Bildet Gruppen und setzt euch in einen Kreis.

Step 2
Jedes Gruppenmitglied überlegt sich kurz einen Satz, der seine persönliche Meinung zum Thema ausdrückt.

Step 3
Wenn alle bereit sind, sagen die Gruppenmitglieder der Reihe nach ihre Meinung.

Step 4
Die anderen Gruppenmitglieder dürfen die Sätze nicht kommentieren.

Think – pair – share

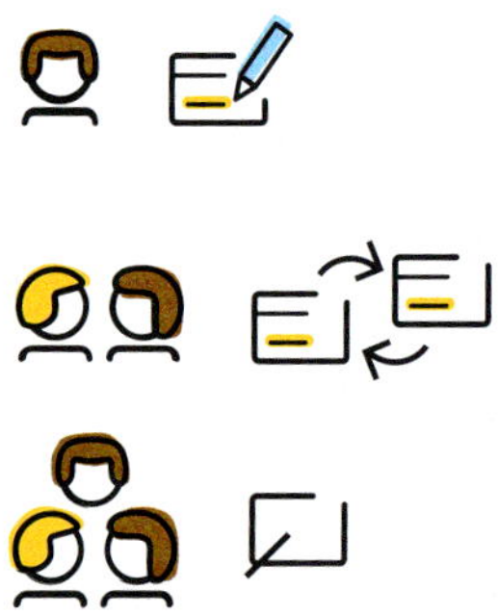

Step 1
Schreibe deine Ideen, Gedanken oder Lösungen zur Aufgabe auf.

Step 2
Tauscht euch zu zweit aus und besprecht eure Notizen.

Step 3
Präsentiert euer Ergebnis anderen Paaren oder der gesamten Klasse.

Tip top

Step 1
Sage zunächst, was dir gut gefallen hat – was „top" war.

Step 2
Sage nun, was noch nicht so gut war, und gib einen Tipp, was man noch verbessern könnte.

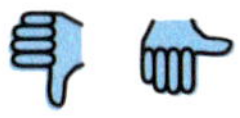

Walking sentences
(Laufende Sätze)

Step 1
Nehmt eine Karte. Ihr findet darauf ein Wort und/oder ein Satzzeichen.

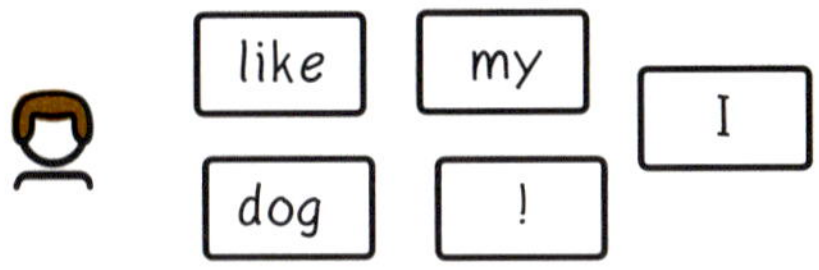

Step 2
Wenn ein Signal ertönt, geht durch die Klasse und bildet vollständige Sätze.
Stellt euch dazu in der richtigen Reihenfolge auf. Haltet eure Karten vor euch, so dass alle sie lesen können.

Step 3
Lest euren Satz vor und schreibt ihn auf.

Writers' conference
(Schreibwerkstatt)

Step 1
Bildet Dreier- oder Vierergruppen.

Step 2
Lest euch eure Sätze/Texte gegenseitig vor.

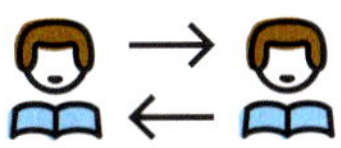

Step 3
Die Zuhörer sagen, was ihnen gefallen hat, und können Verbesserungsvorschläge machen.

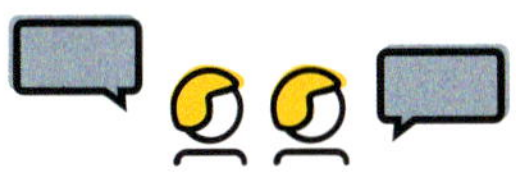

Step 4
Jede Gruppe wählt den besten Text aus und liest ihn der Klasse vor.

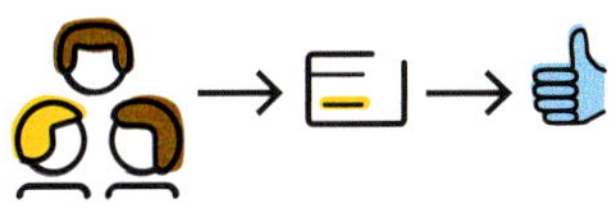

Vocabulary tips

Du kennst schon einige Tipps und Tricks zum Vokabellernen. Erinnerst du dich? Hier gibt es weitere Tipps.

Lerntipp: Englisch im Alltag

Achte auf alle englischen Wörter, die dir begegnen. Ob im Supermarkt, im Fernsehen, in Büchern, auf Werbeplakaten oder auf Schildern am Bahnhof, Flughafen etc.:
Du wirst überrascht sein, wie oft man im Alltag auf die englische Sprache stößt. Das ist ein gutes Training, um noch unbekannte Vokabeln zu lernen. Dazu kannst du dir die Vokabeln aufschreiben oder sie abfotografieren. Nimm sie so oft wie möglich mit, vor allem, wenn du verreist! Die noch unbekannten Wörter kannst du dann zu Hause in einem Wörterbuch nachschlagen. Da du mit jedem Wort eine kleine Geschichte oder bestimmte Situation verbindest (z. B. „Ach ja! Dieses Wort habe ich am Bahnhof gesehen / im Kino gehört."), wirst du es dir leicht merken können!

Wortbildung

Es gibt verschiedene Möglichkeiten, um aus einem Verb ein Nomen abzuleiten.

1. Du kannst die Endung *-ing* anhängen:
   to build → a building
   to feel → a feeling
2. Manche Nomen werden mit der Endung *-er* oder *-or* gebildet.
   Solche Nomen bezeichnen meistens eine Person:
   to play → a player
   to sing → a singer
   to visit → a visitor
3. Es gibt auch die Endung *-ion*:
   to collect → a collection
4. Sehr oft haben auch Verb und Nomen dieselbe Form:
   to answer → an answer
   to drink → a drink

Diese Checkliste kann dir helfen, Fehler zu vermeiden und deine Rechtschreibung zu verbessern. Prüfe alle deine Texte damit.

- **Schreibung:**
- ☐ *gh* wird meist nicht gesprochen. Vergiss es beim Schreiben nicht.
- ☐ *k* kommt vor *t* so gut wie nie vor, z. B. activity – Aktivität, October – Oktober

- **Gleiche Aussprache, unterschiedliche Schreibung:**
- ☐ [iː] z. B. teacher, to meet, tea, Chinese, people, field
- ☐ [uː] z. B. food, fruit, to do, flew, supermarket, barbecue, beautiful

- **Gleiche Aussprache, unterschiedliche Schreibung und Bedeutung:**
- ☐ [iː] z. B. see – sehen, sea – Meer
- ☐ [uː] z. B. two – zwei, too – auch

- **Verdoppelung der Endkonsonanten:**
- ☐ to stop – stopping, stopped
- ☐ to win – winning, winner

- **y wird zu ie:**
- ☐ in der 3. Person Singular: z. B. to worry – he worries; **aber**: to buy – she buys
- ☐ im Plural: z. B. city – cities, party – parties; **aber**: boy – boys
- ☐ bei der Steigerung von Adjektiven: z. B. happy – happier – (the) happiest; easy – easier – (the) easiest

- **Ähnlich und doch anders:**
- ☐ Wortendung *le*: z. B. title – Titel; middle – Mittel
- ☐ *ph* statt *f*: z. B. phone – Telefon; photo – Foto

- **Großschreibung:**
- ☐ Monatsnamen: z. B. January, July, December
- ☐ Wochentage: z. B. Monday, Wednesday, Saturday
- ☐ Eigennamen: z. B. Tom, Lisa, the Brooks, the London Eye, the Thames
- ☐ geografische Namen: Bristol, Greenwich, Germany, Italy

- **Plural:**
- ☐ Der Plural bekommt normalerweise ein *s*: z. B. friend – friends, chair – chairs, film – films
- ☐ Endet ein Wort auf *s* oder *x*, wird *es* angehängt: z. B. bus – buses, box – boxes
- ☐ Manche Wörter haben einen unregelmäßigen Plural: z. B. man – men, child – children, shelf – shelves, mouse – mice

- **Apostroph:**
- ☐ bei Kurzformen: z. B. she is → she's; they are → they're
- ☐ beim Genitiv-s: z. B. Sam's bike, Emma's family, the Jacksons' house, the children's games

- **Wörterbuch:**
- ☐ Prüfe die Schreibung aller Wörter, bei denen du dir nicht ganz sicher bist, indem du sie im Wörterbuch nachschlägst.

Word banks

Online kannst du hören, wie man die Wörter ausspricht.

Word bank: Where I live

→ Find more online ry3j5e

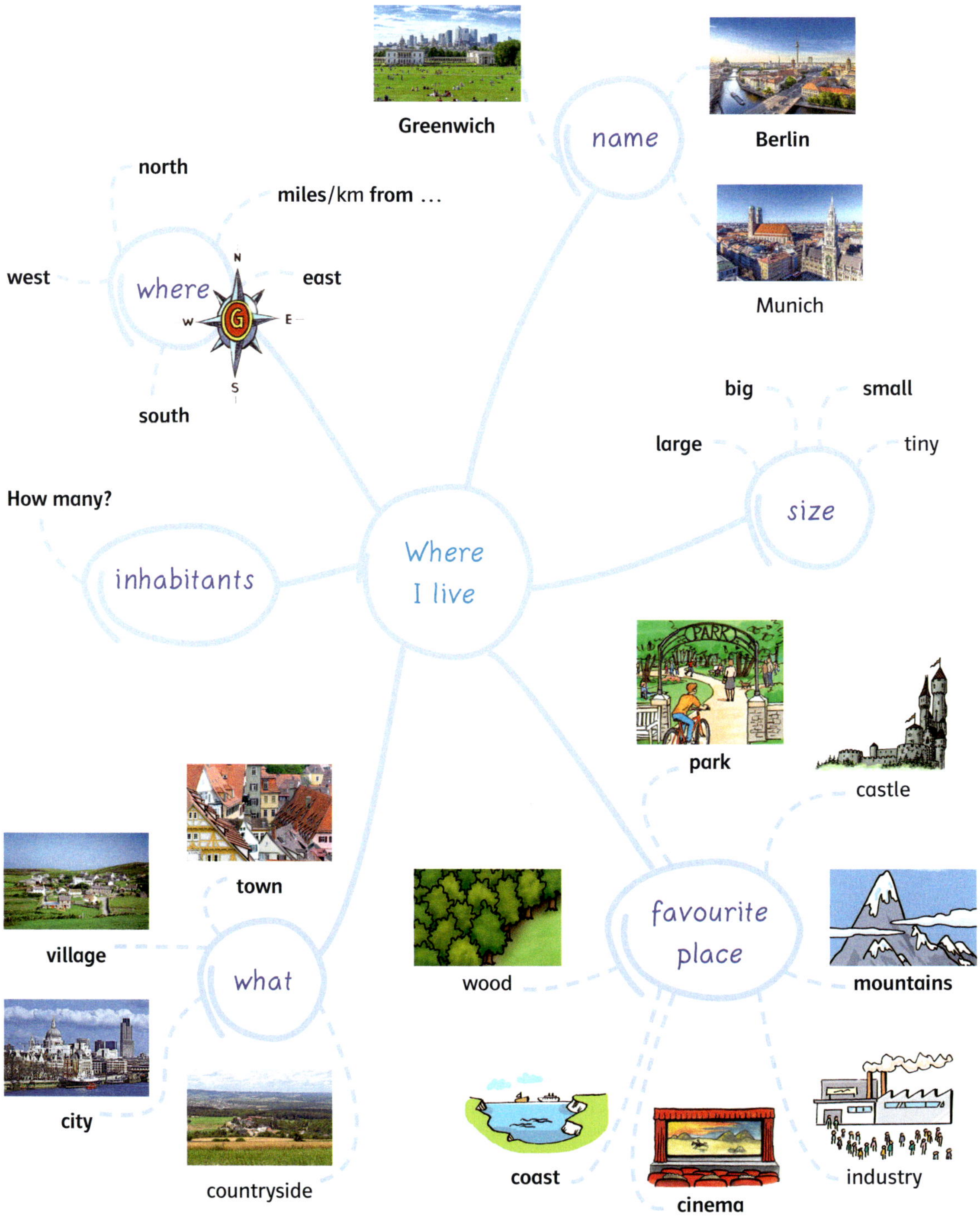

Word bank: **School day** → Find more online ry3j5e

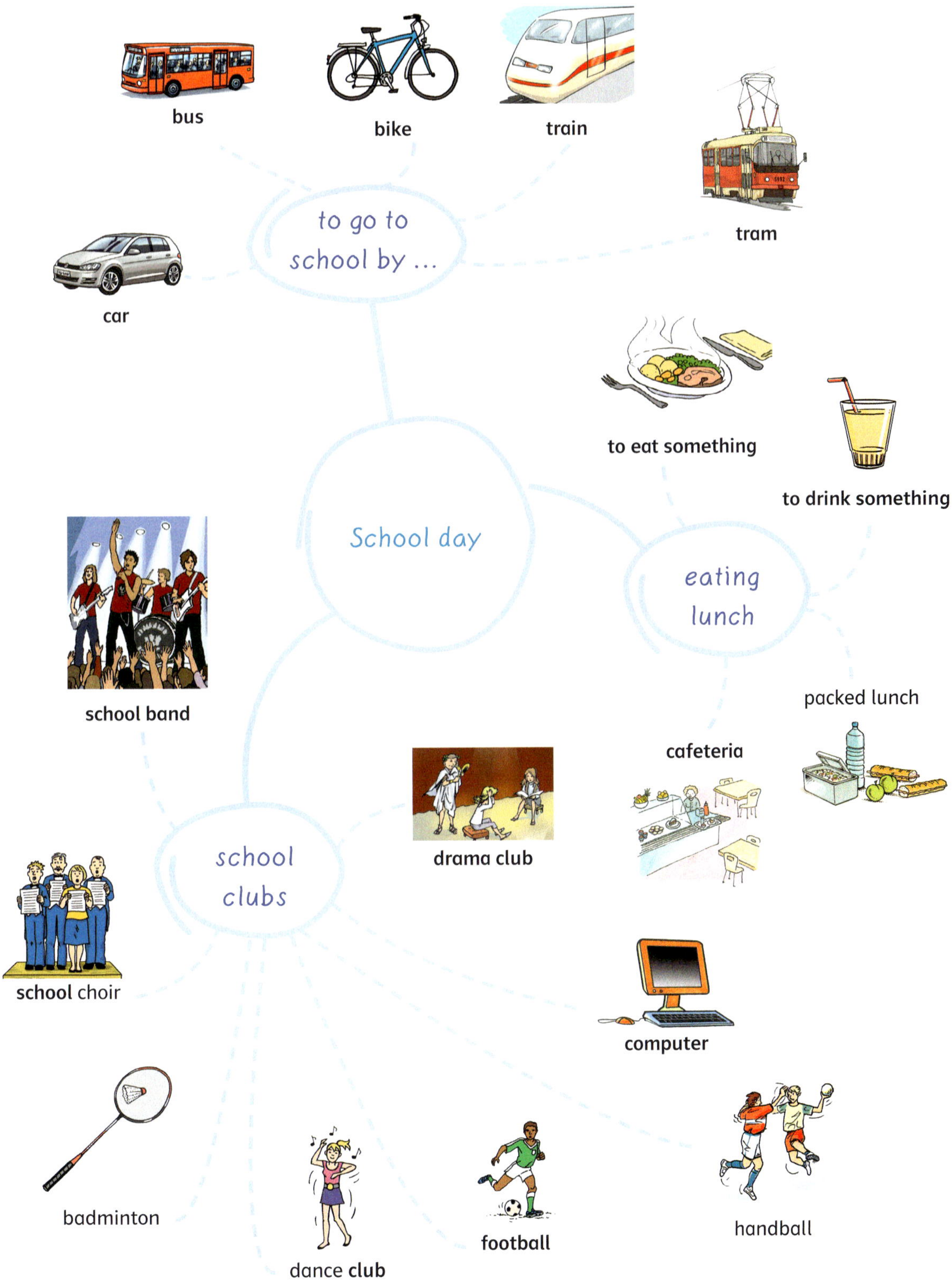

Word bank: **City guide** → Find more online ry3j5e

skyscraper

cathedral

tower

museum

gallery

station

bridge

building

monument

Don't miss ....
Straight ahead **are** ....
You must visit ....
In the distance **you can see** ....
Have a look at / **Look at** ....
Make sure **you visit** ....

I'd like to point out ....
From here ....
... **built it in** ....
It opened **in** ....
It is special because ....

Word bank: **Sports and activities**

→ Find more online ry3j5e

Water sports

swimming

surfing

windsurfing

canoeing

rafting

Ball sports

rugby

football

netball

handball

basketball

Winter sports

skiing

snowboarding

ice skating

Athletics

high jump

long jump

running

Racket sports

tennis

badminton

squash

Equipment

bat

racket

paddle

waterproofs

ball

goggles

helmet

Activities

to ride a bike

to go rock climbing

to do skateboard tricks

to go jogging

to go hiking

Word bank: **What time is it?** → Find more online ry3j5e

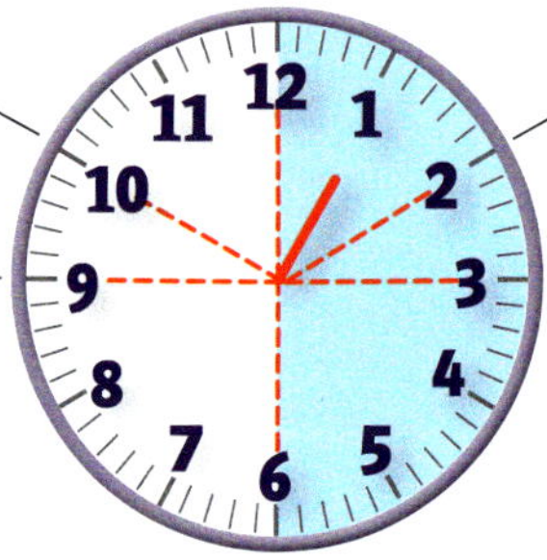

PAST

TO

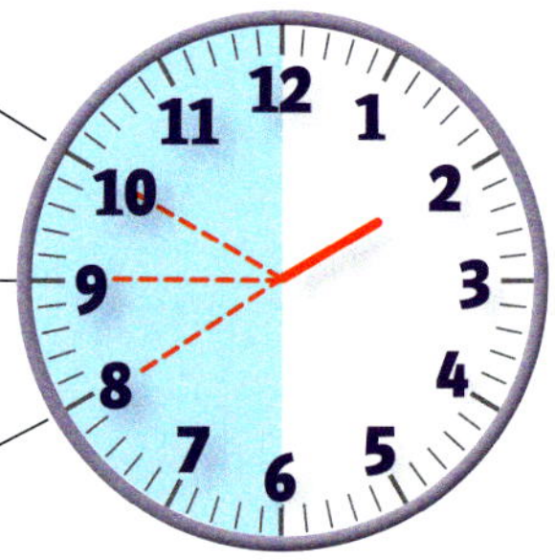

a.m. = 0:00 – 12:00	(in the) morning
p.m. = 12:00 – 0:00	(in the) afternoon
	(in the) evening
	(at) night

a second → a minute → an hour → a day → a week → a month → a year

Word bank: **Have you ever . . . ?** → Find more online ry3j5e

Can I ask you some questions, please?	Yes, of course.
Have you ever lived in a different country?	Yes, I have. No, I haven't.
Have you ever been to . . . ?	I've been to . . . .
Have you ever been to a concert? Have you ever met a film or pop star?	Yes, I have. I've been to / met . . . . No, I haven't.
Have you ever eaten sushi?	Yes, I have. It was yummy/ disgusting/ . . . . No, I haven't, but I'd like to try it. No, I haven't and I don't want to try it.
Thanks for your time. Thanks for the interview. That was really interesting. Have a good day.	You're welcome. No problem. It was interesting.

Word bank: Public transport → Find more online ry3j5e

Public transport

underground

train

bus

tram

taxi

ferry

station

stop

Directions

to turn right

to turn left

to go straight on

at the traffic lights

You should take ....
Use the ... line.
Travel northbound/southbound/westbound/eastbound.
Then ....
It stops at ....
You must/have to buy ....

It costs ....
The bus fare isn't very expensive.
You can buy a single ticket/a return ticket.
Change buses/trains at ....
Check the timetable for the times of the buses.

Word bank: **Giving advice** → Find more online ry3j5e

I have a good idea.

That's great.

Think positive.

That's good news.

That's a good idea.

That sounds good.

That's nice.

That's terrible.

That's horrible.

That's a bad idea.

That sounds awful.

That's not very nice.

Why don't you ...?
You can always ....
Can't you ...?
Maybe you should ....

How about ...?
Call me later.
Let's talk about it later / tomorrow / after school / ....
Let's speak soon.

Word bank: **Picture description / Prepositions** → Find more online ry3j5e

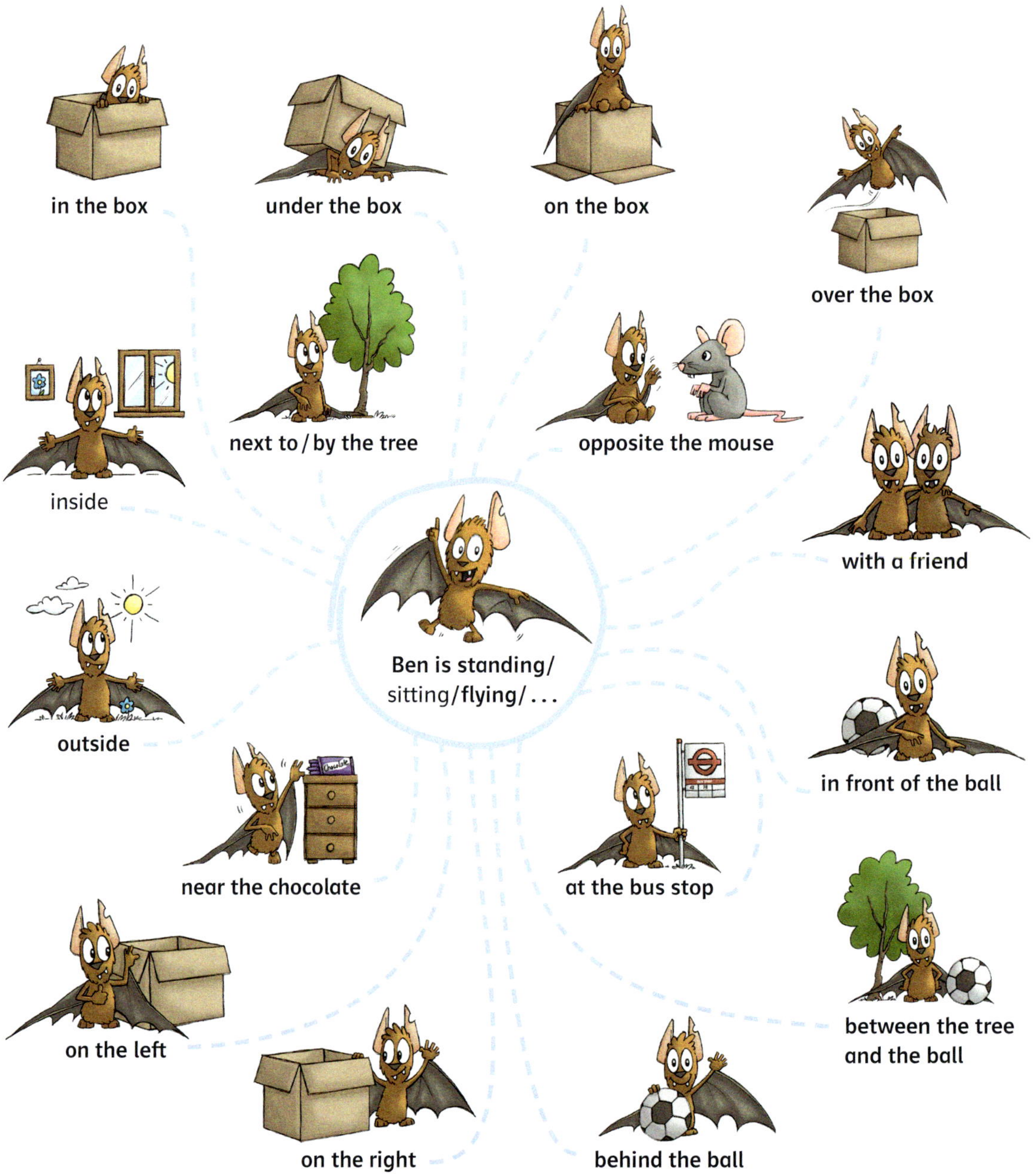

Words for describing pictures:

in the picture	at the top
in the middle	at the bottom
in the foreground	I can see ....
in the background	There is/are ....

Word bank: **Social media and technology** → Find more online ry3j5e

to talk on the phone

to play computer games

to watch TV

to listen to music

Social media and technology

to chat online

to take photos

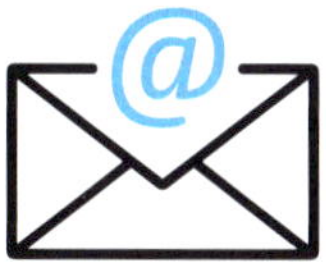
to write an e-mail

to write a message

to surf the internet

to save a file

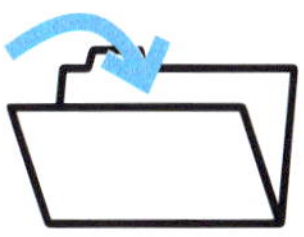

Talking about social media

I'd like to download **this** app.
I change my profile **photo every week.**
Voice messages **are becoming more and more popular.**

The police found the cyberbully.
She posted a funny comment **in the Navajo** forum.
Wayne spends a lot of time on social networks.

Word bank: Summer camp activities and places → Find more online ry3j5e

Activities

to go walking/hiking

to go fishing

to go cycling

to go inline skating

to go rock climbing

to go windsurfing

to go canoeing

to go rafting

to go horse riding

to play volleyball

to play basketball

to do judo

to do handicrafts

to stay on a campsite

to go swimming

Places

countryside

mountains

coast

beach

wood

lake

Vocabulary

Das Vocabulary enthält alle neuen Wörter und Wendungen. Sie stehen in der Reihenfolge, wie sie im Buch vorkommen.

Die Wortliste ist in drei Spalten aufgeteilt:

Links findest du das englische Wort mit der Lautschrift in Klammern. (Die Lautschrift wird ganz unten auf jeder Seite im *Dictionary* erklärt.)

In der mittleren Spalte steht die deutsche Übersetzung.

Rechts findest du Beispielsätze, Hinweise und Tipps, die dir beim Lernen helfen.

Die **fett** gedruckten Wörter musst du lernen.

Symbole und Abkürzungen:

- 👄 Achtung Aussprache!
- ✎ Achtung Schreibweise!
- ↔ ist das Gegenteil von
- → ist verwandt mit
- = entspricht
- *(sg)* Einzahl (Singular)
- *(pl)* Mehrzahl (Plural)
- [R] ähnlich wie im Russischen
- [T] ähnlich wie im Türkischen

Die *Word bank*-Seiten (S. 128 bis 138) helfen dir, die *Task*-Aufgaben in den *Units* zu bearbeiten. Du findest dort nützlichen individuellen Wortschatz zum Thema der *Unit*, der dir hilft, über deine eigene Situation zu sprechen oder zu schreiben. Diese Wörter findest du auch im *Dictionary*.

Wenn du ein Wort nicht weißt und im Wörterbuch nachschlagen willst, schau auf den *Dictionary*-Seiten ab S. 159 nach. Oder bei den *Instructions* auf S. 197.

Zoom in – The British Isles

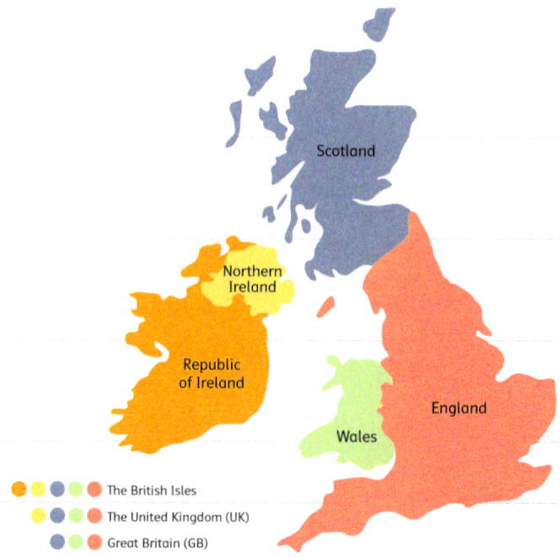

p. 8	**The British Isles** [ðə ˌbrɪtɪʃ ˈaɪlz]	die Britischen Inseln	
	Northern Ireland [ˌnɔːðn ˈaɪələnd]	Nordirland	
	The Republic of Ireland [ðə rɪˌpʌblɪk əv ˈaɪələnd]	Irland	
	Wales [weɪlz]	Wales	
p. 9	**Ireland** [ˈaɪələnd]	Irland	
p. 8	**France** [frɑːns]	Frankreich	[R] Франция [T] Fransa
p. 9	**age** [eɪdʒ]	Alter; Zeitalter	Emily's **age**? – She's fourteen.
	plan [plæn]	Plan	What are your **plans** for today?

Unit 1 Out and about in England

p. 10	**out and about** [ˌaʊt‿ən‿əˈbaʊt]	unterwegs	We are **out and about** in England today.

Intro

	to **go surfing** [ˌɡəʊ ˈsɜːfɪŋ]	surfen gehen	We **went surfing** a lot in Newquay.
p. 11	**theatre** [ˈθɪətə]	Theater	
	play [pleɪ]	Theaterstück	*Romeo and Juliet* is a Shakespeare **play**.
	visit [ˈvɪzɪt]	Besuch; Besichtigung	**visit** → to visit 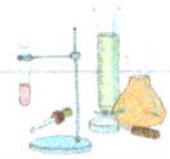
	science [ˈsaɪəns]	Wissenschaft; Naturwissenschaft	
	exhibition [ˌeksɪˈbɪʃn]	Ausstellung	Come and look at the **exhibition**.
	robot [ˈrəʊbɒt]	Roboter; Automat	
	rocket [ˈrɒkɪt]	Rakete	
	to **drive** [draɪv], **drove** [drəʊv]	fahren; treiben	Last weekend we **drove** to Newquay.
	south [saʊθ]	Süd-; Süden	Bavaria is in **south** Germany.
	coast [kəʊst]	Küste	

Topic 1

p. 12	**in the northwest of** [ˌɪn ðə ˈnɔːθwest‿əv]	im Nordwesten von	Manchester is **in the northwest of** England.
	half a million [ˌhɑːf‿ə ˈmɪljən]	eine halbe Million	More than **half a million** people live there.
	traffic [ˈtræfɪk]	Verkehr	There's lots of **traffic** in the city.
	noisy [ˈnɔɪzi]	laut	Cities are usually **noisy**.
	past [pɑːst]	Vergangenheit	In the **past** there was more traffic.
	factory [ˈfæktri]	Fabrik; Werk	
	coal [kəʊl]	Kohle	We need **coal** for the barbecue.
	mine [maɪn]	Bergwerk	You get coal from a coal **mine**.
	west [west]	Westen; West-	My family lives in the **west** of Manchester.
	centre [ˈsentə]	Zentrum; Mitte; Center	My mum works in the **centre** of town.
	about [əˈbaʊt]	*hier:* an	What's the best thing **about** Bavaria?
	north [nɔːθ]	Norden; Nord-	**north** ↔ south
	before [bɪˈfɔː]	vorher; zuvor; schon einmal	**Before**, we lived in the city.
	east [iːst]	Ost-; Osten	Sunderland is on the **east** coast.

goat [gəʊt]	Ziege	
cow [kaʊ]	Kuh	
milk [mɪlk]	Milch	
air [eə]	Luft	I love the **air** in the country.
clean [kli:n]	sauber	**clean** → to clean

Das kenne ich schon

talking about places

in the northwest of [ˌɪn ðə ˈnɔ:θwest‿əv]	im Nordwesten von	to be a long way away [bi: ə ˈlɒŋ ˌweɪ əˈweɪ]	weit weg sein
north [nɔ:θ]	Norden; Nord-	far [fɑ:]	weit
south [saʊθ]	Süden; Süd-	large [lɑ:dʒ]	groß
east [i:st]	Osten; Ost-	small [smɔ:l]	klein
west [west]	Westen; West-	capital (city) [ˈkæpɪtl (sɪti)]	Hauptstadt
quiet [kwaɪət]	leise; ruhig; still	city centre [ˌsɪti ˈsentə]	Stadtzentrum; Stadtmitte
noisy [ˈnɔɪzi]	laut		
traffic [ˈtræfɪk]	Verkehr	environment [ɪnˈvaɪrnmənt]	Umgebung
near [nɪə]	in der Nähe von; nah		

Das kenne ich schon

numbers higher than 1,000

one thousand two hundred 1,200 [wʌn ˌθaʊznd tu: ˈhʌndrəd]	eintausendzweihundert
two thousand five hundred 2,500 [tu: ˌθaʊznd faɪv ˈhʌndrəd]	zweitausendfünfhundert
three thousand seven hundred and sixty-three 3,763 [θri: ˌθaʊznd sevn hʌndrəd‿ən ˈsɪkstiθri:]	dreitausendsiebenhundertdreiundsechzig
fifty thousand 50,000 [fɪfti ˈθaʊznd]	fünfzigtausend
one hundred thousand 100,000 [wʌn ˌhʌndrəd ˈθaʊznd]	einhunderttausend
five hundred thousand/half a million 500,000 [faɪv ˌhʌndrəd ˈθaʊznd/ˌhɑ:f‿ə ˈmɪljən]	fünfhunderttausend/eine halbe Million
seven hundred thousand 700,000 [sevn ˌhʌndrəd ˈθaʊznd]	siebenhunderttausend
a/one million 1,000,000 [ə/wʌn ˈmɪljən]	eine Million

Topic 2

p. 16 **yours** [jɔ:z]	deine; eure; Ihre	There's a hat on the desk. Is it **yours**?
hers [hɜ:z]	ihre	Is that Holly's coat? – No, it isn't **hers**.
mine [maɪn]	meine	Is that your bag? – Yes, it's **mine**.
to take [teɪk]	bringen; *hier:* dauern; brauchen	It **takes** two hours by train.
here [hɪə]	hierher; hierhin	Achtung Schreibweise! h<u>ere</u>

	long [lɒŋ]	lang	**long** ↔ short
	a.m. [ˌeɪ'em]	vormittags *(Uhrzeit)*	10:00 **a.m.** = 10:00 Uhr
	to catch (bus/train) [kætʃ]	nehmen (Bus/Zug); bekommen (Bus/Zug)	I **catch** the number 44 bus to school.
	oh [əʊ]	Null *(bei Uhrzeiten und Telefon-nummern)*	8:05 = It's eight **oh** five.
	drama ['drɑ:mə]	Theater-; Drama; Schauspielerei	R драма
	to act [ækt]	mitspielen; spielen	You don't have to **act**.
	scenery ['si:nri]	Kulissen; Bühnenbild	You can also help make the **scenery**.
	to design [dɪ'zaɪn]	entwerfen; gestalten	We are **designing** the scenery with Mr Day.
	p.m. [ˌpi:'em]	nachmittags *(Uhrzeit)*	10:00 **p.m.** = 22:00 Uhr
	I'm afraid [aɪm‿ə'freɪd]	leider	**I'm afraid** I don't have time.
	occasionally [ə'keɪʒnli]	gelegentlich	I **occasionally** eat in the cafeteria.
	to order ['ɔ:də]	bestellen	Let's **order** three orange juices.
	to sound [saʊnd]	klingen	That **sounds** good. Thank you.
	healthy ['helθi]	gesund	The food doesn't sound very **healthy**.
p. 19	**his** [hɪz]	seine	It's not my DVD, it's **his**.
	theirs [ðeəz]	ihre	This is Dave's and Anna's flat. It's **theirs**.
	ours [aʊəz]	unsere	Can you see the black cat? It's **ours**.

Das kenne ich schon

possessive pronouns

mine [maɪn]	meine	ours [aʊəz]	unsere
yours [jɔ:z]	deine; Ihre	yours [jɔ:z]	eure; Ihre
his [hɪz]	seine	theirs [ðeəz]	ihre
hers [hɜ:z]	ihre		

Text

p. 20	**actor** ['æktə]	Schauspieler; Schauspielerin; Darsteller; Darstellerin	**actor** → to act
	boss [bɒs]	Boss; Chef; Chefin	R босс
	to own [əʊn]	besitzen	He **owns** the Globe Theatre.
	landlord ['lændlɔ:d]	Grundstückseigentümer; Vermieter	The **landlord** wants more money.
	rent [rent]	Miete	The **rent** for the room is £200.
	land [lænd]	Land	Some landlords own a lot of **land**.
	builder ['bɪldə]	Bauarbeiter; Bauarbeiterin	**Builders** build houses.
	to carry ['kæri]	tragen; befördern	The builders **carry** the theatre.

p. 21	**by** [baɪ]	von; an; neben	There's a play **by** Shakespeare at the Globe.
	cannon ['kænən]	Kanone	
	ball [bɔ:l]	Kugel	The cannon **ball** falls on the theatre. 
	fire [faɪə]	Feuer	
	hurt [hɜ:t]	verletzt	Nobody gets **hurt** in the accident.

Das kenne ich schon

jobs

actor ['æktə]	Schauspieler; Schauspielerin; Darsteller; Darstellerin	caretaker ['keəˌteɪkə]	Hausmeister; Hausmeisterin
		chef [ʃef]	Koch; Küchenchef
doctor ['dɒktə]	Arzt; Ärztin	detective [dɪ'tektɪv]	Detektiv; Detektivin
singer ['sɪŋə]	Sänger; Sängerin	police officer [pə'li:s‿ɒfɪsə]	Polizeibeamter; Polizeibeamtin
engineer [ˌendʒɪ'nɪə]	Ingenieur; Ingenieurin; Techniker; Technikerin	farmer ['fɑ:mə]	Bauer; Bäuerin; Landwirt; Landwirtin
teacher ['ti:tʃə]	Lehrer; Lehrerin		
assistant [ə'sɪstnt]	Verkäufer; Verkäuferin	magician [mə'dʒɪʃn]	Zauberkünstler; Zauberkünstlerin

Das kenne ich schon

theatre

drama ['drɑ:mə]	Theater-; Drama; Schauspielerei	stage [steɪdʒ]	Bühne
		actor ['æktə]	Schauspieler; Schauspielerin; Darsteller; Darstellerin
to play [pleɪ]	spielen		
to act [ækt]	mitspielen; spielen		
scenery ['si:nri]	Kulissen; Bühnenbild	play [pleɪ]	Theaterstück

Film

surfing ['sɜ:fɪŋ]	Surfen; Wellenreiten; Surf-	what a … ['wɒt‿ə]	was für ein …
to be right [bi: 'raɪt]	recht haben	brilliant ['brɪliənt]	großartig; hervorragend
how to … ['haʊ tə]	wie man …	surfer ['sɜ:fə]	Surfer; Surferin; Wellenreiter; Wellenreiterin
to surf [sɜ:f]	surfen		
rugby ['rʌgbi]	Rugby	Bye for now. [ˌbaɪ fə 'naʊ]	Bis bald.
wave [weɪv]	Welle		

More about

p. 26	**culture** ['kʌltʃə]	Kultur	Achtung Aussprache!
	gallery ['gæləri]	Halle; Säulenhalle; Galerie	We went in the **gallery** at the museum.
	dinosaur ['daɪnəsɔ:]	Dinosaurier	
	fashion ['fæʃn]	Mode	I love clothes and the newest **fashion**.

	musical ['mju:zɪkl]	Musical; Musiktheaterstück	There are so many **musicals** in London.
	if [ɪf]	wenn; falls	Come with me **if** you like.
	acting ['æktɪŋ]	Schauspielerei; Schauspielen	**acting** → to act
p. 27	**animation** [ˌænɪ'meɪʃn]	Animation; Trickfilm	Achtung Aussprache!
	on TV [ɒn ˌti:'vi:]	im Fernsehen	I watched that film **on TV** on Friday.
	to start [stɑ:t]	gründen	In 1877 he **started** a company.
	animated ['ænɪmeɪtɪd]	animiert	I love **animated** films.
	adult ['ædʌlt]	Erwachsener; Erwachsene	**adult** ↔ kid
	live [laɪv]	Live-	I went to a **live** show at the theatre.
	important [ɪm'pɔ:tnt]	wichtig	Don't forget. It's very **important**!
	British ['brɪtɪʃ]	britisch	Achtung Schreibweise! British
	radio ['reɪdiəʊ]	Radio	Achtung Aussprache!
	hit song ['hɪt ˌsɒŋ]	Hit	The Beatles had lots of **hit songs**.
	popular ['pɒpjələ]	Pop-; beliebt	There are many different **popular** cultures.

Reading skills

p. 28	**ad(vert) (= advertisement)** ['æd(vɜ:t) (əd'vɜ:tɪsmənt)]	Werbung; Anzeige	I saw the **advert** for the new car on TV.
	tour [tʊə]	Tour; Reise	We went on a **tour** of Manchester.
	to rent [rent]	mieten	We **rented** bikes at Piccadilly Gardens.
	technology [tek'nɒlədʒi]	Technik; Technologie	There were exhibitions about **technology**.
	collection [kə'lekʃn]	Sammlung	There's a nice **collection** in the museum.
	artist ['ɑ:tɪst]	Künstler; Künstlerin	L. S. Lowry is a famous Manchester **artist**.
	programme ['prəʊgræm]	Sendung; Programm	What's your favourite **programme**?
p. 29	**brochure** ['brəʊʃə]	Broschüre; Prospekt	R брошюра T broşür
	studio ['stju:diəʊ]	Studio	Achtung Aussprache!

Unit 2 Fun in Wales and Scotland

Intro

p. 32	**Welsh** [welʃ]	Walisisch; walisisch; aus Wales	Teens in Wales learn **Welsh** at school.
	down [daʊn]	hinunter; herunter; entlang; nach unten	Let's ride **down** this mountain.
	zip line ['zɪp ˌlaɪn]	Seilrutsche	One of the longest **zip lines** is in Wales.
	mile [maɪl]	Meile	1 **mile** = 1,609 metres

	until [ʌnˈtɪl]	bis	It's open from 9:00 a.m. **until** 4:00 p.m.
	skiing [ˈskiːɪŋ]	Skifahren; Ski-	
	castle [ˈkɑːsl]	Burg; Schloss	
p. 33	**against** [əˈgenst]	gegen	I fell **against** the tree.
	the English [ði ˈɪŋglɪʃ]	die Engländer	Robert the Bruce fought **the English**.
	competition [ˌkɒmpəˈtɪʃn]	Wettkampf; Wettbewerb	I like the **competitions** on sports day.
	hammer throwing [ˈhæmə ˌθrəʊɪŋ]	Hammerwerfen	I liked the **hammer throwing**.
	hammer [ˈhæmə]	Hammer	
	Scottish [ˈskɒtɪʃ]	schottisch; aus Schottland	**Scottish** → Scotland
	tradition [trəˈdɪʃn]	Tradition; Brauch	Achtung Aussprache!
	bagpipes *(pl)* [ˈbægpaɪps]	Dudelsack	In Scotland people play the **bagpipes**.
	kilt [kɪlt]	Kilt; Schottenrock	A **kilt** is usually for men. 
	skirt [skɜːt]	Rock	
p. 32	**history** [ˈhɪstri]	Geschichte	R история
	Scot [skɒt]	Schotte; Schottin	**Scot** → Scotland

Topic 1

p. 34	**adventure** [ədˈventʃə]	Abenteuer; Erlebnis	Do you like the new **adventure** centre?
	already [ɔːlˈredi]	schon; bereits	Is Jay on the way? – No, he's **already** here!
	to **pack** [pæk]	packen; einpacken	I have to **pack** my things.
	website [ˈwebsaɪt]	Website; Internetseite	We've looked at the centre's **website**. 
	rugby [ˈrʌgbi]	Rugby	
	done [dʌn]	past participle von *to do* (machen, tun)	I have **done** = ich machte/ich habe gemacht
	seen [siːn]	past participle von *to see* (sehen)	I have **seen** = ich sah/ich habe gesehen
	to **need to** [ˈniːd ˌtə]	müssen	We **need to** buy some more eggs.
	strong [strɒŋ]	stark	Rugby is for **strong** people.
	myself [maɪˈself]	mich; selbst	I hurt **myself** last year.
	fit [fɪt]	fit	I'm small but I'm **fit** and strong.
	to **be going to do sth** [biː ˌgəʊɪŋ tə ˈduː]	etw. tun werden	I'**m going to** go rock climbing.
	not ... yet [nɒt ... ˈjet]	noch nicht	I have **not** helped Dad **yet**.
	yet [jet]	schon	Is Beth here **yet**? – No, she's late.
	to **book** [bʊk]	buchen; reservieren	We **booked** the same trip again.
	difficult [ˈdɪfɪklt]	schwierig; schwer; kompliziert	**difficult** ↔ easy

	dangerous [ˈdeɪndʒrəs]	gefährlich	Rock climbing is **dangerous**.
	been [biːn]	past participle von *to be* (sein)	I have **been** = ich war/ich bin gewesen
	always [ˈɔːlweɪz]	schon immer	I've **always** wanted to climb a mountain.
	safe [seɪf]	ungefährlich; sicher	**safe** ↔ dangerous
	careful [ˈkeəfl]	vorsichtig; sorgfältig	Please be **careful**!
	to decide [dɪˈsaɪd]	(sich) entscheiden; beschließen	We have to **decide** where to go.
	to think about [ˌθɪŋk‿əˈbaʊt]	nachdenken über; sich überlegen; denken an	I want to **think about** things first.
	thought [θɔːt]	past participle von *to think* (denken, glauben)	I have **thought** = ich dachte/ich habe gedacht
p. 36	**had** [hæd]	past participle von *to have* (haben, essen)	I have **had** = ich hatte/ich habe gehabt
	made [meɪd]	past participle von *to make* (machen, tun)	I have **made** = ich machte/ich habe gemacht
	taken [ˈteɪkn]	past participle von *to take* (nehmen)	I have **taken** = ich nahm/ich habe genommen
p. 37	**to ski** [skiː]	Ski fahren	I love to **ski**!
	gone [gɒn]	past participle von *to go* (gehen)	I have **gone** = ich ging/ich bin gegangen

Das kenne ich schon

adjectives for free-time activities

fit [fɪt]	fit	safe [seɪf]	ungefährlich; sicher
strong [strɒŋ]	stark	exciting [ɪkˈsaɪtɪŋ]	spannend; aufregend
careful [ˈkeəfl]	vorsichtig; sorgfältig	interesting [ˈɪntrəstɪŋ]	interessant
tired [ˈtaɪəd]	müde	boring [ˈbɔːrɪŋ]	langweilig
difficult [ˈdɪfɪklt]	schwierig; schwer; kompliziert	fast [fɑːst]	schnell
		great [greɪt]	großartig; toll
easy [ˈiːzi]	einfach; leicht	big [bɪg]	groß
dangerous [ˈdeɪndʒrəs]	gefährlich	small [smɔːl]	klein

Das kenne ich schon

irregular verbs in Topic 1

to be [biː], was/were [wɒz/wɜː], been [biːn]	sein
to do [duː], did [dɪd], done [dʌn]	machen; tun
to see [siː], saw [sɔː], seen [siːn]	sehen
to think [θɪŋk], thought [θɔːt], thought [θɔːt]	denken; glauben
to have [hæv], had [hæd], had [hæd]	haben; essen
to take [teɪk], took [tʊk], taken [ˈteɪkn]	nehmen; dauern
to make [meɪk], made [meɪd], made [meɪd]	machen; tun
to go [gəʊ], went [went], gone [gɒn]	gehen; fahren

Topic 2

p. 38	**ever** ['evə]	schon einmal; jemals; überhaupt	Have you **ever** played rugby?
	fun [fʌn]	lustig; spaßig; amüsant	The Highland Games sound **fun**.
	to **be on** [biː‿'ɒn]	auf dem Programm stehen; anstehen; laufen	The Highland dancing **is on** later.
	bought [bɔːt]	past participle von *to buy* (kaufen)	I have **bought** = ich kaufte/ich habe gekauft
	left [left]	übrig	We've got one ticket **left**.
	just [dʒʌst]	gerade (eben); einfach; soeben; nur	I've **just** bought two more tickets.
	over ['əʊvə]	herüber; über; drüben	I'll come **over** at 5:00.
	See you later. [ˌsiː jə 'leɪtə]	Bis später.; Bis dann.	Let's meet at 6:00. – OK. **See you later.**
	to **find out** [ˌfaɪnd‿'aʊt]	herausfinden	**Find out** when the film starts, please.
	line [laɪn]	Zeile; Linie	That's in **line** 7.
p. 40	**another** [ə'nʌðə]	ein anderer; andere; noch ein	She moved to **another** place.

Das kenne ich schon

adverbs of time

already [ɔːl'redi]	schon; bereits	just [dʒʌst]	gerade (eben); soeben
yet [jet]	schon	always ['ɔːlweɪz]	immer; schon immer
never ['nevə]	nie; niemals	still [stɪl]	noch; immer noch
ever ['evə]	schon einmal; jemals	occasionally [ə'keɪʒnli]	gelegentlich

Text

p. 42	**century** ['senʃri]	Jahrhundert	a **century** = 100 years
	battle ['bætl]	Schlacht; Kampf	Years ago, there were many **battles**.
	between [bɪ'twiːn]	zwischen	Ben is **between** the tree and the ball. 
	free [friː]	frei; kostenlos	The Scots wanted to be **free**.
	to **keep out** [ˌkiːp‿'aʊt]	draußen halten	I will **keep** the English **out**.
	army ['ɑːmi]	Armee; Heer	England has a strong **army**.
	lost [lɒst]	past participle von *to lose* (verlieren)	I have **lost** = ich verlor/ich habe verloren
	spider ['spaɪdə]	Spinne	
	web [web]	Netz	
	to **give up** [ˌgɪv‿'ʌp]	aufgeben	The spider never **gives up**.
	must never/not [ˌmʌst 'nevə/'nɒt]	nie/nicht dürfen	I **must never** give up.

p. 43	**won** [wʌn]	past participle von *to win* (gewinnen)	I have **won** = ich gewann/ich habe gewonnen
	to make peace [ˌmeɪk 'pi:s]	Frieden schaffen	Robert the Bruce **made peace** in Scotland.
	brave [breɪv]	tapfer; mutig	Robert the Bruce was a **brave** man.

Film

briefcase ['bri:fkeɪs]	Aktenkoffer; Aktentasche	prop [prɒp]	Requisit
time of year [ˌtaɪm‿əv 'jɪə]	Jahreszeit	reason ['ri:zn]	Grund
		to think [θɪŋk]	finden

More about

p. 48	**to lift** [lɪft]	heben; hochheben; anheben	The men had to **lift** different things.
	heavy events [ˌhevi ɪ'vents]	Heavy Events *(Aktivitäten bei den Highland Games mit schweren Gewichten)*	The **heavy events** are for strong people.
	heavy ['hevi]	schwer; stark; schwierig	The box was very **heavy**.
	dancing ['dɑ:nsɪŋ]	Tanz; Tanzen	**dancing** → to dance
	caber toss ['keɪbə ˌtɒs]	Baumstammwerfen	The **caber toss** is a famous event.
	rarely ['reəli]	selten	**rarely** ↔ often
p. 49	**chain** [tʃeɪn]	Kette	
	to swing [swɪŋ], **swung** [swʌŋ], **swung** [swʌŋ]	schwingen; schwenken	You **swing** the ball above your head.
	as ... as [əz ... əz]	so ... wie	Anna is **as** old **as** Sarah. They're 15.
	stone put ['stəʊn ˌpʊt]	Steinstoßen	The **stone put** is also a heavy event.
	stone [stəʊn]	Stein	
	to use [ju:z]	nehmen; verwenden; benutzen; nutzen	People **use** a stone from the river.
	for example [fər‿ɪg'zɑ:mpl]	zum Beispiel	I like salad, **for example** tomato salad.
	way [weɪ]	Art und Weise	It's a good **way** to spend our holidays.
	possible ['pɒsəbl]	möglich	How is that **possible**?

Presentation skills

p. 50	**presentation** [ˌprezn'teɪʃn]	Präsentation; Referat; Vortrag	We have to do a **presentation** in English.
	university [ˌju:nɪ'vɜ:səti]	Universität	Glasgow has a big **university**.
	twin town [ˌtwɪn 'taʊn]	Partnerstadt	Nuremberg is the **twin town** of Glasgow.

p. 51	**most** [məʊst]	die meisten; die Mehrheit; am meisten	**Most** people like chocolate.

Unit 3 Welcome to Ireland

Intro

p. 52	**euro** ['jʊərəʊ]	Euro *(Währung)*	[R] евро [T] euro
	Irish ['aɪrɪʃ]	irisch; Irisch; aus Irland	There are many famous **Irish** bands.
	orchestra ['ɔ:kɪstrə]	Orchester	[R] оркестр [T] orkestra
p. 53	**half** *(sg)* [hɑ:f], **halves** *(pl)* [hɑ:vz]	(die) Hälfte	**Half** of the class eats in the cafeteria.
	the Irish [ði 'aɪrɪʃ]	die Iren	**the Irish** → Irish
	to celebrate ['seləbreɪt]	feiern	I **celebrate** with my family and friends.
	shamrock ['ʃæmrɒk]	Kleeblatt	
	hurling ['hɜ:lɪŋ]	Hurling *(ähnliche Sportart wie Hockey)*	**Hurling** is an Irish sport.
	Gaelic football [ˌgeɪlɪk 'fʊtbɔ:l]	Gaelic Football	**Gaelic football** is also an Irish sport.
	Gaelic ['geɪlɪk]	gälisch	Irish people love **Gaelic** sports.

Topic 1

p. 54	**workshop** ['wɜ:kʃɒp]	Workshop; Seminar	✎ Achtung Schreibweise! workshop
	public transport [ˌpʌblɪk 'trænspɔ:t]	öffentliche Verkehrsmittel	**public transport**: buses, trams, trains
	timetable ['taɪmˌteɪbl]	Fahrplan	Look at the bus times on the **timetable**.
	to change [tʃeɪndʒ]	umsteigen	We have to **change** at Goldenbridge.
	journey ['dʒɜ:ni]	Fahrt; Reise	The **journey** takes 40 minutes.
	all-day ['ɔ:ldeɪ]	Ganztages-	We need an **all-day** ticket.
	each [i:tʃ]	pro Stück; jeweils; jede	The DVDs are € 10 **each**. = One DVD is € 10.
	single ticket [ˌsɪŋgl 'tɪkɪt]	einfache Fahrkarte	A **single ticket** is for one journey.
	to cost [kɒst], **cost** [kɒst], **cost** [kɒst]	kosten	The tickets **cost** € 1 each.
	return ticket [rɪ'tɜ:n ˌtɪkɪt]	Hin- und Rückfahrkarte	Let's buy a **return ticket**. That's cheaper.
	key [ki:]	Schlüssel	
	to leave [li:v]	hinterlassen; vergessen	I **left** him a message.

notice ['nəʊtɪs]	Aushang; Plakat	I saw your **notice**.
p. 56 to **call** [kɔ:l]	anrufen; rufen; nennen	My grandma **called** on my birthday.

Das kenne ich schon

travel

to travel ['trævl]	fahren; reisen	across [ə'krɒs]	über
past [pɑ:st]	vorbei (an)	on the left [ɒn ðə 'left]	links; auf der linken Seite
to arrive [ə'raɪv]	ankommen	on the right [ɒn ðə 'raɪt]	rechts; auf der rechten Seite
to leave [li:v]	abfahren; weggehen	to take [teɪk]	dauern; brauchen; nehmen
ticket ['tɪkɪt]	Fahrschein; Ticket	to cost [kɒst]	kosten
single ticket [ˌsɪŋgl 'tɪkɪt]	einfache Fahrkarte	stop [stɒp]	Haltestelle; Halt
return ticket [rɪ'tɜ:n ˌtɪkɪt]	Hin- und Rückfahrkarte	timetable ['taɪmˌteɪbl]	Fahrplan
all-day ticket [ˌɔ:ldeɪ 'tɪkɪt]	Ganztagesticket	to change [tʃeɪndʒ]	umsteigen
public transport [ˌpʌblɪk 'trænspɔ:t]	öffentliche Verkehrsmittel	near [nɪə]	in der Nähe von; nah
bus [bʌs]	Bus	to get off [ˌget‿'ɒf]	aussteigen
train [treɪn]	Zug	journey ['dʒɜ:ni]	Fahrt; Reise
tram [træm]	Straßenbahn	map [mæp]	Karte; Plan

Topic 2

p. 58 **to be fed up (with)** [bi: ˌfed‿'ʌp wɪð]	die Nase voll haben (von)	I'**m fed up** with school and homework.
advice [əd'vaɪs]	Rat; Ratschlag	Emily gave me some good **advice**.
not ... any [ˌnɒt ... eni]	kein; keine	She has**n't** got **any** money.
not ... any more [ˌnɒt ... eni 'mɔ:]	nicht mehr	They are**n't** friends **any more**.
bed & breakfast (B & B) [ˌbed‿ən 'brekfəst]	Frühstückspension	We stayed in a **bed & breakfast** in Wales.
to **tell sb to do sth** ['tel tə ˌdu:]	jmdm. etw. auftragen; jmdm. etw. befehlen	Mum always **tells me to tidy my room**.
should [ʃʊd]	sollte	Linda **should** talk to her parents.
can't stand + -ing [ˌkɑ:nt 'stænd ...ɪŋ]	etw. nicht ausstehen können; etw. nicht ertragen	I **can't stand living** in the B & B.
someone ['sʌmwʌn]	jemand	**someone** = somebody
accent ['æksnt]	Akzent	The man had a strong German **accent**.
not ... anything [nɒt ... 'eniθɪŋ]	nichts	I did**n't** understand **anything**.
who [hu:]	der; die; das	There's the man **who** was in the film.

	to **try** [traɪ]	versuchen; probieren; ausprobieren	He's really angry. – I'll **try** to talk to him.
	positive ['pɒzətɪv]	positiv	Try and be **positive**, Linda.
	guest [gest]	Gast	We have **guests** for the weekend.
	anybody ['eniˌbɒdi]	irgendjemand; jemand; jeder	Can **anybody** help me, please?
	that [ðæt]	der; die; das	There's the man **that** helped me yesterday.
	list [lɪst]	Liste	Here is the **list** of things you need.
	chance [tʃɑ:ns]	Möglichkeit; Chance; Gelegenheit	We didn't have the **chance** to visit Big Ben.
	to **think of** ['θɪŋk‿əv]	sich einfallen lassen; denken an/über; sich ausdenken	We can **think of** something good to do.
p. 61	to **walk** [wɔ:k]	gehen; laufen	

Das kenne ich schon

adjectives for feelings

bad [bæd]	schlecht	cool [ku:l]	cool; super
unhappy [ʌn'hæpi]	unglücklich; traurig	special ['speʃl]	besonders; speziell
happy ['hæpi]	glücklich	silly ['sɪli]	albern
positive ['pɒzətɪv]	positiv	awful ['ɔ:fl]	schrecklich; furchtbar
fantastic [fæn'tæstɪk]	fantastisch; großartig	excited [ɪk'saɪtɪd]	aufgeregt; begeistert
nice [naɪs]	schön; nett	strong [strɒŋ]	stark
angry ['æŋgri]	wütend; zornig; verärgert; böse	worried ['wʌrid]	beunruhigt; besorgt
		amazing [ə'meɪzɪŋ]	unglaublich; erstaunlich; toll
sad [sæd]	traurig		
tired ['taɪəd]	müde	pretty ['prɪti]	hübsch

Text

p. 62	**different** ['dɪfrnt]	andere	This is a **different** kind of story.
	gold [gəʊld]	Gold	Guess what? They found **gold**!
	back home [bæk 'həʊm]	zu Hause; daheim	I wanted to be **back home**.
	to **introduce sb to sb** [ˌɪntrə'dju:s]	jmdn. jmdm. vorstellen	I should **introduce myself to** you.
	to **say** [seɪ]	aussprechen	How do you **say** Niamh?
	finally ['faɪnli]	schließlich; zum Schluss	He **finally** found a job in Northampton.
	to **mean** [mi:n], **meant** [ment], **meant** [ment]	bedeuten; meinen	It **meant** we had to move to England.
	whole [həʊl]	ganz	The **whole** city is green.
	card [kɑ:d]	Karte	

	rainbow ['reɪnbəʊ]	Regenbogen	
	each other [ˌiːtʃ‿'ʌðə]	einander; sich; gegenseitig	We send cards and give **each other** sweets.
	gold [gəʊld]	golden; Gold-	My grandma sent a **gold** card.
	paper ['peɪpə]	Papier	Use this **paper** for your list.
	pot [pɒt]	Topf	The **pot** is at the end of the rainbow.
	to feel [fiːl]	sich anfühlen; empfinden; glauben	It nearly **felt** like Ireland.
	even ['iːvn]	noch; sogar	Berlin is big but London is **even** bigger.
p. 63	**poem** ['pəʊɪm]	Gedicht	I read a nice **poem** about summer.
	one(s) [wʌn(z)]	*Platzhalter für ein Nomen*	This scarf is nice, but that **one** is nicer.
	clear [klɪə]	klar; deutlich	The mountains are **clear** to see.
	enough [ɪ'nʌf]	genug; genügend	I have **enough** money for my ticket.
	could [kʊd]	konnte	I **could**n't talk.
	surprise [sə'praɪz]	Überraschung	Her costume for the party is a **surprise**.
p. 62	**headline** ['hedlaɪn]	Überschrift; Schlagzeile	We need a good **headline** for the story.

Das kenne ich schon

prepositions of time

until [ʌn'tɪl]	bis	on [ɒn]	an; am
after ['ɑːftə]	nach	at [æt]	an; um
before [bɪ'fɔː]	vor; bevor	in [ɪn]	im; in; am

Film

during ['djʊərɪŋ]	während	sorry ['sɒri]	bekümmert; traurig

More about

p. 68	**trouble** ['trʌbl]	Problem; Schwierigkeiten; Ärger	There were lots of **troubles** in Ireland.
	island ['aɪlənd]	Insel	
	Protestant ['prɒtɪstnt]	protestantisch; Protestant; Protestantin	Achtung Aussprache!
	Catholic ['kæθlɪk]	Katholik; Katholikin; katholisch	Achtung Schreibweise! Catholic
	religion [rɪ'lɪdʒn]	Religion	There are two **religions** in Ireland.
p. 69	**terrorism** ['terrɪzm]	Terrorismus	There was a lot of **terrorism** in Ireland.
	to die [daɪ]	sterben	He **died** when he was 90 years old.
	then [ðen]	damals	We lived in Wales **then**.
	during ['djʊərɪŋ]	während	I ate my lunch **during** the break.
	since [sɪns]	seit; seitdem	I have lived here **since** March.

	type [taɪp]	Typ; Sorte; Art	There are two **types** of schools in Ireland.
	sign [saɪn]	Zeichen; Anzeichen; Schild	Achtung Schreibweise! sign

Speaking skills

p. 70	**campsite** ['kæmpsaɪt]	Campingplatz; Zeltplatz	
	background ['bækgraʊnd]	Hintergrund	The tree is in the **background**.
	middle ['mɪdl]	Mitte	The car is in the **middle** of the road.
	foreground ['fɔːgraʊnd]	Vordergrund	The dog is in the **foreground**.
p. 71	**to go camping** [ˌgəʊ 'kæmpɪŋ]	campen gehen; zelten gehen	We **went camping** with my cousins.

Unit 4 USA – here we come!

Intro

p. 74	**around** [ə'raʊnd]	*hier:* durch; um	Wayne won a trip **around** the USA.
	valley ['væli]	Tal	
	state [steɪt]	Bundesstaat; Staat	There are 50 **states** in the USA.
	huge [hjuːdʒ]	riesig; riesengroß	**huge** ↔ small
	national park [ˌnæʃnl 'pɑːk]	Nationalpark	The USA has lots of **national parks**.
	America [ə'merɪkə]	Amerika	They speak English in **America**.
	plant [plɑːnt]	Pflanze	
	rafting ['rɑːftɪŋ]	Rafting	You can do **rafting** in the sea or on a river.
	trip [trɪp]	Tour; Trip	We went on a **trip** to the mountains.
p. 75	**US** [ˌjuː'es]	US-amerikanisch	It is a **US** school, not a British school.
	space [speɪs]	Raumfahrt; Weltraum	There are things from **space** at the center.
	center *(AE)* ['sentə]	Zentrum; Mitte; Center	AE: **center** BE: centre
	earth [ɜːθ]	Welt; Erde	
	Native American [ˌneɪtɪv‿ə'merɪkən]	Ureinwohner Amerikas; Ureinwohnerin Amerikas; Indianer; Indianerin; indianisch	**Native Americans** live in the USA.
	native ['neɪtɪv]	eingeboren; einheimisch	The **native** people were there first.
	European [ˌjʊərə'piːən]	Europäer; Europäerin; europäisch; aus Europa	T Avrupalı

	to **settle** ['setl]	siedeln; besiedeln; sich nieder-lassen	Later many Europeans **settled** in America.
	favorite *(AE)* ['feɪvrɪt]	Lieblings-	AE: **favorite** BE: favourite 
	football *(AE)* ['fʊtbɔ:l]	American Football; Football	
	to **go rafting** [ˌgəʊ 'rɑ:ftɪŋ]	raften gehen	I **went rafting** yesterday.

Topic 1

p. 76	**vacation** *(AE)* [və'keɪʃn]	Urlaub; Ferien	AE: **vacation** BE: holiday
	people ['pi:pl]	Volk	I met the Navajo **people** on Tuesday.
	beautiful ['bju:tɪfl]	schön; hübsch; wunderschön	There are **beautiful** beaches in Australia.
	tribe [traɪb]	Stamm; Volksstamm	It is one of the largest **tribes** in the USA.
	reservation [ˌrezə'veɪʃn]	Reservat; Reservierung	A lot of them live in **reservations**.
	to **be interested in** [bi: 'ɪntrəstɪd‿ɪn]	interessiert sein an; sich interes-sieren für	They **are interested in** news from their people.
	social media [ˌsəʊʃl 'mi:diə]	soziale Medien	Many young people use **social media**.
	to **share** [ʃeə]	teilen	I'll **share** my room with you.
	video ['vɪdiəʊ]	Video	There are many cat **videos** on the internet.
	to **post** [pəʊst]	posten; online stellen	I **post** my pictures online.
	themselves [ðəm'selvz]	sich; selbst; sie selbst	They took photos of **themselves**. 
	tablet ['tæblət]	Tablet	
	to **remember** [rɪ'membə]	sich erinnern (an); sich merken	Do you **remember** our trip to London?
	the most important [ðə 'məʊst ɪmˌpɔ:tnt]	die wichtigste	New York is **the most important** city.
	latest ['leɪtɪst]	neueste; aktuell	I always buy the **latest** fashion.
	the least difficult [ðə 'li:st ˌdɪfɪklt]	die einfachste	This website is **the least difficult** to use. 
	newspaper ['nju:sˌpeɪpə]	Zeitung	
	less [les]	weniger	**less** ↔ more
	movie *(AE)* ['mu:vi]	Film	AE: **movie** BE: film
	camp [kæmp]	Camp; Lager	I'm going to go to a football **camp**.
p. 78	**useful** ['ju:sfl]	nützlich; hilfreich; brauchbar	Thanks for your advice. It's very **useful**.

Das kenne ich schon

comparing things

cheap [tʃi:p], cheaper, the cheapest	günstig; billig
big [bɪg], bigger, the biggest	groß
good [gʊd], better, the best	gut
bad [bæd], worse, the worst	schlecht; schlimm
exciting [ɪk'saɪtɪŋ], more exciting, the most exciting	spannend; aufregend
beautiful ['bju:tɪfl], more beautiful, the most beautiful	schön; hübsch; wunderschön
boring ['bɔ:rɪŋ], more boring, the most boring	langweilig
expensive [ɪk'spensɪv], more expensive, the most expensive	teuer

Topic 2

p. 80	**for the 200th time** [fə‿ðə 'tu: hʌndrədθ ˌtaɪm]	zum 200. Mal	I have asked **for the 200th time**.
	which [wɪtʃ]	das; der; die	My house is the house **which** is on the left.
	leader ['li:də]	Leiter; Leiterin	The camp **leader** was Stella Price.
	raft [rɑ:ft]	Raft; Floß	**raft** → rafting
	to paddle ['pædl]	paddeln	We **paddled** down the river in a raft.
	helicopter ['helɪkɒptə]	Helikopter; Hubschrauber	[T] helikopter 
	megaphone ['megəfəʊn]	Megafon	She shouted into the **megaphone**.
	wave [weɪv]	Welle	
	rapid ['ræpɪd]	Stromschnelle	The raft went into the dangerous **rapids**.
	heart [hɑ:t]	Herz	
	to go crazy [ˌgəʊ 'kreɪzi]	durchdrehen; verrückt werden	Wayne's heart **went crazy**.
	rock [rɒk]	Fels; Stein	
	deep [di:p]	tief	The river fell into a **deep** hole.
	current ['kʌrnt]	Strömung	We tried to fight against the **current**.
	to turn over [ˌtɜ:n 'əʊvə]	umkippen; (sich) umdrehen	The raft **turned over** in the river.
	to wake up [ˌweɪk‿'ʌp], **woke up** [ˌwəʊk‿'ʌp], **woken up** [ˌwəʊkn‿'ʌp]	aufwachen; erwachen	I **woke up** at 7 o'clock.
p. 81	**president** ['prezɪdnt]	Präsident; Präsidentin	[R] президент
p. 83	**dollar ($)** ['dɒlə]	Dollar *(amer. Währungseinheit)*	[R] доллар [T] dolar

Das kenne ich schon

ordinal numbers higher than 31st

thirty-second 32nd [ˌθɜːti'seknd]	zweiunddreißigste
thirty-third 33rd [ˌθɜːti'θɜːd]	dreiunddreißigste
fortieth 40th ['fɔːtiəθ]	vierzigste
forty-fifth 45th [ˌfɔːti'fɪfθ]	fünfundvierzigste
fiftieth 50th ['fɪftiəθ]	fünfzigste
fifty-first 51st [ˌfɪfti'fɜːst]	einundfünfzigste
sixtieth 60th ['sɪkstiəθ]	sechzigste
sixty-eighth 68th [ˌsɪksti'eɪtθ]	achtundsechzigste
seventieth 70th ['sevntiəθ]	siebzigste
seventy-fourth 74th [ˌsevnti'fɔːθ]	vierundsiebzigste
eightieth 80th ['eɪtiəθ]	achtzigste
eighty-ninth 89th [ˌeɪti'naɪnθ]	neunundachtzigste
ninetieth 90th ['naɪntiəθ]	neunzigste
ninety-seventh 97th [ˌnaɪnti'sevnθ]	siebenundneunzigste
hundredth 100th ['hʌndrədθ]	hundertste
hundred and sixth 106th [ˌhʌndrəd‿ən 'sɪksθ]	hundertsechste

Das kenne ich schon

'much' or 'many'?

much time [ˌmʌtʃ 'taɪm]	viel Zeit
much money [ˌmʌtʃ 'mʌni]	viel Geld
much fun [ˌmʌtʃ 'fʌn]	viel Spaß
much water [ˌmʌtʃ 'wɔːtə]	viel Wasser
many friends [ˌmeni 'frendz]	viele Freunde
many activities [ˌmeni æk'tɪvətiz]	viele Aktivitäten
many buildings [ˌmeni 'bɪldɪŋz]	viele Gebäude
many people [ˌmeni 'piːpl]	viele Leute; viele Menschen

Text

p. 84	**oval** ['əʊvl]	oval; eiförmig	An American football is **oval**.
	playing field ['pleɪɪŋ ˌfiːld]	Spielfeld	There are two teams on the **playing field**.
	baseball ['beɪsbɔːl]	Baseball	R бейсбол T beyzbol
	to hit [hɪt], **hit** [hɪt], **hit** [hɪt]	treffen; schlagen	The other team tries to **hit** the ball.
	bat [bæt]	Schläger	You use a **bat** to hit the ball.
p. 85	**basket** ['bɑːskɪt]	*hier:* Basketballkorb; Korb	Throw the ball in the **basket**.
	point [pɔɪnt]	Punkt	Make **points** against the other team.
	to bounce [baʊns]	prellen; hüpfen	You can **bounce** the ball in basketball.
	cheerleading ['tʃɪəˌliːdɪŋ]	Cheerleading	**Cheerleading** started in the USA.
	cheerleader ['tʃɪəˌliːdə]	Cheerleader; Cheerleaderin	
	to jump [dʒʌmp]	springen	
	percent (%) [pə'sent]	Prozent	95 **percent** of cheerleaders are girls.
	to motivate ['məʊtɪveɪt]	anspornen; motivieren	Cheerleaders **motivate** the fans.

Film

Go! [gəʊ]	Los!	pal [pæl]	Freund *(ugs.)*
hotel [həʊ'tel]	Hotel	to join [dʒɔɪn]	mitmachen bei
coach [kəʊtʃ]	Trainer; Trainerin	never ['nevə]	noch nie
to surprise [sə'praɪz]	überraschen		

More about

p. 90	**civil rights** *(pl)* [ˌsɪvl 'raɪts]	Bürgerrechte; Grundrechte	King fought for **civil rights** in the 1950s.
	right [raɪt]	Recht	Everyone should have the same **rights**.
	activist ['æktɪvɪst]	Aktivist *(jmd., der sich für etw. engagiert)*; Aktivistin *(jmd., die sich für etw. engagiert)*	Martin Luther King was an **activist**.
	African American [ˌæfrɪkən ə'merɪkən]	Afroamerikaner; Afroamerikanerin	He tried to help the **African Americans**.
	peaceful ['pi:sfl]	friedlich	**peaceful** → peace
	to **protest** [prə'test]	protestieren	He used peaceful ways to **protest**.
	independence [ˌɪndɪ'pendəns]	Unabhängigkeit	They celebrated 100 years of **independence**.
	flag [flæg]	Flagge; Fahne	
	fireworks *(pl)* ['faɪəwɜ:ks]	Feuerwerk	
p. 91	**holiday** ['hɒlədeɪ]	Feiertag	St Patrick's Day is a **holiday** for the Irish.
	to **discover** [dɪ'skʌvə]	entdecken	Columbus didn't really **discover** America.
	Thanksgiving [ˌθæŋks'gɪvɪŋ]	Erntedankfest	**Thanksgiving** is the 4th Thursday in November.
	to **begin** [bɪ'gɪn], **began** [bɪ'gæn], **begun** [bɪ'gʌn]	beginnen; anfangen	I **began** this book yesterday.

Das kenne ich schon

celebrations

to celebrate ['seləbreɪt]	feiern	party ['pɑ:ti]	Party; Feier
fireworks *(pl)* ['faɪəwɜ:ks]	Feuerwerk	procession [prə'seʃn]	Umzug; Festzug
birthday ['bɜ:θdeɪ]	Geburtstag	costume ['kɒstju:m]	Kostüm
dinner ['dɪnə]	Abendessen	carnival ['kɑ:nɪvl]	Karneval; Fasching
barbecue ['bɑ:bɪkju:]	Grillfest	to dance [dɑ:ns]	tanzen
to invite [ɪn'vaɪt]	einladen	present ['preznt]	Geschenk

Writing skills

p. 92	**subject** ['sʌbdʒɪkt]	Betreff	The **subject** is what the e-mail is about.
	profile ['prəʊfaɪl]	Profil; Steckbrief	I saw your **profile** on the internet.

yourself [jɔ:'self]	dich; selbst	Tell me something about **yourself**.
festival ['festɪvl]	Festival; Fest	There is a huge **festival** in June.
café ['kæfeɪ]	Café	Let's have tea in a **café** on Saturday.

Das kenne ich schon

British English/American English

centre ['sentə] *(BE)* center ['sentə] *(AE)*	Zentrum; Mitte; Center	holiday ['hɒlədeɪ] *(BE)* vacation [və'keɪʃn] *(AE)*	Urlaub; Ferien
favourite ['feɪvrɪt] *(BE)* favorite ['feɪvrɪt] *(AE)*	Lieblings-	film [fɪlm] *(BE)* movie ['mu:vi] *(AE)*	Film

Dictionary

Die Abkürzungen geben an, wo das Wort zum ersten Mal vorkommt.
Verwendete Abkürzungen und Zeichen:

U = Unit
* = unregelmäßige Verben

I = Band 1
II = Band 2
III U2, 34 = Band 3, Unit 2, S. 34
<III U1, 13> = nur zum Nachschlagen, gehört nicht zum Lernwortschatz

A

a [ə] ein; eine I
a little (bit) [ə 'lɪtl (bɪt)] ein (kleines) bisschen; ein (klein) wenig II
a lot [ə 'lɒt] viel; sehr I
a lot of [ə 'lɒt‿əv] viel; viele; eine Menge I
a/one hundred ['hʌndrəd] hundert; einhundert I
a/one thousand ['θaʊznd] tausend; eintausend II
a.m. [ˌeɪ'em] vormittags *(Uhrzeit)* III U1, 16
about [ə'baʊt] über I; ungefähr; circa; etwa II; an III U1, 12
to be about [bi: ə'baʊt] handeln von <III U2, 42>
to hang about [ˌhæŋ‿ə'baʊt] herumhängen I
out and about [ˌaʊt‿ən‿ə'baʊt] unterwegs III U1, 10
above [ə'bʌv] über; oberhalb II
Abracadabra! [ˌæbrəkə'dæbrə] Abrakadabra! II
accent ['æksnt] Akzent III U3, 58
accident ['æksɪdnt] Unfall I
across [ə'krɒs] über II
to **act** [ækt] spielen; mitspielen III U1, 16
acting ['æktɪŋ] Schauspielerei; Schauspielen III U1, 26
activist ['æktɪvɪst] Aktivist *(jmd., der sich für etw. engagiert)*; Aktivistin *(jmd., die sich für etw. engagiert)* III U4, 90
activity [æk'tɪvəti] Aktivität I
actor ['æktə] Schauspieler; Schauspielerin; Darsteller; Darstellerin III U1, 20
to **add** [æd] hinzufügen <I>
address [ə'dres] Adresse <III U4, 86>
adjective ['ædʒɪktɪv] Adjektiv; Eigenschaftswort <III U1, 13>
adult ['ædʌlt] Erwachsener; Erwachsene III U1, 27; erwachsen <III U4, 86>
adventure [əd'ventʃə] Abenteuer; Erlebnis III U2, 34
ad(vert) (= advertisement) ['æd(vɜ:t) (əd'vɜ:tɪsmənt)] Werbung; Anzeige III U1, 28
advice [əd'vaɪs] Rat; Ratschlag III U3, 58
I'm **afraid** [aɪm‿ə'freɪd] leider III U1, 16
African American [ˌæfrɪkən ə'merɪkən] Afroamerikaner; Afroamerikanerin III U4, 90
after ['ɑ:ftə] nach I
after that [ˌɑ:ftə 'ðæt] danach I
afternoon [ˌɑ:ftə'nu:n] Nachmittag I
again [ə'gen] noch einmal; wieder I
against [ə'genst] gegen III U2, 33
age [eɪdʒ] Alter; Zeitalter III ZI 9
ago [ə'gəʊ] vor II
to **agree (with)** [ə'gri: (wɪð)] zustimmen; einer Meinung sein (mit) II
first **aid** [ˌfɜ:st 'eɪd] Erste Hilfe <III U4, 86>
air [eə] Luft III U1, 12
all [ɔ:l] alle; ganz I
all of ['ɔ:l‿əv] ganz II
all over [ˌɔ:l‿'əʊvə] in ganz; überall II
all around the world [ɔ:l‿əˌraʊnd ðə 'wɜ:ld] in aller Welt II
All the best, [ɔ:l ðə 'best] Alles Gute II
all-day ['ɔ:ldeɪ] Ganztages- III U3, 54
allergy ['ælədʒi] Allergie <III U4, 86>
alligator ['ælɪgeɪtə] Alligator II
aloud [ə'laʊd] laut <III U2, 35>
alphabet ['ælfəbet] Alphabet <I>
alphabetical [ˌælfə'betɪkl] alphabetisch <II>
already [ɔ:l'redi] schon; bereits III U2, 34
also ['ɔ:lsəʊ] auch I
alternative [ɔ:l'tɜ:nətɪv] alternativ <III U2, 44>
always ['ɔ:lweɪz] immer I; schon immer III U2, 34
amazing [ə'meɪzɪŋ] erstaunlich; unglaublich; toll II
American [ə'merɪkən] amerikanisch; Amerikanisch; aus Amerika; Amerikaner; Amerikanerin II
African American [ˌæfrɪkən ə'merɪkən] Afroamerikaner; Afroamerikanerin III U4, 90
American football [əˌmerɪkən 'fʊtbɔ:l] American Football II
Native American [ˌneɪtɪv‿ə'merɪkən] Ureinwohner Amerikas; Ureinwohnerin Amerikas; Indianer; Indianerin; indianisch III U4, 75
an [æn] ein; eine I
and [ænd] und I
angry ['æŋgri] wütend; zornig; verärgert; böse II
animal ['ænɪml] Tier I

animal rescue shelter [ˌænɪml ˈreskjuː ˌʃeltə] Tierheim I
animated [ˈænɪmeɪtɪd] animiert III U1, 27
animation [ˌænɪˈmeɪʃn] Animation; Trickfilm III U1, 27
announcement [əˈnaʊnsmənt] Durchsage; Ankündigung <II>
another [əˈnʌðə] ein anderer; noch ein; andere III U2, 40
answer [ˈɑːnsə] Antwort II
to **answer** [ˈɑːnsə] antworten; beantworten II
any [ˈeni] irgendwelche; irgendeine I
not ... any more [ˌnɒt ... eni ˈmɔː] nicht mehr III U3, 58
not ... any [ˌnɒt ... eni] kein; keine III U3, 58
anybody [ˈeniˌbɒdi] irgendjemand; jemand; jeder III U3, 58
anything [ˈeniθɪŋ] irgendetwas; etwas III U3, 58
not ... anything [nɒt ... ˈeniθɪŋ] nichts III U3, 58
Anything else? [ˌeniθɪŋ ˈels] Darf es sonst noch etwas sein? I
app [æp] App <III U4, 137>
apple [ˈæpl] Apfel I
April [ˈeɪprl] April I
argument [ˈɑːgjəmənt] Auseinandersetzung; Streit II
arm [ɑːm] Arm II
army [ˈɑːmi] Armee; Heer III U2, 42
around [əˈraʊnd] um ... herum II; durch; um III U4, 74
around the house [əˌraʊnd ðə ˈhaʊs] zu Hause <III U2, 39>
to get around [ˌget əˈraʊnd] herumkommen <III U3, 54>
to walk around [ˌwɔːk‿əˈraʊnd] umherlaufen; herumlaufen <I>
to **arrange** [əˈreɪndʒ] arrangieren <III U2, 33>
to **arrive** [əˈraɪv] ankommen I
Art [ɑːt] Kunst I
article [ˈɑːtɪkl] Artikel; Bericht *(in einer Zeitung)* <III U3, 64>
artist [ˈɑːtɪst] Künstler; Künstlerin III U1, 28
as [æz] wie; als II
... as well as ... [əz ˈwel‿əz] sowohl ... als auch ... II
as ... as [əz ... əz] so ... wie III U2, 49
to **ask** [ɑːsk] fragen I
to ask about [ˈɑːsk əˌbaʊt] fragen nach; sich erkundigen nach II
to ask sb to do sth [ˈɑːsk tə ˌduː] jmdn. bitten, etw. zu tun <III U3, 67>
to ask the way [ˌɑːsk ðə ˈweɪ] nach dem Weg fragen <II>
assistant [əˈsɪstnt] Verkäufer; Verkäuferin I
at [æt] zu; in; an; auf; um; bei I
at home [ət ˈhəʊm] zu Hause; daheim I
at school [ət ˈskuːl] in der Schule I
at the back (of) [ət ðə ˈbæk (ɒv)] hinten (in) <III U3, 55>
at the bottom [æt ðə ˈbɒtəm] unten <III U3, 136>
at the doctor's [ət ðə ˈdɒktəz] beim Arzt II
at the end [ˌət ði ˈend] am Ende II
at the front (of) [ət ðə ˈfrʌnt (ɒv)] vorne (in) <III U1, 24>
at the moment [ət ðə ˈməʊmənt] im Moment; momentan II
at the same time [ət ðə seɪm ˈtaɪm] gleichzeitig; nebenher II
at the seaside [ət ðə ˈsiːsaɪd] am Meer I
at the top [æt ðə ˈtɒp] oben <III U3, 136>
ate [eɪt] simple past von *to eat* II
athletics [æθˈletɪks] Leichtathletik <III U2, 131>
attention [əˈtenʃn] Aufmerksamkeit <III U2, 51>
attic [ˈætɪk] Dachboden I
August [ˈɔːgəst] August I
aunt [ɑːnt] Tante I
autumn [ˈɔːtəm] Herbst II
away [əˈweɪ] weg; entfernt II
to be a long way away [biː ə ˈlɒŋ ˌweɪ əˈweɪ] weit weg sein II
awful [ˈɔːfl] schrecklich; furchtbar I

B

back [bæk] zurück II; Rückseite <III U4, 89>
at the back (of) [ət ðə ˈbæk (ɒv)] hinten (in) <III U3, 55>
back home [bæk ˈhəʊm] zu Hause; daheim III U3, 62
background [ˈbækgraʊnd] Hintergrund III U3, 70
bacon [ˈbeɪkn] Speck I
bad [bæd] schlecht I; schlimm II
That's too bad. [ˌðæts tuː ˈbæd] Schade! II
badminton [ˈbædmɪntən] Badminton; Federball <III U1, 129>
bag [bæg] Tasche; Tüte; Sack I
bagpipes *(pl)* [ˈbægpaɪps] Dudelsack III U2, 33
balcony [ˈbælkəni] Balkon I
ball [bɔːl] Ball I; Kugel III U1, 21
cannon ball [ˈkænən ˌbɔːl] Kanonenkugel III U1, 21
banana [bəˈnɑːnə] Banane I
band [bænd] Band; Musikgruppe II
snack **bar** [ˈsnæk ˌbɑː] Imbissstube; Café I
barbecue [ˈbɑːbɪkjuː] Grill; Grillfest I
to **bark** [bɑːk] bellen II
baseball [ˈbeɪsbɔːl] Baseball III U4, 84
basic [ˈbeɪsɪk] grundlegend <III U2, 51>
basket [ˈbɑːskɪt] Basketballkorb; Korb III U4, 85
basketball [ˈbɑːskɪtbɔːl] Basketball II
bat [bæt] Fledermaus I; Schläger III U4, 84
bathroom [ˈbɑːθrʊm] Bad(ezimmer) II
battle [ˈbætl] Schlacht; Kampf III U2, 42
*to **be** [biː] sein I
to be a long way away [biː ə ˈlɒŋ ˌweɪ əˈweɪ] weit weg sein II
to be about [biː əˈbaʊt] handeln von <III U2, 42>
to be fed up (with) [biː ˌfed‿ˈʌp (wɪð)] die Nase voll haben (von) III U3, 58
to be fun [biː ˈfʌn] Spaß machen; witzig sein II

p pen • **b** bed • **t** ten • **d** dad • **k** cat • **g** grey • **tʃ** chair • **dʒ** job • **f** fan • **v** very • **θ** three • **ð** the

to be going to do sth [bi: ˌgəʊɪŋ tə ˈduː] etw. tun werden III U2, 34
to be good at [bi: ˈgʊd‿ət] gut sein in; gut sein bei I
to be interested in [bi: ˈɪntrəstɪd‿ɪn] sich interessieren für; interessiert sein an III U4, 76
to be late [bi: ˈleɪt] zu spät kommen II
to be lucky [bi:‿ˈlʌki] Glück haben II
to be on [bi:‿ˈɒn] auf dem Programm stehen; anstehen; laufen III U2, 38
to be right [bi: ˈraɪt] recht haben <III U1, 23>
to be scared [bi: ˈskeəd] Angst haben I
to be sick [bi: ˈsɪk] sich übergeben I
beach [biːtʃ] Strand I
bear [beə] Bär II
beautiful [ˈbjuːtɪfl] wunderschön; hübsch; schön III U4, 76
became [bɪˈkeɪm] simple past von *to become* II
because [bɪˈkɒz] weil; da I
*to **become** [bɪˈkʌm] (zu etw.) werden II
bed [bed] Bett I
bed & breakfast (B&B) [ˌbed‿ən ˈbrekfəst] Frühstückspension III U3, 58
to go to bed [ˌgəʊ tə ˈbed] ins Bett gehen I
bedroom [ˈbedrʊm] Kinderzimmer; Schlafzimmer II
been [biːn] past participle von *to be* III U2, 34
before [bɪˈfɔː] vor; bevor II; vorher; zuvor; schon einmal III U1, 12
began [bɪˈgæn] simple past von *to begin* III U4, 91
*to **begin** [bɪˈgɪn] beginnen; anfangen III U4, 91
beginning [bɪˈgɪnɪŋ] Anfang; Beginn II
begun [bɪˈgʌn] past participle von *to begin* III U4, 91
behind [bɪˈhaɪnd] hinter I
to **believe** [bɪˈliːv] glauben II
bell [bel] Glocke II

to **belong** (to) [bɪˈlɒŋ] gehören (zu) <III U4, 91>
below [bɪˈləʊ] unten; unterhalb <III U1, 13>
best [best] am besten; beste; am liebsten II
All the best, [ɔːl ðə ˈbest] Alles Gute II
Best wishes, [ˌbest ˈwɪʃɪz] Viele Grüße; Alles Gute I
better [ˈbetə] besser II
between [bɪˈtwiːn] zwischen III U2, 42
big [bɪg] groß I
big wheel [ˌbɪg ˈwiːl] Riesenrad II
bike [baɪk] Fahrrad I
to go bike riding [ˌgəʊ ˈbaɪk ˌraɪdɪŋ] Fahrrad fahren II
bingo [ˈbɪŋgəʊ] Bingo <III U2, 46>
biography [baɪˈɒgrəfi] Biografie <III U2, 43>
Biology [baɪˈɒlədʒi] Biologie I
date of **birth** [ˌdeɪt‿əv ˈbɜːθ] Geburtsdatum <III U4, 86>
birthday [ˈbɜːθdeɪ] Geburtstag I
black [blæk] schwarz I
blackboard [ˈblækbɔːd] Tafel I
blend [blend] Mischung <III U2, 44>
blog [blɒg] Blog; Internettagebuch I
blue [bluː] blau I
book [bʊk] Buch; Heft I
exercise book [ˈeksəsaɪz ˌbʊk] Übungsheft I
to **book** [bʊk] buchen; reservieren III U2, 34
boring [ˈbɔːrɪŋ] langweilig I
to **borrow** [ˈbɒrəʊ] (sich) ausleihen II
boss [bɒs] Boss; Chef; Chefin III U1, 20
both [bəʊθ] beide <III U2, 40>
a **bottle** of [ə ˈbɒtl‿əv] eine Flasche … II
at the **bottom** [æt ðə ˈbɒtəm] unten <III U3, 136>
bought [bɔːt] simple past von *to buy* I; past participle von *to buy* III U2, 38
to **bounce** [baʊns] prellen; hüpfen III U4, 85
box [bɒks] Box; Kiste; Schachtel I
telephone box [ˈtelɪfəʊn ˌbɒks] Telefonzelle II
boy [bɔɪ] Junge; Bub I

brave [breɪv] tapfer; mutig III U2, 43
bread [bred] Brot I
break [breɪk] Pause I
breakfast [ˈbrekfəst] Frühstück I
bed & breakfast (B&B) [ˌbed‿ən ˈbrekfəst] Frühstückspension III U3, 58
to have breakfast [ˌhæv ˈbrekfəst] frühstücken I
bridge [brɪdʒ] Brücke II
briefcase [ˈbriːfkeɪs] Aktenkoffer; Aktentasche <III U2, 45>
brilliant [ˈbrɪliənt] großartig; hervorragend <III U1, 23>
*to **bring** [brɪŋ] mitbringen; bringen II
British [ˈbrɪtɪʃ] britisch III U1, 27
Britpop [ˈbrɪtpɒp] Britpop *(Musik)* III U1, 27
brochure [ˈbrəʊʃə] Broschüre; Prospekt III U1, 29
brother [ˈbrʌðə] Bruder I
brought [brɔːt] simple past von *to bring* II
brown [braʊn] braun I
speech **bubble** [ˈspiːtʃ ˌbʌbl] Sprechblase <III U3, 67>
*to **build** [bɪld] bauen II
builder [ˈbɪldə] Bauarbeiter; Bauarbeiterin III U1, 20
building [ˈbɪldɪŋ] Gebäude; Bauwerk II
built [bɪlt] simple past von *to build* II
burger [ˈbɜːgə] Hamburger I
bus [bʌs] Bus I
on the bus [ˌɒn ðə ˈbʌs] im Bus II
busy [ˈbɪzi] beschäftigt I
a busy day [ə ˌbɪzi ˈdeɪ] ein ausgefüllter Tag II
but [bʌt] aber I
butter [ˈbʌtə] Butter I
*to **buy** [baɪ] kaufen I
by [baɪ] von; an; neben III U1, 21
by (train) [baɪ (treɪn)] mit (dem Zug) I
Bye. [baɪ] Tschüss. I
Bye for now. [ˌbaɪ fə ˈnaʊ] Bis bald. <III U1, 23>

C

caber [ˈkeɪbə] Baumstamm III U2, 48

caber toss ['keɪbə ˌtɒs] Baumstammwerfen III U2, 48
cabin ['kæbɪn] Hütte <III U4, 86>
café ['kæfeɪ] Café III U4, 92
cafeteria [kæfə'tɪəriə] Cafeteria; Mensa I
cage [keɪdʒ] Käfig II
cake [keɪk] Kuchen I
calculator ['kælkjəleɪtə] Taschenrechner I
phone **call** ['fəʊn ˌkɔ:l] Telefonanruf; Anruf I
to **call** [kɔ:l] anrufen; rufen; nennen III U3, 56
call me ['kɔ:l ˌmi] nenne mich I
caller ['kɔ:lə] Anrufer; Anruferin <II>
came [keɪm] simple past von *to come* I
camp [kæmp] Camp; Lager III U4, 76
camper ['kæmpə] Campteilnehmer; Campteilnehmerin <III U4, 86>
*to go **camping** [ˌgəʊ 'kæmpɪŋ] campen gehen; zelten gehen III U3, 71
campsite ['kæmpsaɪt] Campingplatz; Zeltplatz III U3, 70
can [kæn] können I
can't [kɑ:nt] nicht können I
canal [kə'næl] Kanal III U1, 28
cannon ['kænən] Kanone III U1, 21
cannon ball ['kænən ˌbɔ:l] Kanonenkugel III U1, 21
canoeing [kə'nu:ɪŋ] Kanufahren I
capital (city) ['kæpɪtl] Hauptstadt I
captain ['kæptɪn] Kapitän; Kapitänin; Mannschaftsführer; Mannschaftsführerin II
caption ['kæpʃn] Bildunterschrift; Untertitel <III U1, 21>
car [kɑ:] Auto I
card [kɑ:d] Karte III U3, 62
careful ['keəfl] vorsichtig; sorgfältig III U2, 34
carefully ['keəfli] sorgfältig; vorsichtig <II>
caretaker ['keəˌteɪkə] Hausmeister; Hausmeisterin I
carnival ['kɑ:nɪvl] Karneval; Fasching I
carpet ['kɑ:pɪt] Teppich II
to **carry** ['kæri] tragen; befördern III U1, 20

casting ['kɑ:stɪŋ] Casting; Vorsprechen <III U3, 64>
castle ['kɑ:sl] Burg; Schloss III U2, 32
cat [kæt] Katze I
*to **catch** [kætʃ] fangen II; nehmen; bekommen III U1, 16
cathedral [kə'θi:drl] Kathedrale; Dom <III U1, 130>
Catholic ['kæθlɪk] Katholik; Katholikin; katholisch III U3, 68
caught [kɔ:t] simple past von *to catch* II
to **celebrate** ['seləbreɪt] feiern III U3, 53
celebration [ˌselə'breɪʃn] Feier <III U4, 91>
center *(AE)* ['sentə] Zentrum; Mitte; Center III U4, 75
centre ['sentə] Zentrum; Mitte; Center III U1, 12
city centre [ˌsɪti 'sentə] Stadtzentrum; Stadtmitte II
shopping centre ['ʃɒpɪŋ ˌsentə] Einkaufszentrum I
sports centre ['spɔ:ts ˌsentə] Sportzentrum I
century ['senʃri] Jahrhundert III U2, 42
chain [tʃeɪn] Kette III U2, 49
chair [tʃeə] Stuhl I
champion ['tʃæmpiən] Gewinner; Gewinnerin; Sieger; Siegerin <I>
chance [tʃɑ:ns] Möglichkeit; Chance; Gelegenheit III U3, 58
change [tʃeɪndʒ] Wechselgeld I
to **change** [tʃeɪndʒ] verändern; ändern; wechseln II; umsteigen III U3, 54
chant [tʃɑ:nt] Sprechgesang <I>
charades [ʃə'rɑ:dz] Scharaden <II>
charity ['tʃærɪti] Wohltätigkeitsorganisation; Stiftung; wohltätige Zwecke; Wohltätigkeits- II
chart [tʃɑ:t] Tabelle; Diagramm <I>
to **chat** [tʃæt] chatten; plaudern II
cheap [tʃi:p] günstig; billig II
to **check** [tʃek] überprüfen; kontrollieren II
checklist ['tʃeklɪst] Checkliste <I>
checkout ['tʃekaʊt] Kontrolle <I>
cheerleader ['tʃɪəˌli:də] Cheerleader; Cheerleaderin III U4, 85

cheerleading ['tʃɪəˌli:dɪŋ] Cheerleading III U4, 85
cheese [tʃi:z] Käse I
chef [ʃef] Koch; Küchenchef II
chicken ['tʃɪkɪn] Hähnchen; Huhn I
chicken fried rice ['tʃɪkɪn ˌfraɪd 'raɪs] gebratener Reis mit Hühnerfleisch II
child *(sg)* [tʃaɪld] Kind <III U4, 86>
children *(pl)* ['tʃɪldrən] Kinder I
chimpanzee [ˌtʃɪmpn'zi:] Schimpanse II
Chinese [tʃaɪ'ni:z] chinesisch; Chinesisch; aus China; Chinese; Chinesin II
chips *(pl)* [tʃɪps] Pommes frites I
chocolate ['tʃɒklət] Schokolade I
choir [kwaɪə] Chor <III U1, 129>
*to **choose** [tʃu:z] wählen; auswählen <I>
chorus ['kɔ:rəs] Refrain <I>
Christmas ['krɪsməs] Weihnachten I
Merry Christmas! [ˌmeri 'krɪsməs] Frohe Weihnachten! I
church [tʃɜ:tʃ] Kirche II
cinema ['sɪnəmə] Kino I
city ['sɪti] Stadt; Großstadt I
city centre [ˌsɪti 'sentə] Stadtzentrum; Stadtmitte II
civil rights *(pl)* [ˌsɪvl 'raɪts] Bürgerrechte; Grundrechte III U4, 90
class [klɑ:s] Klasse I
classmate ['klɑ:smeɪt] Klassenkamerad; Klassenkameradin; Mitschüler; Mitschülerin <III U1, 19>
classroom ['klɑ:srʊm] Klassenzimmer I
to **clean** [kli:n] sauber machen; putzen II
clean [kli:n] sauber III U1, 12
clean copy [ˌkli:n 'kɒpi] Reinschrift <III U4, 93>
clear [klɪə] klar; deutlich III U3, 63
That was very clear. [ðæt wɒz veri 'klɪə] Das war sehr klar. <I>
clearly ['klɪəli] deutlich <III U2, 51>
to **climb** [klaɪm] besteigen; klettern; erklettern; steigen II
clock [klɒk] Uhr II
o'clock [ə'klɒk] Uhr *(Zeitangabe bei vollen Stunden)* I

to close [kləʊz] zumachen; schließen I
closed [kləʊzd] geschlossen I
clothes *(pl only)* [kləʊðz] Kleider; Kleidung I
cloud [klaʊd] Wolke II
cloudy ['klaʊdi] bewölkt; wolkig II
club [klʌb] Klub; Treff; Schul-AG I
clue [klu:] Hinweis; Spur I
coach [kəʊtʃ] Trainer; Trainerin <III U4, 87>
coal [kəʊl] Kohle III U1, 12
coast [kəʊst] Küste III U1, 11
coat [kəʊt] Jacke I
zip **code** ['zɪp ˌkəʊd] Postleitzahl <III U4, 86>
cola ['kəʊlə] Cola I
cold [kəʊld] kalt I; Erkältung; Kälte II
collar ['kɒlə] Halsband I
to **collect** [kə'lekt] sammeln <I>
collection [kə'lekʃn] Sammlung III U1, 28
colour ['kʌlə] Farbe I
combination [ˌkɒmbɪ'neɪʃn] Kombination <III U4, 77>
*to **come** [kʌm] kommen I
to come over [ˌkʌm 'əʊvə] herüberkommen; vorbeischauen III U2, 38
comic ['kɒmɪk] Comic(heft) II
comic strip ['kɒmɪk ˌstrɪp] Comic; Bildergeschichte <III U2, 33>
comment ['kɒment] Kommentar <III U4, 137>
company ['kʌmpəni] Unternehmen; Firma; Gesellschaft II
to **compare** [kəm'peə] vergleichen <I>
competition [ˌkɒmpə'tɪʃn] Wettkampf; Wettbewerb III U2, 33
to **complete** [kəm'pli:t] vervollständigen <I>
computer [ˌkəm'pju:tə] Computer I
computing device [kəmˌpju:tɪŋ dɪ'vaɪs] Computergerät <III U4, 79>
concert ['kɒnsət] Konzert I
Congratulations! [kənˌgrætʃə'leɪʃnz] Glückwunsch! II
contact ['kɒntækt] Kontakt I
continent ['kɒntɪnənt] Kontinent; Erdteil II
cook [kʊk] Koch; Köchin <III U4, 86>

to **cook** [kʊk] kochen II
cooking ['kʊkɪŋ] Kochen; Koch- II
cool [ku:l] cool; super I
clean copy [ˌkli:n 'kɒpi] Reinschrift <III U4, 93>
to **copy** ['kɒpi] abschreiben; kopieren <III U1, 13>
to **correct** [kə'rekt] verbessern; richtigstellen; korrigieren II
correct [kə'rekt] richtig; korrekt <I>
*to **cost** [kɒst] kosten III U3, 54
cost [kɒst] simple past, past participle von *to cost* III U3, 54
costume ['kɒstju:m] Kostüm I
could [kʊd] konnte III U3, 63
country ['kʌntri] Land; ländliche Gegend I
countryside ['kʌntrɪsaɪd] Land; Landschaft <III U1, 128>
of **course** [əv 'kɔ:s] natürlich; selbstverständlich II
cousin ['kʌzn] Cousin; Cousine II
cow [kaʊ] Kuh III U1, 12
*to go **crazy** [ˌgəʊ 'kreɪzi] durchdrehen; verrückt werden III U4, 80
cricket ['krɪkɪt] Kricket II
crown jewels *(pl)* [ˌkraʊn 'dʒu:əlz] Kronjuwelen II
culture ['kʌltʃə] Kultur III U1, 26
a **cup** of [ə 'kʌp‿əv] eine Tasse … II
current ['kʌrnt] Strömung III U4, 80
customer ['kʌstəmə] Kunde; Kundin I
cyberbully ['saɪbəˌbʊli] Cybermobber; Cybermobberin <III U4, 137>
cycling ['saɪklɪŋ] Radfahren <III U4, 138>

D

dad [dæd] Papa; Vati I
dance [dɑ:ns] Tanz <III U1, 129>
square dance ['skweə ˌdɑ:ns] Squaredance *(amerikanischer Volkstanz)* II
to **dance** [dɑ:ns] tanzen I
dancer ['dɑ:nsə] Tänzer; Tänzerin I
dancing ['dɑ:nsɪŋ] Tanz; Tanzen III U2, 48
dangerous ['deɪndʒrəs] gefährlich III U2, 34
dark [dɑ:k] dunkel I

date [deɪt] Datum; Zeitpunkt <II>
date of birth [ˌdeɪt‿əv 'bɜ:θ] Geburtsdatum <III U4, 86>
daughter ['dɔ:tə] Tochter I
day [deɪ] Tag I
a busy day [ə ˌbɪzi 'deɪ] ein ausgefüllter Tag II
lucky day [ˌlʌki 'deɪ] Glückstag II
one day ['wʌn deɪ] eines Tages I
sports day ['spɔ:ts ˌdeɪ] Sportfest II
Dear …, [dɪə] Liebe(r) …, *(Anrede in Briefen)* I
December [dɪ'sembə] Dezember I
to **decide** [dɪ'saɪd] (sich) entscheiden; beschließen III U2, 34
deep [di:p] tief III U4, 80
to **describe** [dɪ'skraɪb] beschreiben <III U2, 32>
description [dɪ'skrɪpʃn] Beschreibung <III U3, 136>
design [dɪ'zaɪn] Design; Gestaltung; Entwurf II
DT (Design Technology) [ˌdi:'ti: (dɪˌzaɪn tek'nɒlədʒi)] Technik I
to **design** [dɪ'zaɪn] entwerfen; gestalten III U1, 16
desk [desk] Schreibtisch; Tisch II
detail ['di:teɪl] Detail; Einzelheit <III U1, 11>
detective [dɪ'tektɪv] Detektiv; Detektivin I
computing **device** [kəmˌpju:tɪŋ dɪ'vaɪs] Computergerät <III U4, 79>
dialogue ['daɪəlɒg] Dialog; Gespräch II
diameter [daɪ'æmɪtə] Durchmesser II
diamond ['daɪəmənd] Diamant <II>
diary ['daɪəri] Tagebuch I
dictionary ['dɪkʃnri] Wörterbuch <II>
did [dɪd] simple past von *to do* I
to **die** [daɪ] sterben III U3, 69
different ['dɪfrnt] verschieden; unterschiedlich; anders I; andere III U3, 62
difficult ['dɪfɪklt] schwierig; schwer; kompliziert III U2, 34
dinner ['dɪnə] Mittagessen; Abendessen I
dinosaur ['daɪnəsɔ:] Dinosaurier III U1, 26

directions

giving **directions** [ˌɡɪvɪŋ dɪˈrekʃnz] eine Wegbeschreibung geben; Anweisungen geben <II>
dirty [ˈdɜːti] dreckig; schmutzig I
discount [ˈdɪskaʊnt] Rabatt; Preisnachlass <III U1, 22>
to **discover** [dɪˈskʌvə] entdecken III U4, 91
disgusting [dɪsˈɡʌstɪŋ] ekelhaft; widerlich <III U2, 133>
to empty the **dishwasher** [ˌemti ðə ˈdɪʃwɒʃə] die Spülmaschine ausräumen II
to load the **dishwasher** [ˌləʊd ðə ˈdɪʃwɒʃə] die Spülmaschine einräumen II
in the **distance** [ˌɪn ðə ˈdɪstns] in der Ferne <III U1, 130>
*to **do** [duː] machen; tun I
to do handicrafts [ˌduː ˈhændikrɑːfts] basteln <III U4, 138>
to do homework [ˌduː ˈhəʊmwɜːk] Hausaufgabe(n) machen I
to do magic [ˌduː ˈmædʒɪk] zaubern II
doctor [ˈdɒktə] Arzt; Ärztin II
at the doctor's [ət ðə ˈdɒktəz] beim Arzt II
dog [dɒɡ] Hund I
dollar ($) [ˈdɒlə] Dollar *(amer. Währungseinheit)* III U4, 83
done [dʌn] past participle von *to do* III U2, 34
door [dɔː] Tür II
doorbell [ˈdɔːbel] Türklingel I
down [daʊn] hinunter; herunter; entlang; nach unten III U2, 32
to **download** [ˌdaʊnˈləʊd] herunterladen <III U4, 137>
draft [drɑːft] Entwurf <II>
drama [ˈdrɑːmə] Theater-; Drama; Schauspielerei III U1, 16
drank [dræŋk] simple past von *to drink* II
*to **draw** [drɔː] zeichnen <I>
dream [driːm] Traum I
dress [dres] Kleid I
fancy dress [ˌfænsi ˈdres] Kostüm; Verkleidung I
drink [drɪŋk] Getränk I
*to **drink** [drɪŋk] trinken II
*to **drive** [draɪv] fahren; treiben III U1, 11
drove [drəʊv] simple past von *to drive* III U1, 11
dry [draɪ] trocken II
DT (Design Technology) [ˌdiːˈtiː (dɪˌzaɪn tekˈnɒlədʒi)] Technik I
duo [ˈdʒuːəʊ] Duo <III U2, 44>
during [ˈdjʊərɪŋ] während III U3, 69
DVD [ˌdiːviːˈdiː] DVD I

E

e.g. (= for example) [ˌiːˈdʒiː] z. B. (= zum Beispiel) <II>
each [iːtʃ] pro Stück; jeweils; jede III U3, 54
each one [ˌiːtʃ ˈwʌn] jede <III U4, 83>
each other [ˌiːtʃˈʌðə] einander; sich; gegenseitig III U3, 62
early [ˈɜːli] früh II
earth [ɜːθ] Welt; Erde III U4, 75
east [iːst] Ost-; Osten III U1, 12
eastbound [ˈiːsbaʊnd] in Richtung Osten <III U3, 134>
easy [ˈiːzi] einfach; leicht I
*to **eat** [iːt] essen I
eaten [ˈiːtn] past participle von *to eat* <III U2, 133>
egg [eɡ] Ei I
Eid [iːd] *muslimisches Fest* I
eight [eɪt] acht I
eighteen [ˌeɪˈtiːn] achtzehn I
eighty [ˈeɪti] achtzig I
electronic [ˌelekˈtrɒnɪk] elektronisch <III U2, 44>
electropop [ɪˌlektrəˈpɒp] Elektropop *(Musik)* <III U2, 44>
element [ˈelɪmənt] Element <III U2, 44>
eleven [ɪˈlevn] elf I
e-mail [ˈiːmeɪl] E-Mail II
to **empty** the dishwasher [ˌemti ðə ˈdɪʃwɒʃə] die Spülmaschine ausräumen II
end [end] Ende; Schluss II
at the end [ˌət ði ˈend] am Ende II
end-of-term [ˌend‿əv ˈtɜːm] Schuljahresabschluss <I>
ending [ˈendɪŋ] Schluss <III U3, 67>
energy [ˈenədʒi] Energie; Kraft <III U2, 44>
engineer [ˌendʒɪˈnɪə] Ingenieur; Ingenieurin; Techniker; Technikerin II
English [ˈɪŋɡlɪʃ] Englisch I; englisch; aus England III U2, 33
the English [ði ˈɪŋɡlɪʃ] die Engländer III U2, 33
to **enjoy** [ɪnˈdʒɔɪ] genießen; Gefallen finden an; mögen <III U2, 44>
enough [ɪˈnʌf] genug; genügend III U3, 63
entry [ˈentri] Eintrag; Eintritt <II>
environment [ɪnˈvaɪrnmənt] Umwelt; Umgebung II
equipment [ɪˈkwɪpmənt] Ausrüstung; Zubehör; Ausstattung <III U2, 131>
euro [ˈjʊərəʊ] Euro *(Währung)* III U3, 52
European [ˌjʊərəˈpiːən] Europäer; Europäerin; europäisch; aus Europa III U4, 75
even [ˈiːvn] noch; sogar III U3, 62
evening [ˈiːvnɪŋ] Abend I
in the evening [ɪn ði ˈiːvnɪŋ] abends I
event [ɪˈvent] Veranstaltung; Ereignis II
sporting event [ˈspɔːtɪŋ ɪˌvent] Sportereignis; Sportveranstaltung <III U3, 66>
ever [ˈevə] schon einmal; jemals; überhaupt III U2, 38
every [ˈevri] jede I; alle II
everybody [ˈevriˌbɒdi] jeder; alle <III U4, 86>
everyone [ˈevriwʌn] alle; jeder; zusammen II
everything [ˈevriθɪŋ] alles II
everywhere [ˈevriweə] überallhin; überall II
example [ɪɡˈzɑːmpl] Beispiel III U2, 49
for example [fər‿ɪɡˈzɑːmpl] zum Beispiel III U2, 49
exchange [ɪksˈtʃeɪndʒ] Austausch <III U3, 64>
excited [ɪkˈsaɪtɪd] aufgeregt; begeistert II
exciting [ɪkˈsaɪtɪŋ] spannend; aufregend I

p pen • b bed • t ten • d dad • k cat • g grey • tʃ chair • dʒ job • f fan • v very • θ three • ð the

Excuse me. [ɪk'skjuːz mi] Entschuldigung. II
exercise ['eksəsaɪz] Übung I
exercise book ['eksəsaɪz ˌbʊk] Übungsheft I
exhibition [ˌeksɪ'bɪʃn] Ausstellung III U1, 11
expensive [ɪk'spensɪv] teuer I
experiment [ɪk'sperɪmənt] Versuch; Experiment II
to **explain** [ɪk'spleɪn] erklären <III U4, 85>
eye [aɪ] Auge I

F

face [feɪs] Gesicht I
face painting ['feɪs peɪntɪŋ] Schminken II
fact [fækt] Fakt; Tatsache II
factory ['fæktri] Fabrik; Werk III U1, 12
fair [feə] Fest; Messe; Jahrmarkt II
*to **fall** [fɔːl] fallen; hinfallen I
to fall off [ˌfɔːl_'ɒf] von etw. stürzen; herunterfallen; hinunterfallen II
family ['fæmli] Familie I
family name ['fæmli ˌneɪm] Nachname <III U4, 86>
family tree [ˌfæmli 'triː] Familienstammbaum <I>
famous ['feɪməs] berühmt I
fan [fæn] Fan I
fancy **dress** [ˌfænsi 'dres] Kostüm; Verkleidung I
fantastic [fæn'tæstɪk] fantastisch; großartig II
far [fɑː] weit II
fare [feə] Fahrpreis <III U3, 134>
farm [fɑːm] Bauernhof I
farmer ['fɑːmə] Bauer; Bäuerin; Landwirt; Landwirtin I
fashion ['fæʃn] Mode III U1, 26
fast [fɑːst] schnell II
father ['fɑːðə] Vater I
favorite *(AE)* ['feɪvrɪt] Lieblings- III U4, 75
favourite ['feɪvrɪt] Lieblings- I
February ['februri] Februar I
fed [fed] simple past von *to feed* I
*to be **fed up** (with) [biː ˌfed_'ʌp (wɪð)] die Nase voll haben (von) III U3, 58
*to **feed** [fiːd] füttern I
feedback ['fiːdbæk] Rückmeldung; Feedback <I>
*to **feel** [fiːl] (sich) fühlen II; sich anfühlen; empfinden; glauben III U3, 62
feeling ['fiːlɪŋ] Gefühl <II>
fell [fel] simple past von *to fall* I
felt [felt] simple past von *to feel* II; past participle von *to feel* III U3, 62
female ['fiːmeɪl] weiblich <III U4, 86>
ferry ['feri] Fähre <III U3, 134>
festival ['festɪvl] Fest; Festival III U4, 92
science **fiction** [ˌsaɪəns 'fɪkʃn] Science-Fiction I
playing **field** ['pleɪɪŋ ˌfiːld] Sportplatz II; Spielfeld III U4, 84
fifteen [ˌfɪf'tiːn] fünfzehn I
fifty ['fɪfti] fünfzig I
*to **fight** [faɪt] kämpfen; (sich) streiten II
figure ['fɪgə] Figur; Gestalt II
to save a **file** [ˌseɪv_ə 'faɪl] eine Datei speichern <III U4, 137>
to **fill** [fɪl] füllen <II>
to fill in [ˌfɪl_'ɪn] eintragen; ausfüllen <II>
film [fɪlm] Film I
finally ['faɪnli] schließlich; zum Schluss III U3, 62
*to **find** [faɪnd] finden; herausfinden I
to find out [ˌfaɪnd_'aʊt] herausfinden III U2, 38; erkundigen <I>
fine [faɪn] gut; in Ordnung; schön I
I'm fine. [ˌaɪm 'faɪn] Mir geht es gut. I
to **finish** ['fɪnɪʃ] fertigstellen; vervollständigen I; beenden; fertig machen; erledigen; enden; aufhören II
fire [faɪə] Feuer III U1, 21
fireworks *(pl)* ['faɪəwɜːks] Feuerwerk III U4, 90
first [fɜːst] erste I; zuerst; als Erstes II
first aid [ˌfɜːst 'eɪd] Erste Hilfe <III U4, 86>
first name ['fɜːst ˌneɪm] Vorname <III U4, 86>
the first time [ðə fɜːst 'taɪm] das erste Mal I
fish *(sg)* [fɪʃ], **fish** *(pl)* [fɪʃ] Fisch I
fishing ['fɪʃɪŋ] Angeln; Fischen <III U4, 138>
to **fit** [fɪt] passen <III U3, 55>
fit [fɪt] fit III U2, 34
five [faɪv] fünf I
flag [flæg] Flagge; Fahne III U4, 90
flat [flæt] Wohnung I
flea [fliː] Floh I
flea market ['fliː ˌmɑːkɪt] Flohmarkt I
flew [fluː] simple past von *to fly* II
floor [flɔː] Stockwerk; Etage II
*to **fly** [flaɪ] fliegen II
flyer ['flaɪə] Flyer; Faltblatt <III U3, 54>
food [fuːd] Essen; Lebensmittel I
foot *(sg)* [fʊt], **feet** *(pl)* [fiːt] Fuß II
on foot [ɒn 'fʊt] zu Fuß I
football ['fʊtbɔːl] Fußball I
American football [əˌmerɪkən 'fʊtbɔːl] American Football II
Gaelic football [ˌgeɪlɪk 'fʊtbɔːl] Gaelic Football III U3, 53
football *(AE)* ['fʊtbɔːl] American Football; Football III U4, 75
for [fɔː] für I
for example [fər_ɪg'zɑːmpl] zum Beispiel III U2, 49
for the 200th time [fə_ðə 'tuː hʌndrədθ ˌtaɪm] zum 200. Mal III U4, 80
foreground ['fɔːgraʊnd] Vordergrund III U3, 70
*to **forget** [fə'get] vergessen II
forgot [fə'gɒt] simple past von *to forget* II
form [fɔːm] Form <I>; Formular <III U4, 86>
forty ['fɔːti] vierzig I
forum ['fɔːrəm] Forum <III U4, 137>
fought [fɔːt] simple past von *to fight* II
found [faʊnd] simple past von *to find* II; past participle von *to find* III U2, 38
four [fɔː] vier I
fourteen [ˌfɔː'tiːn] vierzehn I
free [friː] frei; kostenlos III U2, 42
free time [ˌfriː 'taɪm] Freizeit I

free-time [ˌfriːˈtaɪm] Freizeit- <I>

freeze frame [ˈfriːz ˌfreɪm] Standbild <II>

Friday [ˈfraɪdeɪ] Freitag I

chicken **fried** rice [ˈtʃɪkɪn ˌfraɪd ˈraɪs] gebratener Reis mit Hühnerfleisch II

friend [frend] Freund; Freundin I

to make friends [ˌmeɪk ˈfrendz] Freundschaft(en) schließen II

friendly [ˈfrendli] freundlich; sympathisch <III U2, 51>

frisbee [ˈfrɪzbi] Frisbee; Frisbeescheibe I

from [frɒm] aus; von I

at the **front** (of) [ət ðə ˈfrʌnt (ɒv)] vorne (in) <III U1, 24>

in **front** [ɪn ˈfrʌnt] vorn II

in **front** of [ɪn ˈfrʌnt‿əv] vor; davor I

fruit [fruːt] Obst; Frucht I

fun [fʌn] Spaß; Freude I; lustig; spaßig; amüsant III U2, 38

to be fun [biː ˈfʌn] Spaß machen; witzig sein II

funk [fʌŋk] Funk *(Musik)* <III U2, 44>

funny [ˈfʌni] merkwürdig; komisch; lustig I

G

Gaelic [ˈgeɪlɪk] gälisch III U3, 53

Gaelic football [ˌgeɪlɪk ˈfʊtbɔːl] Gaelic Football III U3, 53

gallery [ˈgæləri] Halle; Säulenhalle; Galerie III U1, 26

game [geɪm] Spiel I

to have a game [hæv‿ə ˈgeɪm] spielen <III U2, 46>

gap [gæp] Lücke; Spalt <II>

garden [ˈgɑːdn] Garten I

gave [geɪv] simple past von *to give* I

German [ˈdʒɜːmən] Deutsch I; Deutscher; Deutsche; deutsch; aus Deutschland II

*to **get** [get] bekommen; werden; kommen I; holen <III U1, 22>

to get around [ˌget əˈraʊnd] herumkommen <III U3, 54>

to get doing sth [ˌget ˈduːɪŋ] anfangen, etw. zu tun <III U2, 44>

to get into [ˌget‿ˈɪntə] bilden <I>

to get off [ˌget‿ˈɒf] aussteigen II

to get ready [ˌget ˈredi] sich bereit machen <III U4, 89>

to get up [ˌget‿ˈʌp] aufstehen I

ghost [gəʊst] Geist <II>

girl [gɜːl] Mädchen I

*to **give** [gɪv] geben; schenken I; halten; nennen <III U1, 15>

to give up [ˌgɪv‿ˈʌp] aufgeben III U2, 42

giving directions [ˌgɪvɪŋ dɪˈrekʃnz] eine Wegbeschreibung geben; Anweisungen geben <II>

given [ˈgɪvn] past participle von *to give* III U2, 42

glove [glʌv] Handschuh II

*to **go** [gəʊ] gehen; fahren I

to be going to do sth [biː ˌgəʊɪŋ tə ˈduː] etw. tun werden III U2, 34

to go bike riding [ˌgəʊ ˈbaɪk ˌraɪdɪŋ] Fahrrad fahren II

to go camping [ˌgəʊ ˈkæmpɪŋ] campen gehen; zelten gehen III U3, 71

to go crazy [ˌgəʊ ˈkreɪzi] durchdrehen; verrückt werden III U4, 80

to go rafting [ˌgəʊ ˈrɑːftɪŋ] raften gehen III U4, 75

to go skating [ˌgəʊ ˈskeɪtɪŋ] inlineskaten gehen; Schlittschuhlaufen gehen II

to go surfing [ˌgəʊ ˈsɜːfɪŋ] surfen gehen III U1, 10

to go swimming [ˌgəʊ ˈswɪmɪŋ] schwimmen gehen I

to go tandem bike riding [ˌgəʊ ˈtændəm ˌbaɪk raɪdɪŋ] Tandem fahren II

to go to bed [ˌgəʊ tə ˈbed] ins Bett gehen I

Go! [gəʊ] Los! <III U4, 87>

goat [gəʊt] Ziege III U1, 12

goggles *(pl)* [ˈgɒglz] Brille; Schutzbrille <III U2, 131>

gold [gəʊld] Gold; golden; Gold- III U3, 62

gone [gɒn] past participle von *to go* III U2, 37

good [gʊd] gut I

to be good at [biː ˈgʊd‿ət] gut sein in; gut sein bei I

Goodbye. [gʊdˈbaɪ] Auf Wiedersehen. I

got [gɒt] simple past von *to get* I

to have (got) to [ˈhæv (gɒt) tə] müssen II

to have got [hæv ˈgɒt] haben; besitzen II

GPS (Global Positioning System) [ˌdʒiːpiːˈes] GPS *(ein satellitengestütztes System zur weltweiten Positionsbestimmung)* I

grade *(AE)* [greɪd] Klasse; Jahrgangsstufe; Note II

grammar [ˈgræmə] Grammatik <I>

grandfather [ˈgrænˌfɑːðə] Großvater II

grandma [ˈgrænmɑː] Oma I

grandparents *(pl)* [ˈgrænˌpeərnts] Großeltern II

great [greɪt] großartig; toll I

great-great-grandad [ˌgreɪtgreɪt ˈgrændæd] Ururopa I

green [griːn] grün I

grey [greɪ] grau I

group [gruːp] Gruppe <I>

to **guess** [ges] überlegen; raten; erraten I

Guess what? [ges ˈwɒt] Stellt euch vor!; Stell dir vor! II

guest [gest] Gast III U3, 58

guide [gaɪd] Führer; Führerin <III U1, 130>

guinea pig [ˈgɪni ˌpɪg] Meerschweinchen II

H

had [hæd] simple past von *to have* I; past participle von *to have* III U2, 36

half *(sg)* [hɑːf], **halves** *(pl)* [hɑːvz] (die) Hälfte III U3, 53

half [hɑːf] halb III U1, 12

half past (seven) [ˌhɑːf ˈpɑːst (ˌsevn)] halb (acht) II

half a million [ˌhɑːf‿ə ˈmɪljən] eine halbe Million III U1, 12

half-price [ˌhɑːfˈpraɪs] zum halben Preis <III U1, 22>

Halloween [ˌhæləʊˈiːn] Halloween I

hammer [ˈhæmə] Hammer III U2, 33

hammer throwing ['hæmə ˌθrəʊɪŋ] Hammerwerfen III U2, 33
hamster ['hæmstə] Hamster I
hand [hænd] Hand II
handball ['hændbɔːl] Handball <III U1, 129>
*to do **handicrafts** [ˌduː 'hændikrɑːfts] basteln <III U4, 138>
*to **hang** about [ˌhæŋ‿ə'baʊt] herumhängen I
to **happen** ['hæpn] passieren; geschehen II
That's what happened. [ˌðæts wɒt 'hæpnd] Das ist passiert. II
happy ['hæpi] glücklich I
hard [hɑːd] hart; schwer; schwierig II
hat [hæt] Mütze; Hut II
to **hate** [heɪt] hassen; nicht mögen I
*to **have** [hæv] haben; besitzen; essen; trinken I
to have (got) to ['hæv (gɒt) tə] müssen II
to have a game [hæv‿ə 'geɪm] spielen <III U2, 46>
to have a look (at) [ˌhæv‿ə 'lʊk (ət)] sich anschauen <III U1, 130>
to have a party [ˌhæv‿ə 'pɑːti] eine Party feiern I
to have breakfast [ˌhæv 'brekfəst] frühstücken I
to have got [hæv 'gɒt] haben; besitzen II
to have to ['hæv tə] müssen II
he [hiː] er I
head [hed] Kopf II
headache ['hedeɪk] Kopfweh; Kopfschmerzen II
heading ['hedɪŋ] Überschrift <I>
headline ['hedlaɪn] Überschrift; Schlagzeile III U3, 62
healthy ['helθi] gesund III U1, 16
*to **hear** [hɪə] hören II
heard [hɜːd] simple past von *to hear* II
hearing ['hɪərɪŋ] Gehör II
heart [hɑːt] Herz III U4, 80
heavy ['hevi] schwer; stark; schwierig III U2, 48
heavy events [ˌhevi ɪ'vents] Heavy Events *(Aktivitäten bei den Highland Games mit schweren Gewichten)* III U2, 48
height [haɪt] Höhe II
held [held] simple past von *to hold* II
helicopter ['helɪkɒptə] Helikopter; Hubschrauber III U4, 80
Hello. [hə'ləʊ] Hallo. I
helmet ['helmət] Helm I
help [help] Hilfe I
to **help** [help] helfen I
her [hɜː] ihr I; sie II
here [hɪə] hier I; hierher; hierhin III U1, 16
Here you are. [ˌhɪə ju‿'ɑː] Bitte schön. I
hers [hɜːz] ihre III U1, 16
Hi. [haɪ] Hi.; Hallo. I
high [haɪ] hoch; groß II
high jump ['haɪ ˌdʒʌmp] Hochsprung <III U2, 131>
junior high school [ˌdʒuːniə 'haɪ skuːl] Junior Highschool *(Mittelschule in den USA, in der Regel Klassenstufe 7–9)* II
hiking ['haɪkɪŋ] Wandern <III U2, 131>
him [hɪm] ihm; ihn II
hip-hop ['hɪphɒp] Hip-Hop *(Musik)* III U1, 27
his [hɪz] sein I; seine III U1, 19
historic [hɪ'stɒrɪk] historisch <III U1, 24>
historical [hɪ'stɒrɪkl] historisch; geschichtlich <III U1, 11>
history ['hɪstri] Geschichte III U2, 32
hit song ['hɪt ˌsɒŋ] Hit III U1, 27
*to **hit** [hɪt] treffen; schlagen III U4, 84
hit [hɪt] simple past, past participle von *to hit* III U4, 84
hobby ['hɒbi] Hobby II
*to **hold** [həʊld] halten; festhalten II
hole [həʊl] Loch I
holiday ['hɒlədeɪ] Ferien; Urlaub II; Feiertag III U4, 91
home [həʊm] Zuhause; Heim; nach Hause I
at home [ət 'həʊm] zu Hause; daheim I
back home [bæk 'həʊm] zu Hause; daheim III U3, 62
home town ['həʊm taʊn] Heimatstadt; Heimatort <III U1, 11>
homework ['həʊmwɜːk] Hausaufgabe(n) I
to do homework [ˌduː 'həʊmwɜːk] Hausaufgabe(n) machen I
to **hoover** ['huːvə] staubsaugen II
to **hope** (for) [həʊp (fə)] hoffen (auf) II
horrible ['hɒrəbl] schrecklich; entsetzlich <III U3, 135>
horse [hɔːs] Pferd I
horse riding ['hɔːs ˌraɪdɪŋ] Reiten I
hospital ['hɒspɪtl] Krankenhaus II
hostel ['hɒstl] Herberge; Hostel II
hot [hɒt] heiß I
hot dog ['hɒt ˌdɒg] Hotdog II
hotel [həʊ'tel] Hotel <III U4, 87>
hour [aʊə] Stunde II
house [haʊs] Haus I; House *(Musik)* <III U2, 44>
around the house [əˌraʊnd ðə 'haʊs] zu Hause <III U2, 39>
how [haʊ] wie I
How about ...? [ˌhaʊ‿ə'baʊt] Wie wäre es, wenn ...? <III U3, 135>
How are you? [ˌhaʊ‿'ɑː jə] Wie geht es dir? I
How can I help you? [ˌhaʊ kæn aɪ 'help‿juː] Was kann ich für euch/dich tun? I
How much (is/are) ...? [ˌhaʊ 'mʌtʃ (ɪz/ɑː)] Wie viel (kostet/kosten) ...? I
How old are you? [haʊ‿'əʊld‿ə juː] Wie alt bist du? I
how to ... ['haʊ tə] wie man ... <III U1, 23>
huge [hjuːdʒ] riesig; riesengroß III U4, 74
a/one **hundred** ['hʌndrəd] hundert; einhundert I
hungry ['hʌŋgri] hungrig I
treasure **hunt** ['treʒə ˌhʌnt] Schnitzeljagd; Schatzsuche II
hurling ['hɜːlɪŋ] Hurling *(ähnliche Sportart wie Hockey)* III U3, 53
*to **hurt** [hɜːt] verletzen; wehtun II
hurt [hɜːt] simple past von *to hurt* II; verletzt III U1, 21

I

I [aɪ] ich I

I can't find ... [aɪ kɑːnt ˈfaɪnd] ich kann ... nicht finden I
I don't know. [ˌaɪ dəʊnt ˈnəʊ] Ich weiß (es) nicht! I
I wouldn't like (to) ... [aɪ ˈwʊdnt laɪk (tə)] ich möchte nicht ...; ich würde nicht gerne ... I
I'm afraid [aɪm‿əˈfreɪd] leider III U1, 16
I'm sorry. [aɪm ˈsɒri] Es tut mir leid.; Entschuldigung. II
I'd (= I would) [aɪd] ich würde; ich hätte gern I
I'd like (to) ... (= I would like to) [aɪd ˈlaɪk (tə)] ich möchte ...; ich würde gerne ... I
I'm fine. [ˌaɪm ˈfaɪn] Mir geht es gut. I
ice cream [ˌaɪs ˈkriːm] Eis; Eiscreme II
ice skating [ˈaɪs ˌskeɪtɪŋ] Schlittschuhlaufen <III U2, 131>
idea [aɪˈdɪə] Idee I
if [ɪf] wenn; falls III U1, 26
to **imagine** [ɪˈmædʒɪn] sich vorstellen <II>
important [ɪmˈpɔːtnt] wichtig III U1, 27
the most important [ðə ˈməʊst ɪmˌpɔːtnt] die wichtigste III U4, 76
in [ɪn] im; in; auf; am I
in front [ɪn ˈfrʌnt] vorn II
in person [ɪn ˈpɜːsn] persönlich <III U1, 22>
in the middle of [ɪn ðə ˈmɪdl‿əv] mitten in II
in a park [ɪn‿ə ˈpɑːk] im Park I
in front of [ɪn ˈfrʌnt‿əv] vor; davor I
in the distance [ˌɪn ðə ˈdɪstns] in der Ferne <III U1, 130>
in the evening [ɪn ði‿ˈiːvnɪŋ] abends I
in the northwest of [ˌɪn ðə ˈnɔːθwest‿əv] im Nordwesten von III U1, 12
to **include** [ɪnˈkluːd] beinhalten; enthalten <III U1, 25>
independence [ˌɪndɪˈpendəns] Unabhängigkeit III U4, 90
industry [ˈɪndəstri] Industrie III U1, 28
influence [ˈɪnfluəns] Einfluss <III U2, 44>
to **inform** [ɪnˈfɔːm] informieren <III U2, 51>
information [ˌɪnfəˈmeɪʃn] Information(en) II
inhabitant [ɪnˈhæbɪtnt] Einwohner; Einwohnerin; Bewohner; Bewohnerin <III U1, 128>
inline skating [ˌɪnlaɪn ˈskeɪtɪŋ] Inlineskaten <III U4, 138>
inside [ˌɪnˈsaɪd] drinnen <III U3, 136>
inside cover [ˌɪnsaɪd ˈkʌvə] Umschlaginnenseite <II>
point of **interest** [ˌpɔɪnt‿əv ˈɪntrəst] Sehenswürdigkeit <III U1, 24>
*to be **interested** in [biː ˈɪntrəstɪd‿ɪn] sich interessieren für; interessiert sein an III U4, 76
interesting [ˈɪntrəstɪŋ] interessant I
internet [ˈɪntənet] Internet I
to surf the internet [sɜːf ði ˈɪntənet] im Internet surfen <III U4, 137>
interview [ˈɪntəvjuː] Interview; Befragung <I>; Gespräch <III U3, 70>
to **interview** [ˈɪntəvjuː] befragen; interviewen <II>
into [ˈɪntu] in; in ... hinein II
intro [ˈɪntrəʊ] Auftakt; Einführung <I>
to **introduce** sb to sb [ˌɪntrəˈdjuːs] jmdn. jmdm. vorstellen III U3, 62
introduction [ˌɪntrəˈdʌkʃn] Einleitung; Einführung <III U2, 51>
invitation [ˌɪnvɪˈteɪʃn] Einladung I
to **invite** [ɪnˈvaɪt] einladen II
Irish [ˈaɪrɪʃ] irisch; Irisch; aus Irland III U3, 52
the Irish [ði ˈaɪrɪʃ] die Iren III U3, 53
is [ɪz] ist I
Is something wrong? [ɪz ˈsʌmθɪŋ rɒŋ] Stimmt etwas nicht? II
island [ˈaɪlənd] Insel III U3, 68
it [ɪt] es; er; sie I; ihn; ihm II
it's (= it is) [ɪts] es ist I
It's ten pounds. [ɪts ˌten ˈpaʊndz] Es kostet zehn Pfund. I
its [ɪts] sein; ihr I

J

January [ˈdʒænjuri] Januar I
jeans *(pl)* [dʒiːnz] Jeans I
crown **jewels** *(pl)* [ˌkraʊn ˈdʒuːəlz] Kronjuwelen II
job [dʒɒb] Job I; Aufgabe; Tätigkeit <II>
jogging [ˈdʒɒgɪŋ] Joggen <III U2, 131>
to **join** [dʒɔɪn] mitmachen bei <III U4, 87>
journey [ˈdʒɜːni] Fahrt; Reise III U3, 54
judo [ˈdʒuːdəʊ] Judo <III U4, 138>
juice [dʒuːs] Saft I
July [dʒʊˈlaɪ] Juli I
high **jump** [ˈhaɪ ˌdʒʌmp] Hochsprung <III U2, 131>
long **jump** [ˈlɒŋ ˌdʒʌmp] Weitsprung II
to **jump** [dʒʌmp] springen III U4, 85
June [dʒuːn] Juni I
junior high school [ˌdʒuːniə ˈhaɪ skuːl] Junior Highschool *(Mittelschule in den USA, in der Regel Klassenstufe 7–9)* II
just [dʒʌst] gerade (eben); einfach; soeben; nur III U2, 38
just for fun [ˌdʒʌst fə ˈfʌn] nur (so) zum Spaß <I>

K

*to **keep** [kiːp] halten II; behalten; aufbewahren III U2, 42
to keep in touch [ˌkiːp ɪn ˈtʌtʃ] in Kontakt bleiben II
to keep out [ˌkiːp‿ˈaʊt] draußen halten III U2, 42
kept [kept] simple past von *to keep* II; past participle von *to keep* III U2, 42
key [kiː] Schlüssel III U3, 54
kid [kɪd] Kind I
kilo (kg, kilogram) [ˈkɪləʊ] Kilo (kg, Kilogramm) I
kilometre (km) [kɪˈlɒmɪtə] Kilometer (km) <III U1, 128>
kilt [kɪlt] Kilt; Schottenrock III U2, 33
kind [kaɪnd] Art; Sorte II
king [kɪŋ] König II
newspaper **kiosk** [ˈnjuːspeɪpə ˌkiːɒsk] Zeitungsstand II
kitchen [ˈkɪtʃɪn] Küche II
*to **know** [nəʊ] wissen; kennen I
I don't know. [ˌaɪ dəʊnt ˈnəʊ] Ich weiß (es) nicht! I

L

to label ['leɪbl] beschriften <II>
ladder ['lædə] Leiter I
lake [leɪk] See III U4, 92
lamp [læmp] Lampe II
land [lænd] Land III U1, 20
landlord ['lændlɔ:d] Grundstückseigentümer; Vermieter III U1, 20
landmark ['lænma:k] Wahrzeichen <III U1, 24>
language ['læŋgwɪdʒ] Grammatik; Sprache <I>
lantern ['læntən] Laterne II
laptop ['læptɒp] Laptop I
large [la:dʒ] groß II
to last [la:st] dauern; andauern II
last [la:st] letzte I
late [leɪt] (zu) spät II
  to be late [bi: 'leɪt] zu spät kommen II
later ['leɪtə] später I
  See you later. [ˌsi: jə 'leɪtə] Bis später.; Bis dann. III U2, 38
latest ['leɪtɪst] neueste; aktuell III U4, 76
to laugh [la:f] lachen II
leader ['li:də] Leiter; Leiterin III U4, 80
to learn [lɜ:n] lernen II
*to **leave** [li:v] verlassen; lassen; abfahren; weggehen II; hinterlassen; vergessen III U3, 54
leaving ['li:vɪŋ] Abschieds- II
left [left] links; simple past von *to leave* II; übrig III U2, 38; past participle von *to leave* III U3, 54
  on the left [ɒn ðə 'left] links; auf der linken Seite II
leg [leg] Bein II
less [les] weniger III U4, 76
lesson ['lesn] Schulstunde; Unterricht I
let's (= let us) [lets] lass(t) uns I
life *(sg)* [laɪf], **lives** *(pl)* [laɪvz] Leben II
lift [lɪft] Aufzug II
to lift [lɪft] heben; hochheben; anheben III U2, 48
traffic **light** ['træfɪk ˌlaɪt] Ampel <III U3, 134>
to like [laɪk] mögen; gernhaben I
  like + -ing [ˌlaɪk '…ɪŋ] … gerne I
like [laɪk] wie I
  like this [laɪk 'ðɪs] so; auf diese Weise <I>
line [laɪn] Zeile; Linie III U2, 38
  zip line ['zɪp ˌlaɪn] Seilrutsche III U2, 32
mountain **lion** ['maʊntɪn ˌlaɪən] Puma II
list [lɪst] Liste III U3, 58
  shopping list ['ʃɒpɪŋ ˌlɪst] Einkaufszettel I
to listen (to) ['lɪsn (tə)] anhören; hören; zuhören I
listening ['lɪsnɪŋ] Hörverstehen <I>
  listening skills ['lɪsnɪŋ ˌskɪlz] Fertigkeit Hören <I>
little ['lɪtl] klein I
  a little (bit) [ə 'lɪtl (bɪt)] ein (kleines) bisschen; ein (klein) wenig II
to live [lɪv] wohnen; leben I
live [laɪv] Live- III U1, 27
living room ['lɪvɪŋ ˌrʊm] Wohnzimmer II
to load the dishwasher [ˌləʊd ðə 'dɪʃwɒʃə] die Spülmaschine einräumen II
local ['ləʊkl] örtlich; lokal; hiesig II
locked [lɒkt] abgeschlossen I
lonely ['ləʊnli] einsam <III U3, 63>
long [lɒŋ] lang III U1, 16
  to be a long way away [bi: ə 'lɒŋ ˌweɪ ə'weɪ] weit weg sein II
  long jump ['lɒŋ ˌdʒʌmp] Weitsprung II
longer ['lɒŋgə] länger I
*to have a **look** (at) [ˌhæv‿ə 'lʊk (ət)] sich anschauen <III U1, 130>
to look [lʊk] schauen; aussehen; sehen; nachschauen I
  to look after [ˌlʊk‿'a:ftə] aufpassen auf; hüten; sich kümmern um II
  to look at ['lʊk‿ət] anschauen I
*to **lose** [lu:z] verlieren II
lost [lɒst] simple past von *to lose* II; past participle von *to lose* III U2, 42
a **lot** [ə 'lɒt] viel; sehr I
a **lot of** [ə 'lɒt‿əv] viel; viele; eine Menge I
lots of ['lɒts‿əv] jede Menge; viel; viele I
loud [laʊd] laut I
Love, [lʌv] Liebe Grüße; Herzliche Grüße I
to love [lʌv] lieben; gern mögen I
lovely ['lʌvli] schön; hübsch <III U2, 44>
lucky ['lʌki] glücklich; Glück bringend II
  to be lucky [bi:‿'lʌki] Glück haben II
  lucky day [ˌlʌki 'deɪ] Glückstag II
lunch [lʌnʃ] Mittagessen I
  packed lunch [ˌpækt 'lʌnʃ] Lunchpaket; Vesper <III U1, 129>
lunchtime ['lʌnʃtaɪm] Mittagspause; Mittagszeit I

M

made [meɪd] simple past von *to make* II; past participle von *to make* III U2, 36
magazine [ˌmægə'zi:n] Zeitschrift <I>
*to do **magic** [ˌdu: 'mædʒɪk] zaubern II
magician [mə'dʒɪʃn] Zauberkünstler; Zauberkünstlerin II
main [meɪn] wichtigste <III U1, 29>
*to **make** [meɪk] erstellen; basteln; machen; tun I; bilden; ausmachen <II>
  to make friends [ˌmeɪk 'frendz] Freundschaft(en) schließen II
  to make peace [ˌmeɪk 'pi:s] Frieden schaffen III U2, 43
  to make sure [ˌmeɪk 'ʃɔ:] dafür sorgen; sich versichern <III U1, 130>
male [meɪl] männlich <III U4, 86>
mall [mɔ:l] Einkaufspassage; Einkaufszentrum II
man *(sg)* [mæn], **men** *(pl)* [men] Mann I
many ['meni] viele I
map [mæp] Karte; Plan II
March [ma:tʃ] März I
market ['ma:kɪt] Markt I
  flea market ['fli: ˌma:kɪt] Flohmarkt I
match [mætʃ] Spiel; Match I
to match [mætʃ] zuordnen <I>
Maths [mæθs] Mathe I
May [meɪ] Mai I
maybe ['meɪbi] vielleicht II
me [mi:] ich; mich; mir I

meal [miːl] Essen; Mahlzeit II
*__to mean__ [miːn] bedeuten; meinen III U3, 62
meaning ['miːnɪŋ] Bedeutung <III U3, 55>
meant [ment] simple past, past participle von *to mean* III U3, 62
medal ['medl] Medaille II
media ['miːdiə] Medien <II>
  social media [ˌsəʊʃl 'miːdiə] soziale Medien III U4, 76
mediation [ˌmiːdi'eɪʃn] Sprachmittlung <I>
  mediation skills [ˌmiːdi'eɪʃn ˌskɪlz] Fertigkeit Sprachmittlung <I>
*to **meet** [miːt] kennenlernen; treffen I; (sich) treffen II
megaphone ['megəfəʊn] Megafon III U4, 80
melodic [mə'lɒdɪk] melodisch; wohlklingend <III U2, 44>
Merry Christmas! [ˌmeri 'krɪsməs] Frohe Weihnachten! I
mess [mes] Durcheinander; Unordnung I
message ['mesɪdʒ] Nachricht; SMS II
  voice message ['vɔɪs ˌmesɪdʒ] Sprachnachricht <III U4, 137>
met [met] simple past von *to meet* II
metre ['miːtə] Meter II
middle ['mɪdl] Mittelteil <III U3, 67>; Mitte III U3, 70
  in the middle of [ɪn ðə 'mɪdl‿əv] mitten in II
mild [maɪld] mild II
mile [maɪl] Meile III U2, 32
milk [mɪlk] Milch III U1, 12
million ['mɪljən] Million I
  half a million [ˌhɑːf‿ə 'mɪljən] eine halbe Million III U1, 12
mind map ['maɪnd ˌmæp] Wörternetz <I>
Never **mind.** [ˌnevə 'maɪnd] Macht nichts.; Schon gut.; Mach dir nichts draus. II
mine [maɪn] Bergwerk III U1, 12
mine [maɪn] meine III U1, 16
minute ['mɪnɪt] Minute I
mirror ['mɪrə] Spiegel <III U2, 51>
to **miss** [mɪs] verpassen; vermissen II
mistake [mɪ'steɪk] Fehler <III U3, 67>
to **mix** [mɪks] mischen <III U3, 66>
model ['mɒdl] Vorlage; Muster <I>
modern ['mɒdn] modern I
at the **moment** [ət ðə 'məʊmənt] im Moment; momentan II
Monday ['mʌndeɪ] Montag I
money ['mʌni] Geld I
  to raise money [ˌreɪz 'mʌni] Geld sammeln; Geld aufbringen II
month [mʌnθ] Monat II
monument ['mɒnjəmənt] Denkmal <III U1, 130>
more [mɔː] mehr; weitere II
morning ['mɔːnɪŋ] Morgen; Vormittag I
  this morning [ðɪs 'mɔːnɪŋ] heute Morgen II
most [məʊst] die meisten; die Mehrheit; am meisten III U2, 51
  the most important [ðə 'məʊst ɪmˌpɔːtnt] die wichtigste III U4, 76
mother ['mʌðə] Mutter I
to **motivate** ['məʊtɪveɪt] anspornen; motivieren III U4, 85
mountain ['maʊntɪn] Berg II
  mountain lion ['maʊntɪn ˌlaɪən] Puma II
mouse *(sg)* [maʊs], **mice** *(pl)* [maɪs] Maus I
mouth [maʊθ] Mund II
to **move** [muːv] umziehen II
movie *(AE)* ['muːvi] Film III U4, 76
Mr ['mɪstə] Herr *(Anrede)* I
Mrs ['mɪsɪz] Frau *(Anrede)* I
much [mʌtʃ] viel I
mud [mʌd] Schlamm; Matsch I
muffin ['mʌfɪn] Muffin II
mum [mʌm] Mama; Mutti I
museum [mjuː'ziːəm] Museum II
music ['mjuːzɪk] Musik I
musical ['mjuːzɪkl] Musical; Musiktheaterstück III U1, 26
Muslim ['mʊzlɪm] Muslim; Muslimin I
must [mʌst] müssen II
  must never/not [ˌmʌst 'nevə/'nɒt] nie/nicht dürfen III U2, 42
my [maɪ] mein I
  My name is … [maɪ 'neɪm‿ɪz] Ich heiße … I
myself [maɪ'self] mich; selbst III U2, 34

N

name [neɪm] Name I
  family name ['fæmli ˌneɪm] Nachname <III U4, 86>
  first name ['fɜːst ˌneɪm] Vorname <III U4, 86>
to **name** [neɪm] benennen <I>; nennen <III U4, 85>
narrator [nə'reɪtə] Erzähler; Erzählerin I
national ['næʃnl] National-; national III U4, 74
  national park [ˌnæʃnl 'pɑːk] Nationalpark III U4, 74
native ['neɪtɪv] eingeboren; einheimisch III U4, 75
  Native American [ˌneɪtɪv‿ə'merɪkən] Ureinwohner Amerikas; Ureinwohnerin Amerikas; Indianer; Indianerin; indianisch III U4, 75
near [nɪə] in der Nähe von I; nah II
nearly ['nɪəli] fast; beinahe II
neck [nek] Hals; Nacken II
to **need** [niːd] brauchen I
  to need to ['niːd ˌtə] müssen III U2, 34
neighbour ['neɪbə] Nachbar; Nachbarin I
netball ['netbɔːl] Korbball I
social **network** [ˌsəʊʃl 'netwɜːk] soziales Netzwerk <III U4, 79>
never ['nevə] nie; niemals II; noch nie <III U4, 87>
  Never mind. [ˌnevə 'maɪnd] Macht nichts.; Schon gut.; Mach dir nichts draus. II
new [njuː] neu I
news [njuːz] Nachricht(en); Neuigkeit(en) II
newspaper ['njuːsˌpeɪpə] Zeitung III U4, 76
  newspaper kiosk ['njuːspeɪpə ˌkiːɒsk] Zeitungsstand II
next [nekst] nächste I; als Nächstes II
  next to ['nekst tə] neben I
nice [naɪs] schön; nett I
  Nice to meet you. [ˌnaɪs tə 'miːt juː] Schön, dich kennenzulernen. I
night [naɪt] Nacht I
nine [naɪn] neun I
nineteen [ˌnaɪn'tiːn] neunzehn I

ninety ['naɪnti] neunzig I
no [nəʊ] kein; keine; nein I
no one ['nəʊ wʌn] niemand I
nobody ['nəʊbədi] niemand II
noise [nɔɪz] Geräusch I
noisy ['nɔɪzi] laut III U1, 12
north [nɔ:θ] Norden; Nord- III U1, 12
northbound ['nɔ:θbaʊnd] in Richtung Norden <III U3, 134>
northwest [ˌnɔ:θ'west] Nordwesten III U1, 12
in the northwest of [ˌɪn ðə 'nɔ:θwest‿əv] im Nordwesten von III U1, 12
nose [nəʊz] Nase II
not [nɒt] nicht I
not ... any more [ˌnɒt ... eni 'mɔ:] nicht mehr III U3, 58
not ... anything [nɒt ... 'eniθɪŋ] nichts III U3, 58
not ... yet [nɒt ... 'jet] noch nicht III U2, 34
not ... any [ˌnɒt ... eni] kein; keine III U3, 58
notes *(pl)* [nəʊts] Notizen <I>
to take notes [ˌteɪk 'nəʊts] sich Notizen machen <I>
nothing ['nʌθɪŋ] nichts II
notice ['nəʊtɪs] Aushang; Plakat III U3, 54
November [nə'vembə] November I
now [naʊ] jetzt; nun I
Bye for now. [ˌbaɪ fə 'naʊ] Bis bald. <III U1, 23>
number ['nʌmbə] Zahl; Nummer I

O

o'clock [ə'klɒk] Uhr *(Zeitangabe bei vollen Stunden)* I
occasionally [ə'keɪʒnli] gelegentlich III U1, 16
October [ɒk'təʊbə] Oktober I
odd one out [ˌɒd wʌn‿'aʊt] das Wort, das nicht in die Gruppe passt <I>
of [ɒv] von I
of course [əv 'kɔ:s] natürlich; selbstverständlich II
ticket **office** ['tɪkɪt ˌɒfɪs] Kartenverkaufsstelle <III U1, 11>
police **officer** [pə'li:s‿ɒfɪsə] Polizeibeamter; Polizeibeamtin I
often ['ɒfn] oft; häufig II
oh [əʊ] Null *(bei Uhrzeiten und Telefonnummern)* III U1, 16
oil [ɔɪl] Öl II
OK (okay) [əʊ'keɪ] okay I
old [əʊld] alt I
on [ɒn] auf; an; am I; mit II
to be on [bi:‿'ɒn] auf dem Programm stehen; anstehen; laufen III U2, 38
on TV [ɒn ˌti:'vi:] im Fernsehen III U1, 27
to put on [ˌpʊt‿'ɒn] anziehen II
to try on [ˌtraɪ 'ɒn] anprobieren II
on foot [ɒn 'fʊt] zu Fuß I
on Saturdays [ɒn 'sætədeɪz] samstags I
on the bus [ˌɒn ðə 'bʌs] im Bus II
on the left [ɒn ðə 'left] links; auf der linken Seite II
on the right [ɒn ðə 'raɪt] rechts; auf der rechten Seite II
once [wʌns] einmal; einst II
once upon a time [ˌwʌns əpɒn‿ə 'taɪm] es war einmal II
one [wʌn] eins; ein I
a/one hundred ['hʌndrəd] hundert; einhundert I
a/one thousand ['θaʊznd] tausend; eintausend II
no one ['nəʊ wʌn] niemand I
one day ['wʌn deɪ] eines Tages I
one(s) [wʌn(z)] *Platzhalter für ein Nomen* III U3, 63
each one [ˌi:tʃ 'wʌn] jede <III U4, 83>
online [ɒn'laɪn] online; Online- II
only ['əʊnli] nur I
to **open** ['əʊpn] öffnen; aufmachen I; eröffnen <III U1, 130>
open ['əʊpn] geöffnet I
opposite ['ɒpəzɪt] Gegenteil <I>; gegenüber II
or [ɔ:] oder I
orange ['ɒrɪndʒ] orange; Orange I
orchestra ['ɔ:kɪstrə] Orchester III U3, 52
order ['ɔ:də] Reihenfolge <I>
word order ['wɜ:d‿ˌɔ:də] Wortstellung; Satzstellung <II>
to **order** ['ɔ:də] bestellen III U1, 16
to **organize** ['ɔ:gənaɪz] organisieren I
other ['ʌðə] andere II
each other [ˌi:tʃ‿'ʌðə] einander; sich; gegenseitig III U3, 62
others ['ʌðəz] anderen II
our [aʊə] unser I
ours [aʊəz] unsere III U1, 19
*to keep **out** [ˌki:p‿'aʊt] draußen halten III U2, 42
out and about [ˌaʊt‿ən‿ə'baʊt] unterwegs III U1, 10
out of ... ['aʊt‿əv] aus ... heraus I
outside [ˌaʊt'saɪd] außerhalb; außen; draußen; im Freien II
oval ['əʊvl] oval; eiförmig III U4, 84
over ['əʊvə] vorbei <II>; herüber; über; drüben III U2, 38
all over [ˌɔ:l‿'əʊvə] in ganz; überall II
to come over [ˌkʌm 'əʊvə] herüberkommen; vorbeischauen III U2, 38
to turn over [ˌtɜ:n 'əʊvə] umkippen; (sich) umdrehen III U4, 80
to **own** [əʊn] besitzen III U1, 20
own [əʊn] eigene II

P

p.m. [ˌpi:'em] nachmittags *(Uhrzeit)* III U1, 16
to **pack** [pæk] packen; einpacken III U2, 34
packed lunch [ˌpækt 'lʌnʃ] Lunchpaket; Vesper <III U1, 129>
paddle ['pædl] Paddel <III U2, 131>
to **paddle** ['pædl] paddeln III U4, 80
page [peɪdʒ] Seite <I>
to **paint** [peɪnt] bemalen; malen; streichen II
face **painting** ['feɪs peɪntɪŋ] Schminken II
wall **painting** ['wɔ:l peɪntɪŋ] Wandmalerei II
pair [peə] Paar <II>
pal [pæl] Freund *(ugs.)* <III U4, 87>
paper ['peɪpə] Papier III U3, 62
paragraph ['pærəgra:f] Abschnitt; Absatz; Paragraf <III U3, 62>
parent ['peərnt] Elternteil <III U4, 86>
parents *(pl)* ['peərnts] Eltern I
park [pa:k] Park I

national park [ˌnæʃnl ˈpɑːk] Nationalpark III U4, 74
theme park [ˈθiːm ˌpɑːk] Freizeitpark II
part [pɑːt] Teil; Rolle II
to take part (in) [ˌteɪk ˈpɑːt (ɪn)] mitmachen (bei); teilnehmen (an) II
partner [ˈpɑːtnə] Partner; Partnerin I
party [ˈpɑːti] Party; Feier I
to have a party [ˌhæv‿ə ˈpɑːti] eine Party feiern I
to **pass** on [ˌpɑːs‿ˈɒn] weitergeben <III U4, 75>
past [pɑːst] Vergangenheit III U1, 12
past [pɑːst] vorbei (an) I; nach *(bei Uhrzeitangaben)* II
half past (seven) [ˌhɑːf ˈpɑːst (ˌsevn)] halb (acht) II
quarter to/past [ˈkwɔːtə tə/pɑːst] Viertel vor/nach II
*to **pay** [peɪ] bezahlen <III U4, 86>
PE (Physical Education) [ˌpiːˈiː (ˌfɪzɪkl edʒʊˈkeɪʃn)] Sportunterricht I
peace [piːs] Frieden III U2, 43
to make peace [ˌmeɪk ˈpiːs] Frieden schaffen III U2, 43
peaceful [ˈpiːsfl] friedlich III U4, 90
pen [pen] Stift; Füller I
pencil [ˈpensl] Bleistift I
people [ˈpiːpl] Volk III U4, 76
people *(pl only)* [ˈpiːpl] Leute; Menschen I
percent (%) [pəˈsent] Prozent III U4, 85
present **perfect** [ˌpreznt ˈpɜːfɪkt] das Perfekt <III U2, 36>
person [ˈpɜːsn] Mensch; Person II
in person [ɪn ˈpɜːsn] persönlich <III U1, 22>
pet [pet] Haustier I
phone [fəʊn] Telefon; Handy I
phone call [ˈfəʊn ˌkɔːl] Telefonanruf; Anruf I
to **phone** [fəʊn] anrufen; telefonieren II
photo [ˈfəʊtəʊ] Foto I
to take photos (of) [ˌteɪk ˈfəʊtəʊz (əv)] Fotos machen; fotografieren II
phrase [freɪz] Wortverbindung; Satzteil; Satz; Redewendung <III U1, 13>
picnic [ˈpɪknɪk] Picknick I
picture [ˈpɪktʃə] Bild I
picture-based [ˈpɪktʃəbeɪst] bildbezogen <III U3, 70>
a **piece** of [ə ˈpiːs‿əv] ein Stück … II
pier [pɪə] Pier II
pink [pɪŋk] pink; rosa I
pizza [ˈpiːtsə] Pizza I
place [pleɪs] Platz; Stelle; Ort I
plan [plæn] Plan III ZI 9
to **plan** [plæn] planen <II>
planner [ˈplænə] Kalender; Planer II
plant [plɑːnt] Pflanze III U4, 74
play [pleɪ] Theaterstück III U1, 11
to **play** [pleɪ] spielen I
player [ˈpleɪə] Spieler; Spielerin II
playground [ˈpleɪgraʊnd] Schulhof; Pausenhof; Spielplatz I
playing field [ˈpleɪɪŋ ˌfiːld] Sportplatz II; Spielfeld III U4, 84
please [pliːz] bitte I
plum [plʌm] Pflaume I
poem [ˈpəʊɪm] Gedicht III U3, 63
point [pɔɪnt] Punkt III U4, 85
point of interest [ˌpɔɪnt‿əv ˈɪntrəst] Sehenswürdigkeit <III U1, 24>
starting point [ˈstɑːtɪŋ ˌpɔɪnt] Ausgangspunkt <III U3, 55>
to **point** [pɔɪnt] zeigen <I>
to point out [ˌpɔɪnt‿ˈaʊt] zeigen; darauf hinweisen <III U1, 130>
police officer [pəˈliːs‿ɒfɪsə] Polizeibeamter; Polizeibeamtin I
swimming **pool** [ˈswɪmɪŋ ˌpuːl] Schwimmbad I
pop [pɒp] Pop *(Musik)* II
popular [ˈpɒpjələ] Pop-; beliebt III U1, 27
positive [ˈpɒzətɪv] positiv III U3, 58
possible [ˈpɒsəbl] möglich III U2, 49
to **post** [pəʊst] posten; online stellen III U4, 76
postcard [ˈpəʊstkɑːd] Postkarte I
poster [ˈpəʊstə] Poster II
pot [pɒt] Topf III U3, 62
pound (£) [paʊnd] Pfund *(brit. Währungseinheit)* I
practice [ˈpræktɪs] Training; Übung I
to **practise** [ˈpræktɪs] üben; trainieren <II>
preferred [prɪˈfɜːd] bevorzugt <III U4, 86>
preposition [ˌprepəˈzɪʃn] Präposition <III U3, 136>
present [ˈpreznt] Geschenk I
present perfect [ˌpreznt ˈpɜːfɪkt] das Perfekt <III U2, 36>
present progressive [ˌpreznt prəˈgresɪv] Verlaufsform der Gegenwart <II>
to **present** [prɪˈzent] präsentieren <I>
presentation [ˌpreznˈteɪʃn] Präsentation; Referat; Vortrag III U2, 50
presentation skills [ˌpreznˈteɪʃn ˌskɪlz] Fertigkeit Präsentieren <III U2, 50>
president [ˈprezɪdnt] Präsident; Präsidentin III U4, 81
pretty [ˈprɪti] hübsch II
price [praɪs] Preis I
prize [praɪz] Preis; Gewinn II
problem [ˈprɒbləm] Problem I
procession [prəˈseʃn] Umzug; Festzug II
profile [ˈprəʊfaɪl] Profil; Steckbrief III U4, 92
programme [ˈprəʊgræm] Sendung; Programm III U1, 28
present **progressive** [ˌpreznt prəˈgresɪv] Verlaufsform der Gegenwart <II>
project [ˈprɒdʒekt] Projekt II
prop [prɒp] Requisit <III U2, 45>
to **protest** [prəˈtest] protestieren III U4, 90
Protestant [ˈprɒtɪstnt] protestantisch; Protestant; Protestantin III U3, 68
public transport [ˌpʌblɪk ˈtrænspɔːt] öffentliche Verkehrsmittel III U3, 54
to **pull** [pʊl] ziehen I
pullover [ˈpʊləʊvə] Pullover I
to **push** [pʊʃ] schieben I
stone **put** [ˈstəʊn ˌpʊt] Steinstoßen III U2, 49
*to **put** [pʊt] setzen; legen; stellen I; bringen; stecken II
to put in [ˌpʊt‿ˈɪn] einsetzen <I>
to put on [ˌpʊt‿ˈɒn] anziehen II
put [pʊt] simple past von *to put* I

Q

quarter to/past ['kwɔ:tə tə/pɑ:st] Viertel vor/nach II
queen [kwi:n] Königin II
question ['kwestʃən] Frage I
queue [kju:] Warteschlange II
quiet [kwaɪət] leise; ruhig; still II
quite [kwaɪt] ziemlich; ganz; völlig II
quiz [kwɪz] Rätsel <I>; Quiz; Ratespiel <III U4, 79>

R

rabbit ['ræbɪt] Kaninchen I
raccoon [rə'ku:n] Waschbär I
race [reɪs] Wettrennen; Rennen; Wettlauf II
sack race ['sæk ˌreɪs] Sackhüpfen II
racket ['rækɪt] Schläger <III U2, 131>
radio ['reɪdiəʊ] Radio III U1, 27
raffle ['ræfl] Gewinnspiel; Tombola II
raft [rɑ:ft] Raft; Floß III U4, 80
rafting ['rɑ:ftɪŋ] Rafting III U4, 74
to go rafting [ˌgəʊ 'rɑ:ftɪŋ] raften gehen III U4, 75
to **rain** [reɪn] regnen I
rainbow ['reɪnbəʊ] Regenbogen III U3, 62
rainy ['reɪni] regnerisch II
to **raise** money [ˌreɪz 'mʌni] Geld sammeln; Geld aufbringen II
ran [ræn] simple past von *to run* II
rang [ræŋ] simple past von *to ring* II
rap [ræp] Rap I
rapid ['ræpɪd] Stromschnelle III U4, 80
rarely ['reəli] selten III U2, 48
*to **read** [ri:d] lesen; vorlesen II
read [red] simple past von *to read* II
reading ['ri:dɪŋ] Lesen <I>
reading skills ['ri:dɪŋ ˌskɪlz] Fertigkeit Lesen <I>
ready ['redi] bereit; fertig I
to get ready [ˌget 'redi] sich bereit machen <III U4, 89>
really ['rɪəli] wirklich; eigentlich I
reason ['ri:zn] Grund <III U3, 62>
to **record** [rɪ'kɔ:d] aufnehmen; aufzeichnen <I>
red [red] rot I
registration [ˌredʒɪ'streɪʃn] Überprüfung der Anwesenheit I; Anmeldung <III U4, 86>
registration form [redʒɪ'streɪʃn ˌfɔ:m] Anmeldeformular <III U4, 86>
religion [rɪ'lɪdʒn] Religion III U3, 68
religious [rɪ'lɪdʒəs] religiös; gläubig <III U1, 24>
to **remember** [rɪ'membə] sich erinnern (an); sich merken III U4, 76; daran denken <III U2, 41>
rent [rent] Miete III U1, 20
to **rent** [rent] mieten III U1, 28
to **repeat** [rɪ'pi:t] wiederholen <I>
report [rɪ'pɔ:t] Bericht <II>
to **report** (on) [rɪ'pɔ:t (ɒn)] berichten (über) <III U2, 39>
animal **rescue shelter** [ˌænɪml 'reskju: ˌʃeltə] Tierheim I
reservation [ˌrezə'veɪʃn] Reservat; Reservierung III U4, 76
rest [rest] Rest II
restaurant ['restrɒnt] Restaurant II
result [rɪ'zʌlt] Ergebnis <I>
return ticket [rɪ'tɜ:n ˌtɪkɪt] Hin- und Rückfahrkarte III U3, 54
*to **rewrite** [ˌri:'raɪt] umschreiben; neu schreiben <III U1, 19>
to **rhyme** [raɪm] (sich) reimen <III U1, 17>
rhyming ['raɪmɪŋ] Reim- <III U1, 17>
rice [raɪs] Reis II
chicken fried rice ['tʃɪkɪn ˌfraɪd 'raɪs] gebratener Reis mit Hühnerfleisch II
ride [raɪd] Fahrt; Fahrgeschäft; Ritt II
*to **ride** [raɪd] fahren; reiten I
horse **riding** ['hɔ:s ˌraɪdɪŋ] Reiten I
right [raɪt] Recht III U4, 90
civil rights *(pl)* [ˌsɪvl 'raɪts] Bürgerrechte; Grundrechte III U4, 90
right [raɪt] richtig; korrekt I; rechts; rechte II
to be right [bi: 'raɪt] recht haben <III U1, 23>
on the right [ɒn ðə 'raɪt] rechts; auf der rechten Seite II
You're right. [jɔ:‿'raɪt] Du hast recht. I
*to **ring** [rɪŋ] klingeln; läuten I
river ['rɪvə] Fluss I
road [rəʊd] Straße I
robot ['rəʊbɒt] Roboter; Automat III U1, 11
rock [rɒk] Fels; Stein III U4, 80; Rock *(Musik)* <III U2, 44>
rock climbing ['rɒk ˌklaɪmɪŋ] Klettern I
rocket ['rɒkɪt] Rakete III U1, 11
role play ['rəʊl ˌpleɪ] Rollenspiel <I>
roller coaster ['rəʊlə ˌkəʊstə] Achterbahn II
room [ru:m] Zimmer; Raum I
round [raʊnd] reihum <III U1, 25>
rubber ['rʌbə] Radiergummi I
rubbish ['rʌbɪʃ] Müll; Abfall I
rugby ['rʌgbi] Rugby III U2, 34
rule [ru:l] Regel <I>
ruler ['ru:lə] Lineal I
*to **run** [rʌn] laufen; rennen; fahren II; betreiben; leiten; führen <III U4, 86>
to run away [ˌrʌn‿ə'weɪ] weglaufen II

S

sack race ['sæk ˌreɪs] Sackhüpfen II
sad [sæd] traurig I
safe [seɪf] ungefährlich; sicher III U2, 34
said [sed] simple past von *to say* I; past participle von *to say* III U3, 62
salad ['sæləd] Salat I
the **same** [ðə 'seɪm] der gleiche; derselbe; gleich; genauso II
at the same time [ət ðə seɪm 'taɪm] gleichzeitig; nebenher II
sandwich ['sænwɪdʒ] Sandwich; belegtes Brot I
sang [sæŋ] simple past von *to sing* II
Saturday ['sætədeɪ] Samstag I
on Saturdays [ɒn 'sætədeɪz] samstags I
to **save** [seɪv] retten; sparen II
to save a file [ˌseɪv‿ə 'faɪl] eine Datei speichern <III U4, 137>
saw [sɔ:] simple past von *to see* I
saxophone ['sæksəfəʊn] Saxofon I
*to **say** [seɪ] nennen; sagen; nachsprechen; sprechen I; aussprechen III U3, 62

to scan [skæn] nach Details durchsuchen; scannen <III U1, 29>
to scare [skeə] erschrecken <II>
*to be **scared** [bi: 'skeəd] Angst haben I
scarf *(sg)* [skɑ:f], **scarves** *(pl)* [skɑ:vz] Schal; Tuch II
scary ['skeəri] unheimlich; gruselig; beängstigend I
scene [si:n] Szene <II>
scenery ['si:nri] Kulissen; Bühnenbild III U1, 16
school [sku:l] Schule I
at school [ət 'sku:l] in der Schule I
junior high school [ˌdʒu:niə 'haɪ sku:l] Junior Highschool *(Mittelschule in den USA, in der Regel Klassenstufe 7–9)* II
school trip [ˌsku:l 'trɪp] Klassenfahrt; Schulausflug II
science ['saɪəns] Wissenschaft; Naturwissenschaft III U1, 11
science fiction [ˌsaɪəns 'fɪkʃn] Science-Fiction I
Scot [skɒt] Schotte; Schottin III U2, 32
Scottish ['skɒtɪʃ] schottisch; aus Schottland III U2, 33
sea [si:] Meer I
to search [sɜ:tʃ] durchsuchen; suchen; durchstöbern <III U2, 43>
at the **seaside** [ət ðə 'si:saɪd] am Meer I
season ['si:zn] Jahreszeit; Saison II
second ['seknd] Sekunde <I>; zweite II
second-hand [ˌsekn'hænd] gebraucht; secondhand; aus zweiter Hand I
*to **see** [si:] sehen I
See you. ['si: ju:] Wir sehen uns.; Bis bald.; Tschüss. II
Let me see. [ˌlet mi 'si:] Lass mich mal schauen. I
See you later. [ˌsi: jə 'leɪtə] Bis später.; Bis dann. III U2, 38
See you soon. [ˌsi: ju: 'su:n] Bis bald. I
seen [si:n] past participle von *to see* III U2, 34
*to **sell** [sel] verkaufen I
*to **send** [send] schicken; senden I
sent [sent] simple past von *to send* I
sentence ['sentəns] Satz <I>
September [sep'tembə] September I
series *(no pl)* ['sɪəri:z] Serie <III U3, 64>
serious ['sɪəriəs] ernst; schwer II
to settle ['setl] siedeln; besiedeln; sich niederlassen III U4, 75
seven ['sevn] sieben I
seventeen [ˌsevn'ti:n] siebzehn I
seventy ['sevnti] siebzig I
shamrock ['ʃæmrɒk] Kleeblatt III U3, 53
to share [ʃeə] teilen III U4, 76
shark [ʃɑ:k] Hai I
she [ʃi:] sie I
sheep *(sg)* [ʃi:p], **sheep** *(pl)* [ʃi:p] Schaf I
shelf *(sg)* [ʃelf], **shelves** *(pl)* [ʃelvz] Regal; Regalbrett II
animal rescue **shelter** [ˌænɪml 'reskju: ˌʃeltə] Tierheim I
ship [ʃɪp] Schiff I
shirt [ʃɜ:t] Hemd; Shirt I
shoe [ʃu:] Schuh I
shop [ʃɒp] Geschäft; Laden I
sports shop ['spɔ:ts ˌʃɒp] Sportgeschäft II
shopping ['ʃɒpɪŋ] Einkaufen I
shopping centre ['ʃɒpɪŋ ˌsentə] Einkaufszentrum I
shopping list ['ʃɒpɪŋ ˌlɪst] Einkaufszettel I
short [ʃɔ:t] kurz II
shorts *(pl)* [ʃɔ:ts] Shorts; kurze Hose II
should [ʃʊd] sollte III U3, 58
to shout [ʃaʊt] rufen; schreien I
show [ʃəʊ] Show; Aufführung I
*to **show** [ʃəʊ] zeigen II
*to be **sick** [bi: 'sɪk] sich übergeben I
side [saɪd] Seite II
sight [saɪt] Sehenswürdigkeit II
sign [saɪn] Zeichen; Anzeichen; Schild III U3, 69
signature ['sɪgnətʃə] Unterschrift <III U4, 86>
silly ['sɪli] albern II
simple past [ˌsɪmpl 'pɑ:st] einfache Vergangenheit <II>
simple present [ˌsɪmpl 'preznt] einfache Gegenwart; Präsens <II>
since [sɪns] seit; seitdem III U3, 69
*to **sing** [sɪŋ] singen I
singer ['sɪŋə] Sänger; Sängerin I
single ticket [ˌsɪŋgl 'tɪkɪt] einfache Fahrkarte III U3, 54
sister ['sɪstə] Schwester I
*to **sit** [sɪt] sitzen <III U3, 136>
*to **sit** (down) [ˌsɪt ('daʊn)] sich setzen; sich hinsetzen I
situation [ˌsɪtju'eɪʃn] Situation <II>
six [sɪks] sechs I
sixteen [ˌsɪk'sti:n] sechzehn I
sixty ['sɪksti] sechzig I
size [saɪz] Größe II
to skate [skeɪt] inlineskaten; Schlittschuh laufen II
skateboard ['skeɪtbɔ:d] Skateboard I
skater ['skeɪtə] Skater; Skaterin I
*to go **skating** [ˌgəʊ 'skeɪtɪŋ] inlineskaten gehen; Schlittschuhlaufen gehen II
ice **skating** ['aɪs ˌskeɪtɪŋ] Schlittschuhlaufen <III U2, 131>
inline **skating** [ˌɪnlaɪn 'skeɪtɪŋ] Inlineskaten <III U4, 138>
to ski [ski:] Ski fahren III U2, 37
skiing ['ski:ɪŋ] Skifahren; Ski- III U2, 32
mediation **skills** [ˌmi:di'eɪʃn ˌskɪlz] Fertigkeit Sprachmittlung <I>
to skim [skɪm] überfliegen <III U1, 29>
skirt [skɜ:t] Rock III U2, 33
skyscraper ['skaɪˌskreɪpə] Wolkenkratzer <III U1, 130>
*to **sleep** [sli:p] schlafen II
slept [slept] simple past von *to sleep* II
slowly ['sləʊli] langsam <III U2, 51>
small [smɔ:l] klein I
smurf [smɜ:f] Schlumpf I
snack bar ['snæk ˌbɑ:] Imbissstube; Café I
snow [snəʊ] Schnee II
snowboard ['snəʊbɔ:d] Snowboard I
snowboarding ['snəʊbɔ:dɪŋ] Snowboarden <III U2, 131>
snowy ['snəʊi] schneereich; verschneit II
so [səʊ] also; deshalb I; so; dermaßen II

soccer *(AE)* ['sɒkə] Fußball II
social media [ˌsəʊʃl 'miːdiə] soziale Medien III U4, 76
social network [ˌsəʊʃl 'netwɜːk] soziales Netzwerk <III U4, 79>
sold [səʊld] simple past von *to sell* II
some [sʌm] etwas; einige; ein paar I
somebody ['sʌmbədi] jemand I
someone ['sʌmwʌn] jemand III U3, 58
something ['sʌmθɪŋ] etwas I
Is something wrong? [ɪz 'sʌmθɪŋ rɒŋ] Stimmt etwas nicht? II
sometimes ['sʌmtaɪmz] manchmal I
song [sɒŋ] Lied I
hit song ['hɪt ˌsɒŋ] Hit III U1, 27
soon [suːn] bald II
See you soon. [ˌsiː juː 'suːn] Bis bald. I
sorry ['sɒri] bekümmert; traurig <III U3, 65>
Sorry. ['sɒri] Tut mir leid.; Entschuldigung. I
I'm sorry. [aɪm 'sɒri] Es tut mir leid.; Entschuldigung. II
to **sort** [sɔːt] sortieren <III U3, 59>
soul [səʊl] Soul *(Musik)* <III U2, 44>
sound [saʊnd] Laut; Geräusch; Ton <I>; Klang; Sound <III U4, 82>
to **sound** [saʊnd] klingen III U1, 16
south [saʊθ] Süd-; Süden III U1, 11
southbound ['saʊθbaʊnd] in Richtung Süden <III U3, 134>
souvenir [ˌsuːvn'ɪə] Souvenir; Andenken II
space [speɪs] Raumfahrt; Weltraum III U4, 75
*to **speak** [spiːk] sprechen I
speaking ['spiːkɪŋ] Sprechen <I>
speaking skills ['spiːkɪŋ ˌskɪlz] Fertigkeit Sprechen <I>
special ['speʃl] besonders; speziell I
speech bubble ['spiːtʃ ˌbʌbl] Sprechblase <III U3, 67>
spelling ['spelɪŋ] Rechtschreibung I
*to **spend** [spend] verbringen *(Zeit)*; ausgeben *(Geld)* II
spent [spent] simple past von *to spend* II
spider ['spaɪdə] Spinne III U2, 42
sport [spɔːt] Sport III U1, 28
sports centre ['spɔːts ˌsentə] Sportzentrum I
sports day ['spɔːts ˌdeɪ] Sportfest II
sports shop ['spɔːts ˌʃɒp] Sportgeschäft II
sports *(pl only)* [spɔːts] Sportarten I
sporting event ['spɔːtɪŋ ɪˌvent] Sportereignis; Sportveranstaltung <III U3, 66>
spring [sprɪŋ] Frühling II
to **spy** [spaɪ] sehen I
square dance ['skweə ˌdɑːns] Square-dance *(amerikanischer Volkstanz)* II
squash [skwɒʃ] Squash <III U2, 131>
stadium ['steɪdiəm] Stadion I
stage [steɪdʒ] Bühne II
stall [stɔːl] Stand; Bude I
*to **stand** [stænd] stehen II
can't stand + -ing [ˌkɑːnt 'stænd …ɪŋ] etw. nicht ausstehen können; etw. nicht ertragen III U3, 58
star [stɑː] Star I
start [stɑːt] Start; Anfang; Beginn <I>
to **start** [stɑːt] anfangen; beginnen; starten I; gründen III U1, 27
starting point ['stɑːtɪŋ ˌpɔɪnt] Ausgangspunkt <III U3, 55>
state [steɪt] Bundesstaat; Staat III U4, 74
statement ['steɪtmənt] Aussagesatz; Aussage; Behauptung; Erklärung; Stellungnahme <III U3, 54>
station ['steɪʃn] Bahnhof; Station <III U1, 130>
train station ['treɪn ˌsteɪʃn] Bahnhof <III U3, 57>
to **stay** [steɪ] bleiben; übernachten I
step [step] Schritt; Stufe II
still [stɪl] noch; immer noch II
stone [stəʊn] Stein III U2, 49
stone put ['stəʊn ˌpʊt] Steinstoßen III U2, 49
stood [stʊd] simple past von *to stand* II; past participle von *to stand* III U3, 58
stop [stɒp] Haltestelle; Halt II
to **stop** [stɒp] beenden; aufhören; anhalten II
storm [stɔːm] Sturm I
story ['stɔːri] Geschichte I
straight ahead [ˌstreɪt ə'hed] geradeaus <III U1, 130>
straight on [streɪt_'ɒn] geradeaus II
strawberry ['strɔːbri] Erdbeere I
street [striːt] Straße I
stressed [strest] betont <III U2, 35>
comic **strip** ['kɒmɪk ˌstrɪp] Comic; Bildergeschichte <III U2, 33>
strong [strɒŋ] stark III U2, 34
*to be **stuck** [biː 'stʌk] feststecken; stecken bleiben I
student ['stjuːdnt] Schüler; Schülerin I
studio ['stjuːdiəʊ] Studio III U1, 29
study skills [ˌstʌdi 'skɪlz] Fertigkeit Lern- und Arbeitstechniken <I>
subject ['sʌbdʒɪkt] Schulfach I; Betreff III U4, 92
suddenly ['sʌdnli] plötzlich; auf einmal I
summary ['sʌmri] Zusammenfassung <III U1, 27>
summer ['sʌmə] Sommer II
sun [sʌn] Sonne II
Sunday ['sʌndeɪ] Sonntag I
sunny ['sʌni] sonnig II
supermarket ['suːpəˌmɑːkɪt] Supermarkt I
sure [ʃɔː] sicher II
to make sure [ˌmeɪk 'ʃɔː] dafür sorgen; sich versichern <III U1, 130>
to **surf** [sɜːf] surfen <III U1, 23>
to surf the internet [sɜːf ði 'ɪntənet] im Internet surfen <III U4, 137>
surfer ['sɜːfə] Surfer; Surferin; Wellenreiter; Wellenreiterin <III U1, 23>
surfing ['sɜːfɪŋ] Surfen; Wellenreiten; Surf- <III U1, 23>
to go surfing [ˌgəʊ 'sɜːfɪŋ] surfen gehen III U1, 10
surprise [sə'praɪz] Überraschung III U3, 63
to **surprise** [sə'praɪz] überraschen <III U4, 87>
surprised [sə'praɪzd] überrascht II
survey ['sɜːveɪ] Umfrage <III U1, 19>
sushi ['suːʃi] Sushi <III U2, 133>
sweet [swiːt] Süßigkeit; Bonbon I
*to **swim** [swɪm] schwimmen I
*to go **swimming** [ˌgəʊ 'swɪmɪŋ] schwimmen gehen I

swimming

swimming pool ['swɪmɪŋ ˌpu:l] Schwimmbad I

*to **swing** [swɪŋ] schwingen; schwenken III U2, 49

swung [swʌŋ] simple past, past participle von *to swing* III U2, 49

T

table ['teɪbl] Tisch; Tabelle <I>

tablet ['tæblət] Tablet III U4, 76

tail [teɪl] Schwanz I

*to **take** [teɪk] mitnehmen; nehmen I; hinbringen II; dauern; brauchen; bringen III U1, 16

to take notes [ˌteɪk 'nəʊts] sich Notizen machen <I>

to take out [ˌteɪk‿'aʊt] hinausbringen II

to take part (in) [ˌteɪk 'pɑ:t (ɪn)] mitmachen (bei); teilnehmen (an) II

to take photos (of) [ˌteɪk 'fəʊtəʊz (əv)] Fotos machen; fotografieren II

to take the dog for a walk [ˌteɪk ðə dɒg fɔ:r‿ə 'wɔ:k] den Hund ausführen I

to take turns [ˌteɪk 'tɜ:nz] sich abwechseln <I>

to take up [ˌteɪk 'ʌp] einnehmen <III U1, 25>

taken ['teɪkn] past participle von *to take* III U2, 36

talent ['tælənt] Talent; Begabung I

talk [tɔ:k] Vortrag; Gespräch; Unterhaltung <III U1, 15>

to **talk** (to) [tɔ:k (tə)] reden (mit); sprechen (mit) I

tall [tɔ:l] hoch; groß II

tandem ['tændəm] Tandem II

task [tɑ:sk] Aufgabe; Auftrag <I>

taxi ['tæksi] Taxi <III U3, 134>

tea [ti:] Tee; Abendessen I

teacher ['ti:tʃə] Lehrer; Lehrerin I

team [ti:m] Mannschaft; Team; Gruppe I

techno ['teknəʊ] Techno *(Musik)* III U1, 27

technology [tek'nɒlədʒi] Technik; Technologie III U1, 28

DT (Design Technology) [ˌdi:'ti: (dɪˌzaɪn tek'nɒlədʒi)] Technik I

teddy ['tedi] Teddybär I

teen [ti:n] Jugend-; Teenager; Teenagerin; Jugendlicher; Jugendliche II

teenager ['ti:nˌeɪdʒə] Teenager; Jugendlicher; Jugendliche <III ZI, 9>

telephone ['telɪfəʊn] Telefon <III U4, 86>

telephone box ['telɪfəʊn ˌbɒks] Telefonzelle II

*to **tell** [tel] erzählen; sagen I

to tell sb to do sth ['tel tə ˌdu:] jmdm. etw. auftragen; jmdm. etw. befehlen III U3, 58

ten [ten] zehn I

tennis ['tenɪs] Tennis I

tent [tent] Zelt II

terrible ['terəbl] schrecklich; furchtbar <III U3, 135>

terrorism ['terrɪzm] Terrorismus III U3, 69

to **test** [test] testen; prüfen II

text [tekst] Text <I>

than [ðæn] als II

Thank you. ['θæŋk ju] Danke. I

Thanks. [θæŋks] Danke. I

Thanksgiving [ˌθæŋks'gɪvɪŋ] Erntedankfest III U4, 91

that [ðæt] das; dieses; jene I; die; der III U3, 58; dass II

after that [ˌɑ:ftə 'ðæt] danach I

that's why ['ðæts waɪ] deshalb; deswegen II

That's too bad. [ˌðæts tu: 'bæd] Schade! II

the [ðə] die; der; das I

theatre ['θɪətə] Theater III U1, 11

their [ðeə] ihr I

theirs [ðeəz] ihre III U1, 19

them [ðem] sie *(Pl.)* I; ihnen II

theme [θi:m] Thema; Motto <I>

theme park ['θi:m ˌpɑ:k] Freizeitpark II

themselves [ðəm'selvz] sich; selbst; sie selbst III U4, 76

then [ðen] dann; danach I; damals III U3, 69

there [ðeə] da; dort; dorthin; dahin I

there are [ðeər‿'ɑ:] da sind; es gibt I

there's (= there is) [ðeəz] da ist; dort ist; es gibt I

these [ði:z] diese II

they [ðeɪ] sie *(Pl.)* I

thing [θɪŋ] Sache; Ding I

*to **think** [θɪŋk] denken; glauben II; finden <III U2, 45>

to think about [ˌθɪŋk‿ə'baʊt] nachdenken über; sich überlegen; denken an III U2, 34

to think of ['θɪŋk‿əv] denken an/über; sich einfallen lassen; sich ausdenken III U3, 58

third [θɜ:d] dritte II

thirteen [θɜ:'ti:n] dreizehn I

thirty ['θɜ:ti] dreißig I

this [ðɪs] das; dies I

this morning [ðɪs 'mɔ:nɪŋ] heute Morgen II

like this [laɪk 'ðɪs] so; auf diese Weise <I>

those [ðəʊz] jene II

thought [θɔ:t] simple past von *to think* II; past participle von *to think* III U2, 34

a/one **thousand** ['θaʊznd] tausend; eintausend II

three [θri:] drei I

threw [θru:] simple past von *to throw* II

*to **throw** [θrəʊ] werfen II

Thursday ['θɜ:zdeɪ] Donnerstag I

ticket ['tɪkɪt] Ticket; Eintrittskarte; Fahrschein II

return ticket [rɪ'tɜ:n ˌtɪkɪt] Hin- und Rückfahrkarte III U3, 54

single ticket [ˌsɪŋgl 'tɪkɪt] einfache Fahrkarte III U3, 54

ticket office ['tɪkɪt ˌɒfɪs] Kartenverkaufsstelle <III U1, 11>

to **tidy** ['taɪdi] aufräumen; in Ordnung bringen II

tidy ['taɪdi] ordentlich <II>

time [taɪm] Zeit; Uhrzeit; Mal I

at the same time [ət ðə seɪm 'taɪm] gleichzeitig; nebenher II

free time [ˌfri: 'taɪm] Freizeit I

time of year [ˌtaɪm‿əv 'jɪə] Jahreszeit <III U2, 45>

for the 200th time [fə ðə 'tu: hʌndrədθ ˌtaɪm] zum 200. Mal III U4, 80

the first time [ðə fɜ:st 'taɪm] das erste Mal I

timetable ['taɪmˌteɪbl] Stundenplan I; Fahrplan III U3, 54

tiny ['taɪni] klein; winzig <III U1, 128>

tip [tɪp] Tipp; Ratschlag <I>

tired ['taɪəd] müde I

title ['taɪtl] Titel; Überschrift <I>

to [tu:] zu; nach; in I; um zu; an; auf <II>; bis <III U1, 27>; vor *(bei Uhrzeitangaben)* III U3, 54

quarter to/past ['kwɔ:tə tə/pɑ:st] Viertel vor/nach II

today [tə'deɪ] heute I

together [tə'geðə] zusammen I

told [təʊld] simple past von *to tell* I; past participle von *to tell* III U3, 58

tomato *(sg)* [tə'mɑ:təʊ], **tomatoes** *(pl)* [tə'mɑ:təʊz] Tomate I

tomorrow [tə'mɒrəʊ] morgen II

too [tu:] auch; zu I

took [tʊk] simple past von *to take* II

tooth *(sg)* [tu:θ], **teeth** *(pl)* [ti:θ] Zahn II

top [tɒp] Spitze; oberer Teil; oberes Ende II

at the top [æt ðə 'tɒp] oben <III U3, 136>

topic ['tɒpɪk] Thema <I>

torch [tɔ:tʃ] Taschenlampe I

caber **toss** ['keɪbə ˌtɒs] Baumstammwerfen III U2, 48

to **toss** [tɒs] werfen III U2, 48

*to keep in **touch** [ˌki:p ɪn 'tʌtʃ] in Kontakt bleiben II

tour [tʊə] Tour; Reise III U1, 28

tourist ['tʊərɪst] Tourist; Touristin II

tower ['taʊə] Turm II

town [taʊn] Stadt I

home town ['həʊm taʊn] Heimatstadt; Heimatort <III U1, 11>

twin town [ˌtwɪn 'taʊn] Partnerstadt III U2, 50

tradition [trə'dɪʃn] Tradition; Brauch III U2, 33

traffic ['træfɪk] Verkehr III U1, 12

traffic light ['træfɪk ˌlaɪt] Ampel <III U3, 134>

train [treɪn] Zug I

train station ['treɪn ˌsteɪʃn] Bahnhof <III U3, 57>

trained [treɪnd] geschult <III U4, 86>

trainer ['treɪnə] Turnschuh II

tram [træm] Straßenbahn I

transport ['trænspɔ:t] Verkehr; Transport II

public transport [ˌpʌblɪk 'trænspɔ:t] öffentliche Verkehrsmittel III U3, 54

to **travel** ['trævl] fahren; reisen II

treasure hunt ['treʒə ˌhʌnt] Schnitzeljagd; Schatzsuche II

tree [tri:] Baum I

tribe [traɪb] Stamm; Volksstamm III U4, 76

trick [trɪk] Kunststück; Trick I; Streich II

trip [trɪp] Ausflug; Fahrt; Reise I; Tour; Trip III U4, 74

school trip [ˌsku:l 'trɪp] Klassenfahrt; Schulausflug II

trouble ['trʌbl] Problem; Schwierigkeiten; Ärger III U3, 68

trumpet ['trʌmpɪt] Trompete II

to **try** [traɪ] versuchen; probieren; ausprobieren III U3, 58

to try on [ˌtraɪ 'ɒn] anprobieren II

T-shirt ['ti:ʃɜ:t] T-Shirt II

Tuesday ['tju:zdeɪ] Dienstag I

tunnel ['tʌnl] Tunnel III ZI 8

to **turn** [tɜ:n] abbiegen II

to turn over [ˌtɜ:n 'əʊvə] umkippen; (sich) umdrehen III U4, 80

Turn the music down. [ˌtɜ:n ðə mju:zɪk 'daʊn] Mach die Musik leiser. I

*to take **turns** [ˌteɪk 'tɜ:nz] sich abwechseln <I>

TV [ˌti:'vi:] Fernseher I; Fernsehen; Fernseh- III U1, 27

on TV [ɒn ˌti:'vi:] im Fernsehen III U1, 27

to watch TV [ˌwɒtʃ ti:'vi:] fernsehen I

twelve [twelv] zwölf I

twenty ['twenti] zwanzig I

twenty-one [ˌtwenti'wʌn] einundzwanzig I

twin town [ˌtwɪn 'taʊn] Partnerstadt III U2, 50

two [tu:] zwei I

type [taɪp] Sorte; Art; Typ III U3, 69

to **type** [taɪp] tippen <III U3, 67>

typical ['tɪpɪkl] typisch; charakteristisch <I>

U

umpire ['ʌmpaɪə] Schiedsrichter; Schiedsrichterin <III U4, 89>

uncle ['ʌŋkl] Onkel I

under ['ʌndə] unter I

underground ['ʌndəgraʊnd] U-Bahn I

*to **understand** [ˌʌndə'stænd] verstehen II

understood [ˌʌndə'stʊd] simple past von *to understand* II

unhappy [ʌn'hæpi] unglücklich; traurig II

uniform ['ju:nɪfɔ:m] Uniform I

unique [ju:'ni:k] einzigartig <III U2, 44>

unit ['ju:nɪt] Lektion; Kapitel <I>

university [ˌju:nɪ'vɜ:səti] Universität III U2, 50

until [ʌn'tɪl] bis III U2, 32

up [ʌp] hinauf; oben; hoch II

to **upload** [ʌp'ləʊd] hochladen II

US [ˌju:'es] US-amerikanisch III U4, 75

us [ʌs] uns; wir II

use [ju:s] Gebrauch; Nutzen; Verwendung <III U4, 77>

to **use** [ju:z] benutzen; verwenden; nehmen; nutzen III U2, 49

useful ['ju:sfl] nützlich; hilfreich; brauchbar III U4, 78

usually ['ju:ʒli] normalerweise; gewöhnlich II

V

vacation *(AE)* [və'keɪʃn] Urlaub; Ferien III U4, 76

valley ['væli] Tal III U4, 74

vegetarian [ˌvedʒɪ'teəriən] Vegetarier; Vegetarierin I

verb [vɜ:b] Verb <II>

very ['veri] sehr I

video ['vɪdiəʊ] Video III U4, 76
viewing ['vju:ɪŋ] Hör-/Sehverstehen <I>
viewing skills ['vju:ɪŋ ˌskɪlz] Fertigkeit Hör-/Sehverstehen <I>
village ['vɪlɪdʒ] Dorf I
visit ['vɪzɪt] Besuch; Besichtigung III U1, 11
to **visit** ['vɪzɪt] besuchen I
visitor ['vɪzɪtə] Besucher; Besucherin II
vocabulary [və'kæbjəlri] Vokabular; Wortschatz <III U3, 55>
voice [vɔɪs] Stimme <III U2, 44>
voice message ['vɔɪs ˌmesɪdʒ] Sprachnachricht <III U4, 137>
volleyball ['vɒlibɔ:l] Volleyball <III U4, 138>

W

to **wait** (for) [weɪt (fə)] warten (auf) II
*to **wake** up [ˌweɪk_'ʌp] aufwachen; erwachen III U4, 80
walk [wɔ:k] Wanderung; Spaziergang I
to **walk** [wɔ:k] gehen; laufen III U3, 61
to walk around [ˌwɔ:k_ə'raʊnd] umherlaufen; herumlaufen <I>
walking ['wɔ:kɪŋ] Wandern <III U4, 138>
wall [wɔ:l] Wand; Mauer II
wall painting ['wɔ:l peɪntɪŋ] Wandmalerei II
to **want** (to) [wɒnt (tə)] wollen; mögen I
wardrobe ['wɔ:drəʊb] Kleiderschrank II
warm [wɔ:m] warm II
warm-up ['wɔ:mʌp] Aufwärmtraining; Aufwärmen II
was [wɒz] simple past von *to be* I
wash [wɒʃ] Wäsche II
to **wash** [wɒʃ] (sich) waschen; spülen II
to **watch** [wɒtʃ] anschauen; ansehen I; zuschauen; zusehen; beobachten II
to watch TV [ˌwɒtʃ ti:'vi:] fernsehen I
water ['wɔ:tə] Wasser I
waterproofs ['wɔ:təpru:fs] Regenbekleidung <III U2, 131>
wave [weɪv] Welle III U4, 80
wax [wæks] Wachs II
way [weɪ] Weg I; Art und Weise III U2, 49
to ask the way [ˌɑ:sk ðə 'weɪ] nach dem Weg fragen <II>
to be a long way away [bi: ə 'lɒŋ ˌweɪ ə'weɪ] weit weg sein II
we [wi:] wir I
*to **wear** [weə] tragen; anhaben I
weather ['weðə] Wetter; Witterung II
web [web] Netz III U2, 42
website ['websaɪt] Website; Internetseite III U2, 34
Wednesday ['wenzdeɪ] Mittwoch I
week [wi:k] Woche I
weekend ['wi:kend] Wochenende I
welcome (to) ['welkəm (tə)] willkommen (bei/in) I
You're welcome. [jɔ: 'welkəm] Gern geschehen. <III U2, 133>
well [wel] gut II
Well, … [wel] Na ja, …; Also … II
… as well as … [əz 'wel_əz] sowohl … als auch … II
Well done! [ˌwel 'dʌn] Gut gemacht! II
Welsh [welʃ] Walisisch; walisisch; aus Wales III U2, 32
went [went] simple past von *to go* I
were [wɜ:] simple past von *to be* I
west [west] Westen; West- III U1, 12
westbound ['wesbaʊnd] in Richtung Westen <III U3, 134>
wet [wet] nass I
what [wɒt] was; welche I
what a … ['wɒt_ə] was für ein … <III U1, 23>
What about …? [ˌwɒt_ə'baʊt] Und …?; Was ist mit …? II
What colour is …? [ˌwɒt 'kʌlər_ɪz] Welche Farbe hat …? I
What time is it? [ˌwɒt 'taɪm_ɪz_ɪt] Wie viel Uhr ist es?; Wie spät ist es? I
What's the weather like? [ˌwɒts ðə 'weðə laɪk] Wie ist das Wetter? II
What's your name? [ˌwɒts jə 'neɪm] Wie heißt du? I
wheel [wi:l] Rad II
big wheel [ˌbɪg 'wi:l] Riesenrad II
wheelchair ['wi:ltʃeə] Rollstuhl I
when [wen] wann I; wenn; als II
where [weə] wo; wohin; woher I
which [wɪtʃ] welche; was II; das; der; die III U4, 80
white [waɪt] weiß I
who [hu:] wer I; der; die; das III U3, 58
whole [həʊl] ganz III U3, 62
whose [hu:z] wessen <III U1, 19>
why [waɪ] warum I
that's why ['ðæts waɪ] deshalb; deswegen II
will [wɪl] werden II
*to **win** [wɪn] siegen; gewinnen I
wind [wɪnd] Wind I
window ['wɪndəʊ] Fenster I
windsurfing ['wɪndsɜ:fɪŋ] Windsurfen <III U2, 131>
windy ['wɪndi] windig II
winner ['wɪnə] Sieger; Siegerin; Gewinner; Gewinnerin I
winter ['wɪntə] Winter I
Best **wishes**, [ˌbest 'wɪʃɪz] Viele Grüße; Alles Gute I
with [wɪð] mit I; bei II
without [wɪ'ðaʊt] ohne II
wizard ['wɪzəd] Zauberer II
woke up [ˌwəʊk_'ʌp] simple past von *to wake up* III U4, 80
woken up [ˌwəʊkn_'ʌp] past participle von *to wake up* III U4, 80
wolf *(sg)* [wʊlf], **wolves** *(pl)* [wʊlvz] Wolf II
woman *(sg)* ['wʊmən], **women** *(pl)* ['wɪmɪn] Frau I
won [wʌn] simple past von *to win* II; past participle von *to win* III U2, 43
won't (= will not) [wəʊnt] nicht werden II
wood [wʊd] Holz I; Wald <III U1, 128>
wooden ['wʊdn] Holz- <III U4, 86>
woof [wʊf] wau I
wool [wʊl] Wolle I
word [wɜ:d] Wort II
word order ['wɜ:d_ɔ:də] Wortstellung; Satzstellung <II>
wore [wɔ:] simple past von *to wear* I
work [wɜ:k] Arbeit II

to **work** [wɜːk] arbeiten I
workshop [ˈwɜːkʃɒp] Workshop; Seminar III U3, 54
world [wɜːld] Welt I
all around the world [ɔːl‿əˌraʊnd ðə ˈwɜːld] in aller Welt II
worried [ˈwʌrid] beunruhigt; besorgt II
to **worry** [ˈwʌri] sich Sorgen machen I
Don't worry. [ˌdəʊnt ˈwʌri] Mach dir keine Sorgen. I
worse [wɜːs] schlechter; schlimmer II
worst [wɜːst] schlimmste; schlechteste II
Would you like (to) …? [ˌwʊd jə ˈlaɪk (tə)] Möchtest du …?; Würdest du gern …? I
I wouldn't like (to) … [aɪ ˈwʊdnt laɪk (tə)] ich möchte nicht …; ich würde nicht gerne … I
I'd (= I would) [aɪd] ich würde; ich hätte gern I

*to **write** [raɪt] schreiben I
to write down [ˌraɪt ˈdaʊn] aufschreiben <III U1, 29>
writing [ˈraɪtɪŋ] Schreiben <I>
writing skills [ˈraɪtɪŋ ˌskɪlz] Fertigkeit Schreiben <II>
wrong [rɒŋ] falsch I
wrote [rəʊt] simple past von *to write* II

Y

year [jɪə] Klasse; Jahrgangsstufe; Jahr I
time of year [ˌtaɪm‿əv ˈjɪə] Jahreszeit <III U2, 45>
yellow [ˈjeləʊ] gelb I
yes [jes] ja I
yesterday [ˈjestədeɪ] gestern I
yet [jet] schon III U2, 34
not … yet [nɒt … ˈjet] noch nicht III U2, 34
you [juː] du; Sie; ihr; dich; euch; dir; Ihnen I
You're welcome. [jɔː ˈwelkəm] Gern geschehen. <III U2, 133>
young [jʌŋ] jung II
your [jɔː] dein; euer; Ihr I
yours [jɔːz] deine; eure; Ihre III U1, 16
Yours, [jɔːz] Dein *(Grußformel in Briefen oder E-Mails)* II
yourself [jɔːˈself] dich; selbst III U4, 92
youth [juːθ] Jugend- I
yummy [ˈjʌmi] lecker II

Z

zero [ˈzɪərəʊ] null I
zip line [ˈzɪp ˌlaɪn] Seilrutsche III U2, 32
zip code [ˈzɪp ˌkəʊd] Postleitzahl <III U4, 86>
to **zoom** in [ˈzuːm‿ɪn] heranzoomen <I>

Boys' names

Alex [ˈælɪks] III U1, 20
Andy [ˈændi] <III U1, 23>
Ashley [ˈæʃli] III U3, 58
Atsa [ˈætsə] III U4, 76
Dylan [ˈdɪlən] III ZI 9
George [dʒɔːdʒ] III U1, 16
Greg [greg] <III U1, 23>
Josh [dʒɒʃ] <III U1, 23>
Joshua [ˈdʒɒʃuə] III U4, 92
Mark [mɑːk] III U2, 34
Marley [ˈmɑːli] <III U3, 65>
Nathan [ˈneɪθn] <III U3, 65>
Patrick [ˈpætrɪk] III ZI 9
Ryan [raɪən] III U4, 92
Sam [sæm] III U1, 13
Sean [ʃɔːn] <III U3, 65>
Shay [ʃeɪ] III U3, 56
Stuart [stʃʊət] III U2, 38
Tom [tɒm] III U1, 12
Wayne [weɪn] III U4, 74

Girls' names

Alicia [əˈlɪʃə] <III U2, 45>
Alison [ˈælɪsn] III ZI 9
Beth [beθ] III U2, 34
Billy [ˈbɪli] III U3, 62
Carmen [ˈkɑːmen] <III U4, 87>
Carol [ˈkærl] III U1, 17
Caroline [ˈkærlaɪn] III U1, 13
Ellie [ˈeli] III U1, 13
Fiona [fiˈəʊnə] III U2, 38
Jackie [ˈdʒæki] III U3, 56
Julie [ˈdʒuːli] III U3, 58
Kirsty [ˈkɜːsti] III U2, 38
Laura [ˈlɔːrə] <III U2, 45>
Leah [ˈliːə] III U4, 92
Lisa [ˈliːsə] III U3, 54
Mandy [ˈmændi] <III U1, 23>
Maya [ˈmaɪə] <III U1, 23>
Niamh [niːv] III U3, 62
Nisha [ˈnɪʃə] III U3, 62
Sarah [ˈseərə] III U1, 10
Sonya [ˈsɒnjə] III U3, 62
Sophie [ˈsəʊfi] III ZI 9
Susan [ˈsuːzn] <III U4, 86>

Surnames

McCoy [məˈkɔɪ] III U1, 16
Price [praɪs] III U4, 80
Thompson [ˈtɒmsn] <III U4, 86>

Place names

Africa [ˈæfrɪkə] Afrika II
Alabama [ˌæləˈbæmə] *Bundesstaat in den USA* III U4, 75
America [əˈmerɪkə] Amerika III U4, 74
Antarctica [ænˈtɑːktɪkə] Antarktis II
Australia [ɒsˈtreɪliə] Australien I
Bannockburn [ˈbænəkbɜːn] *Ort in Schottland* III U2, 43
Boston [ˈbɒstn] *Stadt in den USA* III U4, 75
Brighton [ˈbraɪtn] *Küstenstadt in Südostengland* III U1, 11
Bristol [ˈbrɪstl] *Stadt in Südwestengland* III U1, 27
Britain [ˈbrɪtn] Großbritannien II
The **British Isles** [ðə ˌbrɪtɪʃ ˈaɪlz] die Britischen Inseln III ZI 8
California (CA) [ˌkælɪˈfɔːniə] Kalifornien <III U4, 86>
Canada [ˈkænədə] Kanada I
Cardiff [ˈkɑːdɪf] *Hauptstadt von Wales* III U2, 32
Cork [kɔːk] *Stadt in Irland* III U3, 58
Cornwall [ˈkɔːnwɔːl] *Grafschaft in Südwestengland* <III U1, 23>
D.C. (District of Columbia) [ˌdiːˈsiː (ˌdɪstrɪkt‿əv kəˈlʌmbiə)] *Bundesdistrikt in den USA* III U4, 74
Dallas [ˈdæləs] *Großstadt in den USA* III U4, 79
Delaware [ˈdeləweə] *Bundesstaat in den USA* III U4, 79
Donegal [ˌdɒnɪˈgɔːl] *Stadt in Irland* III U3, 62
Dublin [ˈdʌblɪn] *Hauptstadt von Irland* III U3, 53
Edinburgh [ˈedɪnbrə] *Hauptstadt von Schottland* III U2, 33
England [ˈɪŋglənd] England I
Europe [ˈjʊərəp] Europa II
France [frɑːns] Frankreich III ZI 8
Germany [ˈdʒɜːməni] Deutschland I
Glasgow [ˈglɑːzgəʊ] *Stadt in Schottland* III U2, 50
Great Britain [ˌgreɪt ˈbrɪtn] Großbritannien I
Greenwich [ˈgrenɪdʒ] *Stadtteil im Südosten Londons* I
Huntsville [ˈhʌntsvɪl] *Stadt in den USA* III U4, 75
India [ˈɪndiə] Indien I
Ireland [ˈaɪələnd] Irland III ZI 9
Istanbul [ˌɪstænˈbʊl] *Großstadt in der Türkei* I
Jamaica [dʒəˈmeɪkə] Jamaika II
Kensington [ˈkenzɪŋtən] *Stadtteil im Westen Londons* III U1, 26
London [ˈlʌndən] *Hauptstadt von England* I
Los Angeles (LA) [lɒsˈændʒəliːz] *Großstadt in den USA* III U4, 75
Maine [meɪn] *Bundesstaat in den USA* III U4, 79
Manchester [ˈmæntʃɪstə] *Stadt in Nordengland* II
Michigan [ˈmɪʃɪgən] *Bundesstaat in den USA* III U4, 76
Moscow [ˈmɒskəʊ] Moskau I
Munich [ˈmjuːnɪk] München <III U1, 128>
New York [ˌnjuːˈjɔːk] *Großstadt in den USA* III U4, 74
Newquay [ˈnjuːki] *Küstenstadt in England* III U1, 10
Northampton [ˌnɔːˈθæmtən] *Stadt in Mittelengland* III U3, 62
Northern Ireland [ˌnɔːðn‿ˈaɪələnd] Nordirland III ZI 8
Nuremberg [ˈnjʊərəmbɜːg] Nürnberg III U2, 50
Orlando [ɔːˈlændəʊ] *Stadt in den USA* III U4, 92
Oxford [ˈɒksfəd] *Stadt in England* III U1, 10
Poland [ˈpəʊlənd] Polen II
The **Republic of Ireland** [ðə rɪˌpʌblɪk‿əv‿ˈaɪələnd] Irland III ZI 8
Rhode Island [ˌrəʊdˈaɪlənd] *Bundesstaat in den USA* III U4, 79
Russia [ˈrʌʃə] Russland I
Salford [ˈsɔːlfəd] *Stadt in Nordengland* III U1, 28
Scotland [ˈskɒtlənd] Schottland I
Stapleton [ˈsteɪpltən] *Dorf in Nordengland* III U1, 12

Stirling [ˈstɜːlɪŋ] *Stadt in Schottland* III U2, 38

Sunderland [ˈsʌndlənd] *Küstenstadt in England* III U1, 12

Swansea [ˈswɒnzi] *Stadt in Wales* <III U2, 44>

Thailand [ˈtaɪlænd] Thailand I

Turkey [ˈtɜːki] Türkei I

UK (United Kingdom) [ˌjuːˈkeɪ (juːˌnaɪtɪd ˈkɪŋdəm)] Vereinigtes Königreich von Großbritannien und Nordirland II

United States [juːˌnaɪtɪdˈsteɪts] Vereinigte Staaten II

USA (United States of America) [ˌjuːesˈeɪ (juːˌnaɪtɪd ˌsteɪts‿əv əˈmerɪkə)] USA (Vereinigte Staaten von Amerika) I

Wales [weɪlz] Wales III ZI 8

Washington, D.C. [ˌwɒʃɪŋtən ˌdiːˈsiː] *Hauptstadt der USA* III U4, 74

Other names

Aardman Animations [ˌɑːdmən ænɪˈmeɪʃnz] *britische Filmproduktionsgesellschaft* III U1, 27

Abbey Street [ˈæbi ˌstriːt] *Straße in Dublin* III U3, 54

Aladdin [əˈlædɪn] *Name eines Musicals* <III U1, 22>

Amazing Walls Centre [əˌmeɪzɪŋ ˌwɔːlz ˈsentə] *Name einer Kletterhalle* III U2, 34

Baker Middle School [ˌbeɪkə ˈmɪdl ˌskuːl] *Schulname* III U4, 92

BBC (= British Broadcasting Corporation) [ˌbiːbiːˈsiː] *britische Rundfunkanstalt* III U1, 28

BBC Breakfast [ˌbiːbiːsiː ˈbrekfəst] *Name einer Fernsehsendung* III U1, 28

BBC Sport [ˌbiːbiːsiː ˈspɔːt] *Sportprogramm der BBC* III U1, 28

The **Beatles** [ðə ˈbiːtlz] *britische Band* III U1, 27

Bell High School [ˌbel ˈhaɪ skuːl] *Schulname* <III U4, 86>

Black Mountains [ˌblæk ˈmaʊntɪnz] *Hügelgruppe in Wales* III U2, 34

Blackhorse [ˈblækhɔːs] *Haltestelle in Dublin* III U3, 55

Brave Men [ˈbreɪv ˌmen] *Bandname* <III U2, 44>

Brecon Beacons [ˌbrekn ˈbiːknz] *Bergkette in Wales* <III U2, 44>

Bridge Street [ˈbrɪdʒ ˌstriːt] *Straßenname* III U3, 56

George H. W. **Bush** [ˌdʒɔːdʒ eɪtʃdʌbljuː ˈbʊʃ] *Präsident der USA (1989–1993)* III U4, 81

Cardiff Castle [ˈkɑːdɪf ˌkɑːsl] *Burg in Wales* III U2, 32

Celtic [ˈseltɪk] *Name einer Fußballmannschaft* III U2, 50

Celtic Park Stadium [ˈseltɪk ˌpɑːk ˌsteɪdiəm] *Name eines Fußballstadions* III U2, 51

The **Channel Tunnel** [ðə ˌtʃænl ˈtʌnl] Kanaltunnel III ZI 8

Chelsea [ˈtʃelsi] *Name einer Fußballmannschaft* <III U4, 87>

Chicken Run [ˈtʃɪkɪn ˌrʌn] *Animationsfilm* III U1, 27

Bill **Clinton** [ˌbɪl ˈklɪntən] *Präsident der USA (1993–2001)* III U4, 81

Clyde Arc [ˈklaɪd ˌɑːk] *Brücke in Glasgow* III U2, 50

Colorado River [ˌkɒlrɑːdəʊ ˈrɪvə] *Fluss in den USA* III U4, 75

Christopher **Columbus** [ˌkrɪstəfə kəˈlʌmbəs] *Entdecker* III U4, 91

Columbus Day [kəˌlʌmbəs ˈdeɪ] *Feiertag in den USA* III U4, 91

Croke Park [ˈkrəʊk ˌpɑːk] *Name eines Stadions* III U3, 53

Crystal Falls [ˌkrɪstl ˈfɔːlz] *Wasserfall in den USA* III U4, 76

Daisy [ˈdeɪzi] *Tiername* III U1, 12

Edward I [ˌedwəd ðə ˈfɜːst] *König von England (1272–1307)* III U2, 42

European Union [jʊərəˌpiːən ˈjuːnjən] Europäische Union III U3, 52

George's Dock [ˈdʒɔːdʒɪz ˌdɒk] *Haltestelle in Dublin* III U3, 55

Geronimo [dʒəˈrɒnɪməʊ] *Name eines Ureinwohners Amerikas* III U4, 79

The **Globe Theatre** [ðə ˌgləʊb ˈθɪətə] Globe-Theater III U1, 11

Goldenbridge [ˌgəʊldnˈbrɪdʒ] *Haltestelle in Dublin* III U3, 54

Grand Canyon [ˌgrænd ˈkænjən] *Sehenswürdigkeit in den USA* III U4, 74

Grand Canyon National Park [grænd ˌkænjən ˌnæʃnl ˈpɑːk] *Nationalpark in den USA* III U4, 74

Highland dancing [ˌhaɪlənd ˈdɑːnsɪŋ] *schottische Form des Schautanzes* III U2, 33

Highland Games [ˌhaɪlənd ˈgeɪmz] *traditionelle schottische Veranstaltungen mit sportlichen Wettkämpfen* III U2, 33

Independence Day [ɪndɪˈpendəns ˌdeɪ] *amerikanischer Unabhängigkeitstag* III U4, 90

Irish Sea [ˌaɪrɪʃ ˈsiː] Irische See III U3, 63

Kenny [ˈkeni] *Tiername* III U1, 14

Martin Luther **King** [ˌmɑːtɪn ˌluːθə ˈkɪŋ] *Bürgerrechtler* III U4, 90

LA Chargers [ˌeleɪ ˈtʃɑːdʒəz] *Name eines Footballteams* III U4, 75

Lake Apopka [ˌleɪk æˈpɒpkə] *See in den USA* III U4, 92

Larry [ˈlæri] *Tiername* III U4, 92

Layla [ˈleɪlə] *Sängerin* <III U2, 44>

Leicester Square [ˈlestə ˌskweə] *Platz in London* III U1, 26

The **Lion King** [ðə ˈlaɪən kɪŋ] *Name eines Musicals* III U1, 26

Liverpool [ˈlɪvəpuːl] *Name einer Fußballmannschaft* <III U4, 87>

Peter **Lord** [ˌpiːtə ˈlɔːd] *Mitbegründer von Aardman Animations* III U1, 27

L. S. **Lowry** [ˌeles ˈlaʊri] *englischer Künstler* III U1, 28

Lowry Arts Centre [ˌlaʊri ˈɑːts ˌsentə] *Sehenswürdigkeit in Salford* III U1, 28

Malcolm III [ˌmælkəm ðə ˈθɜːd] *König von Schottland (1058–1093)* III U2, 48

Mamma Mia! [məˌmɑː ˈmiə] *Name eines Musicals* III U1, 26

Manchester City [ˌmæntʃɪstə ˈsɪti] *Name einer Fußballmannschaft* III U1, 12

Manchester Ship Canal [ˌmæntʃɪstə ˈʃɪp kəˌnæl] *Kanal in Nordwestengland* III U1, 28

Martin Luther King Day [ˌmɑːtɪn ˌluːθə ˌkɪŋ ˈdeɪ] *Feiertag in den USA zu Ehren Martin Luther Kings* III U4, 90

Media City [ˌmiːdiə ˈsɪti] *Sehenswürdigkeit in Salford* III U1, 28

Monument Valley [ˌmɒnjəmənt ˈvæli] *Sehenswürdigkeit in den USA* III U4, 75

Mount Snowdon [ˌmaʊnt ˈsnəʊdn] *höchster Berg in Wales* III U2, 32

Mountain Camp Woodside [ˌmaʊntɪn kæmp ˈwʊdsaɪd] *Name eines Feriencamps* <III U4, 86>

Museum of Science and Industry [mjuːˌziːəm əv ˌsaɪəns ən ˈɪndəstri] *Museum in Manchester* III U1, 28

Napa Valley [ˌnæpə ˈvæli] *Weinregion in den USA* III U4, 75

Natural History Museum [ˌnætʃrl ˈhɪstri mjuːˌziːəm] *Naturhistorisches Museum in London* III U1, 26

Navajo [ˈnævəhəʊ] *Indianervolk in den USA* III U4, 75

O'Connell Street [əˈkɒnl ˌstriːt] *Straße in Dublin* III U3, 54

Barack **Obama** [ˌbærək əʊˈbɑːmə] *Präsident der USA (2009–2017)* III U4, 81

Old Trafford Museum [əʊld ˈtræfəd mjuːˌziːəm] *Museum in Manchester* III U1, 28

Old Trafford Stadium [əʊld ˈtræfəd ˌsteɪdiəm] *Name eines Fußballstadions* III U1, 28

Nick **Park** [ˌnɪk ˈpɑːk] *Trickfilmer* III U1, 27

Park Rd [ˌpɑːk ˈrəʊd] *Straßenname* <III U4, 86>

Penfriends Worldwide [ˌpenfrendz wɜːldˈwaɪd] *Name einer internationalen Brieffreundschaftsseite* III U4, 92

The **Phantom of the Opera** [ðə ˌfæntəm‿əv ði‿ˈɒprə] *Name eines Musicals* III U1, 26

Piccadilly Gardens [pɪkəˌdɪli ˈgɑːdnz] *Park in Manchester* III U1, 28

Pocahontas [ˌpɒkəˈhɒntəs] *Name einer Ureinwohnerin Amerikas* III U4, 79

Rangers [ˈreɪndʒəz] *Name einer Fußballmannschaft* III U2, 50

Ronald **Reagan** [ˌrɒnld ˈreɪgn] *Präsident der USA (1981–1989)* III U4, 81

Red Line [ˈred ˌlaɪn] *Straßenbahnlinie in Dublin* III U3, 54

Rhyme [raɪm] *Bandname* <III U2, 44>

River Thames [ˌrɪvə ˈtemz] *Fluss in London* III U1, 20

Riverside Museum [ˈrɪvəsaɪd mjuːˌziːəm] *Museum in Glasgow* III U2, 51

Robert the Bruce [ˈrɒbət ðə ˌbruːs] *König von Schottland (1306–1329)* III U2, 33

Romeo and Juliet [ˌrəʊmiəʊ‿ən ˈdʒuːliət] Romeo und Julia III U1, 11

Science Museum [ˈsaɪəns mjuːˌziːəm] *Museum in London* III U1, 11

Scottish Football Museum [skɒtɪʃ ˈfʊtbɔːl mjuːˌziːəm] *Museum in Glasgow* III U2, 51

William **Shakespeare** [ˌwɪljəm ˈʃeɪkspɪə] *englischer Schriftsteller* III U1, 11

Shaun the Sheep [ˌʃɔːn ðə ˈʃiːp] *Animationsserie* III U1, 27

Silicon Valley [ˌsɪlɪkən ˈvæli] *Sitz vieler Computerfirmen in den USA* III U4, 75

16th St. [sɪkˌstiːnθ ˈstriːt] *Straßenname* <III U4, 86>

The **Spire** [ðə ˈspaɪə] *Monument und Wahrzeichen von Dublin* III U3, 54

Spirit [ˈspɪrɪt] *Bandname* <III U2, 44>

David **Sproxton** [ˌdeɪvɪd ˈsprɒkstn] *Mitbegründer von Aardman Animations* III U1, 27

Squanto [ˈskwɒntəʊ] *Name eines Ureinwohners Amerikas* III U4, 79

St Patrick's Day [sn ˈpætrɪks ˌdeɪ] *Feiertag in Irland am 17. März* III U3, 53

Statue of Liberty [ˌstætʃuː‿əv ˈlɪbəti] *Freiheitsstatue in New York* III U4, 74

Street Brothers [ˈstriːt ˌbrʌðəz] *Bandname* <III U2, 44>

Super Bowl [ˈsuːpə ˌbəʊl] *Meisterschaftsendspiel der American-Football-Profiliga* III U4, 84

Tara Street [ˈtɑːrə ˌstriːt] *Straße in Dublin* III U3, 55

Taste of Style [ˌteɪst‿əv ˈstaɪl] *Bandname* <III U2, 44>

Tigerboy III [ˈtaɪgəˌbɔɪ ˈθriː] *Filmname* III U3, 61

Trinity [ˈtrɪnəti] *Haltestelle in Dublin* III U3, 55

Donald **Trump** [ˌdɒnld ˈtrʌmp] *Präsident der USA (seit 2017)* III U4, 81

US Space and Rocket Center [ˌjuːes ˌspeɪs‿ən ˈrɒkɪt ˌsentə] *Raumfahrtmuseum in den USA* III U4, 75

Victoria and Albert Museum [vɪkˌtɔːriə ənd‿ˌælbət mjuːˈziːəm] *Museum in London* III U1, 26

Visions [ˈvɪʒnz] *Name einer Schauspielschule* III U3, 54

Wallace and Gromit [ˌwɒlɪs‿ən ˈgrɒmɪt] *Animationsfilmreihe* III U1, 27

Western Commuter Line [ˌwestən kəˈmjuːtə ˌlaɪn] *Nahverkehrszuglinie in Dublin* III U3, 53

A

abbiegen to turn II
Abend evening I
Abendessen dinner; tea I
abends in the evening I
Abenteuer adventure III U2, 34
aber but I
abfahren to leave II
Abfall rubbish I
abgeschlossen locked I
Abrakadabra! Abracadabra! II
Abschieds- leaving II
acht eight I
Achterbahn roller coaster II
achtzehn eighteen I
achtzig eighty I
Afroamerikaner African American III U4, 90
Afroamerikanerin African American III U4, 90
Aktivist *(jmd., der sich für etw. engagiert)* activist III U4, 90
Aktivistin *(jmd., die sich für etw. engagiert)* activist III U4, 90
Aktivität activity I
aktuell latest III U4, 76
Akzent accent III U3, 58
albern silly II
alle all I; everyone; every II
alles everything II
Alles Gute Best wishes, I; All the best, II
Alligator alligator II
als as; than; when II
als Nächstes next II
also so I
Also … Well, … II
alt old I
Alter age III ZI 9
am in; on I
am Ende at the end II
Amerikaner American II
Amerikanerin American II
Amerikanisch American II
amerikanisch American II
amüsant fun III U2, 38
an on; at I; to II; about III U1, 12; by III U1, 21
andauern to last II
Andenken souvenir II
andere other II; different III U3, 62; another III U2, 40
anderen others II
ein **anderer** another III U2, 40
ändern to change II
anders different I
Anfang beginning II
anfangen to start I; to begin III U4, 91
sich **anfühlen** to feel III U3, 62
Angst haben to be scared I
anhaben to wear I
anhalten to stop II
anheben to lift III U2, 48
anhören to listen (to) I
Animation animation III U1, 27
animiert animated III U1, 27
ankommen to arrive I
anprobieren to try on II
Anruf phone call I
anrufen to phone II; to call III U3, 56
anschauen to look at; to watch I
ansehen to watch I
anspornen to motivate III U4, 85
anstehen to be on III U2, 38
Antwort answer II
antworten to answer II
Anzeichen sign III U3, 69
Anzeige ad(vert) (= advertisement) III U1, 28
anziehen to put on II
Apfel apple I
April April I
Arbeit work II
arbeiten to work I
Ärger trouble III U3, 68
Arm arm II
Armee army III U2, 42
Art kind II; type III U3, 69
Art und Weise way III U2, 49
Arzt doctor II
Ärztin doctor II
auch too; also I
auf in; on; at I
auf einmal suddenly I
Auf Wiedersehen. Goodbye. I
auf der linken Seite on the left II
auf der rechten Seite on the right II
aufbewahren to keep III U2, 42
Geld **aufbringen** to raise money II
Aufführung show I
aufgeben to give up III U2, 42
aufgeregt excited II
aufhören to finish; to stop II
aufmachen to open I
aufpassen auf to look after II
aufräumen to tidy II
aufregend exciting I
aufstehen to get up I
jmdm. etw. **auftragen** to tell sb to do sth III U3, 58
aufwachen to wake up III U4, 80
Aufwärmen warm-up II
Aufwärmtraining warm-up II
Aufzug lift II
Auge eye I
August August I
aus from I
sich **ausdenken** to think of III U3, 58
Auseinandersetzung argument II
Ausflug trip I
den Hund **ausführen** to take the dog for a walk I
ausgeben *(Geld)* to spend II
ein **ausgefüllter** Tag a busy day II
Aushang notice III U3, 54
(sich) **ausleihen** to borrow II
ausprobieren to try III U3, 58
die Spülmaschine **ausräumen** to empty the dishwasher II
aussehen to look I
außen outside II
außerhalb outside II
aussprechen to say III U3, 62
etw. nicht **ausstehen** können can't stand + -ing III U3, 58
aussteigen to get off II
Ausstellung exhibition III U1, 11
Auto car I
Automat robot III U1, 11

B

Bad(ezimmer) bathroom II
bald soon II
Balkon balcony I
Ball ball I
Banane banana I
Band band II
Bär bear II
Baseball baseball III U4, 84

Basketball basketball II
Basketballkorb basket III U4, 85
basteln to make II
Bauarbeiter builder III U1, 20
Bauarbeiterin builder III U1, 20
bauen to build II
Bauer farmer I
Bäuerin farmer I
Bauernhof farm I
Baum tree I
Baumstamm caber III U2, 48
Baumstammwerfen caber toss III U2, 48
Bauwerk building II
beängstigend scary I
beantworten to answer II
bedeuten to mean III U3, 62
beenden to finish; to stop II
jmdm. etw. **befehlen** to tell sb to do sth III U3, 58
befördern to carry III U1, 20
Begabung talent I
begeistert excited II
Beginn beginning II
beginnen to start I; to begin III U4, 91
behalten to keep III U2, 42
bei at I; with II
Bein leg II
beinahe nearly II
Beispiel example III U2, 49
  zum Beispiel for example III U2, 49
bekommen to get I
bekommen to catch III U1, 16
beliebt popular III U1, 27
bellen to bark II
bemalen to paint II
benutzen to use III U2, 49
beobachten to watch II
bereit ready I
bereits already III U2, 34
Berg mountain II
Bergwerk mine III U1, 12
berühmt famous I
beschäftigt busy I
beschließen to decide III U2, 34
Besichtigung visit III U1, 11
besiedeln to settle III U4, 75
besitzen to have I; to have got II; to own III U1, 20
besonders special I
besorgt worried II
besser better II
beste best II
  am besten best II
besteigen to climb II
bestellen to order III U1, 16
Besuch visit III U1, 11
besuchen to visit I
Besucher visitor II
Besucherin visitor II
Betreff subject III U4, 92
Bett bed I
  ins Bett gehen to go to bed I
beunruhigt worried II
bevor before II
bewölkt cloudy II
Bild picture I
billig cheap II
Biologie Biology I
bis until III U2, 32
  Bis bald. See you soon. I; See you. II
  Bis dann. See you later. III U2, 38
  Bis später. See you later. III U2, 38
ein (kleines) **bisschen** a little (bit) II
bitte please I
  Bitte schön. Here you are. I
blau blue I
bleiben to stay I
  stecken bleiben to be stuck I
Bleistift pencil I
Blog blog I
Bonbon sweet I
böse angry II
Boss boss III U1, 20
Box box I
Brauch tradition III U2, 33
brauchbar useful III U4, 78
brauchen to need I; to take III U1, 16
braun brown I
bringen to bring II; to take III U1, 16
britisch British III U1, 27
Britpop *(Musik)* Britpop III U1, 27
Broschüre brochure III U1, 29
Brot bread I
  belegtes Brot sandwich I
Brücke bridge II
Bruder brother I
Bub boy I
Buch book I
buchen to book III U2, 34
Bude stall I
Bühne stage II
Bühnenbild scenery III U1, 16
Bundesstaat state III U4, 74
Burg castle III U2, 32
Bürgerrechte civil rights *(pl)* III U4, 90
Bus bus I
Butter butter I

C

Café snack bar I; café III U4, 92
Cafeteria cafeteria I
Camp camp III U4, 76
campen gehen to go camping III U3, 71
Campingplatz campsite III U3, 70
Center centre III U1, 12; center *(AE)* III U4, 75
Chance chance III U3, 58
chatten to chat II
Cheerleader cheerleader III U4, 85
Cheerleaderin cheerleader III U4, 85
Cheerleading cheerleading III U4, 85
Chef boss III U1, 20
Chefin boss III U1, 20
Chinese Chinese II
Chinesin Chinese II
Chinesisch Chinese II
chinesisch Chinese II
circa about II
Cola cola I
Comic(heft) comic II
Computer computer I
cool cool I
Cousin cousin II
Cousine cousin II

D

da there; because I
Dachboden attic I
daheim at home I; back home III U3, 62
dahin there I
damals then III U3, 69
danach then; after that I
Danke. Thanks.; Thank you. I
dann then I
  Bis dann. See you later. III U2, 38
Darsteller actor III U1, 20
Darstellerin actor III U1, 20
das the; this; that I; who III U3, 58; which III U4, 80

dass that I I
dauern to last II; to take III U1, 16
davor in front of I
dein your I
Dein *(Grußformel in Briefen oder E-Mails)* Yours, II
deine yours III U1, 16
denken to think II
denken an to think about III U2, 34
denken an/über to think of III U3, 58
der the I; that; who III U3, 58; which III U4, 80
dermaßen so II
derselbe the same II
deshalb so I
Design design II
Detektiv detective I
Detektivin detective I
deutlich clear III U3, 63
Deutsch German I
deutsch German II
Deutsche German II
Deutscher German II
Dezember December I
Dialog dialogue II
dich you I; yourself III U4, 92
die the I; that; who III U3, 58; which III U4, 80
Dienstag Tuesday I
dies this I
diese these II
dieses that I
Ding thing I
Dinosaurier dinosaur III U1, 26
dir you I
Dollar *(amer. Währungseinheit)* dollar ($) III U4, 83
Donnerstag Thursday I
Dorf village I
dort there I
dorthin there I
Drama drama III U1, 16
draußen outside II
draußen halten to keep out III U2, 42
dreckig dirty I
drei three I
dreißig thirty I
dreizehn thirteen I
dritte third II
drüben over III U2, 38
du you I
Dudelsack bagpipes *(pl)* III U2, 33
dunkel dark I
durch around III U4, 74
durchdrehen to go crazy III U4, 80
Durcheinander mess I
Durchmesser diameter II
nie/nicht **dürfen** must never/not III U2, 42

E

Ei egg I
eiförmig oval III U4, 84
eigene own II
eigentlich really I
ein one; a; an I
einander each other III U3, 62
eine a; an I
einfach easy I; just III U2, 38
einfache Fahrkarte single ticket III U3, 54
die einfachste the least difficult III U4, 76
sich **einfallen** lassen to think of III U3, 58
eingeboren native III U4, 75
einheimisch native III U4, 75
einhundert a/one hundred I
einige some I
Einkaufen shopping I
Einkaufspassage mall II
Einkaufszentrum shopping centre I; mall II
Einkaufszettel shopping list I
einladen to invite II
Einladung invitation I
einmal once II
schon einmal before III U1, 12; ever III U2, 38
einpacken to pack III U2, 34
die Spülmaschine **einräumen** to load the dishwasher II
eins one I
einst once II
eintausend a/one thousand II
Eintrittskarte ticket II
einundzwanzig twenty-one I
Eis ice cream II
Eiscreme ice cream II
elf eleven I
Eltern parents *(pl)* I
E-Mail e-mail II
empfinden to feel III U3, 62
Ende end II
am Ende at the end II
oberes Ende top II
enden to finish II
die **Engländer** the English III U2, 33
Englisch English I
englisch English III U2, 33
entdecken to discover III U4, 91
entfernt away II
entlang down III U2, 32
(sich) **entscheiden** to decide III U2, 34
Entschuldigung. Sorry. I; I'm sorry.; Excuse me. II
entwerfen to design III U1, 16
Entwurf design II
er it; he I
Erdbeere strawberry I
Erde earth III U4, 75
Erdteil continent II
Ereignis event II
sich **erinnern** (an) to remember III U4, 76
Erkältung cold II
erklettern to climb II
sich **erkundigen** nach to ask about II
Erlebnis adventure III U2, 34
erledigen to finish II
ernst serious II
Erntedankfest Thanksgiving III U4, 91
erraten to guess I
erstaunlich amazing II
erste first I
das erste Mal the first time I
als **Erstes** first II
etw. nicht **ertragen** can't stand + -ing III U3, 58
erwachen to wake up III U4, 80
Erwachsene adult III U1, 27
Erwachsener adult III U1, 27
erzählen to tell I
Erzähler narrator I
Erzählerin narrator I
es it I
Es tut mir leid. I'm sorry. II
es war einmal once upon a time II
Essen food I; meal II
essen to eat; to have I
Etage floor II

etwa about II
etwas something; some I; anything III U3, 58
euch you I
euer your I
eure yours III U1, 16
Euro *(Währung)* euro III U3, 52
Europäer European III U4, 75
Europäerin European III U4, 75
europäisch European III U4, 75
Experiment experiment II

F

Fabrik factory III U1, 12
Fahne flag III U4, 90
fahren to go; to ride I; to run; to travel II; to drive III U1, 11
  Fahrrad fahren to go bike riding II
  Ski fahren to ski III U2, 37
  Tandem fahren to go tandem bike riding II
Fahrgeschäft ride II
einfache **Fahrkarte** single ticket III U3, 54
Fahrplan timetable III U3, 54
Fahrrad bike I
  Fahrrad fahren to go bike riding II
Fahrschein ticket II
Fahrt trip I; ride II; journey III U3, 54
Fakt fact II
fallen to fall I
falls if III U1, 26
falsch wrong I
Familie family I
Fan fan I
fangen to catch II
fantastisch fantastic II
Farbe colour I
Fasching carnival I
fast nearly II
Februar February I
Feier party I
feiern to celebrate III U3, 53
  eine Party feiern to have a party I
Feiertag holiday III U4, 91
Fels rock III U4, 80
Fenster window I
Ferien holiday II; vacation *(AE)* III U4, 76
Fernseh- TV III U1, 27
Fernsehen TV III U1, 27
  im Fernsehen on TV III U1, 27
fernsehen to watch TV I
Fernseher TV I
fertig ready I
  fertig machen to finish II
fertigstellen to finish I
Fest fair II; festival III U4, 92
festhalten to hold II
Festival festival III U4, 92
feststecken to be stuck I
Festzug procession II
Feuer fire III U1, 21
Feuerwerk fireworks *(pl)* III U4, 90
Figur figure II
Film film I; movie *(AE)* III U4, 76
finden to find I
Firma company II
Fisch fish I
fit fit III U2, 34
Flagge flag III U4, 90
eine **Flasche** … a bottle of II
Fledermaus bat I
fliegen to fly II
Floh flea I
Flohmarkt flea market I
Floß raft III U4, 80
Fluss river I
Foto photo I
  Fotos machen to take photos (of) II
fotografieren to take photos (of) II
Frage question I
fragen to ask I
  fragen nach to ask about II
Frau woman I
Frau *(Anrede)* Mrs I
frei free III U2, 42
  im Freien outside II
Freitag Friday I
Freizeit free time I
Freizeitpark theme park II
Freude fun I
Freund friend I
Freundin friend I
Freundschaft(en) schließen to make friends II
Frieden peace III U2, 43
  Frieden schaffen to make peace III U2, 43
friedlich peaceful III U4, 90
Frisbee frisbee I
Frisbeescheibe frisbee I
Frohe Weihnachten! Merry Christmas! I
Frucht fruit I
früh early II
Frühling spring II
Frühstück breakfast I
frühstücken to have breakfast I
Frühstückspension bed & breakfast (B & B) III U3, 58
(sich) **fühlen** to feel II
Füller pen I
fünf five I
fünfzehn fifteen I
fünfzig fifty I
für for I
furchtbar awful I
Fuß foot II
  zu Fuß on foot I
Fußball football I; soccer *(AE)* II
füttern to feed I

G

Galerie gallery III U1, 26
gälisch Gaelic III U3, 53
ganz all I; all of; quite II; whole III U3, 62
  in ganz all over II
Ganztages- all-day III U3, 54
Garten garden I
Gast guest III U3, 58
Gebäude building II
geben to give I
gebratener Reis mit Hühnerfleisch chicken fried rice II
gebraucht second-hand I
Geburtstag birthday I
Gedicht poem III U3, 63
gefährlich dangerous III U2, 34
gegen against III U2, 33
gegenseitig each other III U3, 62
gegenüber opposite II
gehen to go I; to walk III U3, 61
  campen gehen to go camping III U3, 71
  inlineskaten gehen to go skating II
  ins Bett gehen to go to bed I
  raften gehen to go rafting III U4, 75
  Schlittschuhlaufen gehen to go skating II

zelten gehen to go camping III U3, 71
Gehör hearing II
gelb yellow I
Geld money I
Geld aufbringen to raise money II
Geld sammeln to raise money II
Gelegenheit chance III U3, 58
gelegentlich occasionally III U1, 16
genauso the same II
genug enough III U3, 63
genügend enough III U3, 63
geöffnet open I
gerade (eben) just III U2, 38
geradeaus straight on II
Geräusch noise I
... **gerne** like + -ing I
gernhaben to like I
Geschäft shop I
geschehen to happen II
Geschenk present I
Geschichte story I; history III U2, 32
geschlossen closed I
Gesellschaft company II
Gesicht face I
Gespräch dialogue II
Gestalt figure II
gestalten to design III U1, 16
Gestaltung design II
gestern yesterday I
gesund healthy III U1, 16
Getränk drink I
Gewinn prize II
gewinnen to win I
Gewinner winner I
Gewinnerin winner I
Gewinnspiel raffle II
gewöhnlich usually II
glauben to think; to believe II; to feel III U3, 62
gleich the same II
der **gleiche** the same II
gleichzeitig at the same time II
Glocke bell II
Glück bringend lucky II
Glück haben to be lucky II
glücklich happy I; lucky II
Glückstag lucky day II
Glückwunsch! Congratulations! II
Gold gold III U3, 62
Gold- gold III U3, 62
golden gold III U3, 62
grau grey I
Grill barbecue I
Grillfest barbecue I
groß big I; large; high; tall II
großartig great I; fantastic II
Größe size II
Großeltern grandparents *(pl)* II
Großstadt city I
Großvater grandfather II
grün green I
gründen to start III U1, 27
Grundrechte civil rights *(pl)* III U4, 90
Grundstückseigentümer landlord III U1, 20
Gruppe team I
gruselig scary I
Viele **Grüße** Best wishes, I
günstig cheap II
gut fine; good I; well II
gut sein in to be good at I
Gut gemacht! Well done! II
gut sein bei to be good at I
Mir geht es gut. I'm fine. I
Alles **Gute** Best wishes, I; All the best, II

H

haben to have I; to have got II
Angst haben to be scared I
Glück haben to be lucky II
Hähnchen chicken I
Hai shark I
halb half III U1, 12
eine halbe Million half a million III U1, 12
halb (acht) half past (seven) II
(die) **Hälfte** half III U3, 53
Halle gallery III U1, 26
Hallo. Hello.; Hi. I
Hals neck II
Halsband collar I
Halt stop II
halten to hold; to keep II
draußen halten to keep out III U2, 42
Haltestelle stop II
Hamburger burger I
Hammer hammer III U2, 33
Hammerwerfen hammer throwing III U2, 33
Hamster hamster I
Hand hand II
aus zweiter Hand second-hand I
Handschuh glove II
Handy phone I
hart hard II
hassen to hate I
häufig often II
Hauptstadt capital (city) I
Haus house I
nach Hause home I
zu Hause at home I; back home III U3, 62
Hausaufgabe(n) homework I
Hausaufgabe(n) machen to do homework I
Hausmeister caretaker I
Hausmeisterin caretaker I
Haustier pet I
heben to lift III U2, 48
Heer army III U2, 42
Heft book I
Heim home I
heiß hot I
Ich **heiße** ... My name is ... I
helfen to help I
Helikopter helicopter III U4, 80
Helm helmet I
Hemd shirt I
herausfinden to find I; to find out III U2, 38
Herberge hostel II
Herbst autumn II
Herr *(Anrede)* Mr I
herüber over III U2, 38
herüberkommen to come over III U2, 38
herumhängen to hang about I
herunter down III U2, 32
herunterfallen to fall off II
Herz heart III U4, 80
Herzliche Grüße Love, I
heute today I
heute Morgen this morning II
hier here I
hierher here III U1, 16
hierhin here III U1, 16
hiesig local II
Hilfe help I
hilfreich useful III U4, 78

Hin- und Rückfahrkarte return ticket III U3, 54
hinauf up II
hinausbringen to take out II
hinbringen to take II
in ... **hinein** into II
hinfallen to fall I
sich **hinsetzen** to sit (down) I
hinter behind I
Hintergrund background III U3, 70
hinterlassen to leave III U3, 54
hinunter down III U2, 32
hinunterfallen to fall off II
Hinweis clue I
Hip-Hop *(Musik)* hip-hop III U1, 27
Hit hit song III U1, 27
Hobby hobby II
hoch high; up; tall II
hochheben to lift III U2, 48
hochladen to upload II
hoffen (auf) to hope (for) II
Höhe height II
Holz wood I
hören to listen (to) I; to hear II
kurze **Hose** shorts *(pl)* II
Hostel hostel II
Hotdog hot dog II
hübsch pretty II; beautiful III U4, 76
Hubschrauber helicopter III U4, 80
Huhn chicken I
gebratener Reis mit **Hühnerfleisch** chicken fried rice II
Hund dog I
  den Hund ausführen to take the dog for a walk I
hundert a/one hundred I
hungrig hungry I
hüpfen to bounce III U4, 85
Hut hat II
hüten to look after II

I

ich I; me I
  ich hätte gern I'd (= I would) I
  ich möchte ... I'd like (to) ... (= I would like to) I
  ich würde I'd (= I would) I
  ich würde gerne ... I'd like (to) ... (= I would like to) I
  ich würde nicht gerne ... I wouldn't like (to) ... I
Idee idea I
ihm it; him II
ihn it; him II
Ihnen you I
ihnen them II
ihr you; her; their; its I
Ihr your I
Ihre yours III U1, 16
ihre hers III U1, 16; **theirs** III U1, 19
im in I
  im Fernsehen on TV III U1, 27
  im Freien outside II
  im Moment at the moment II
  im Nordwesten von in the north-west of III U1, 12
Imbissstube snack bar I
immer always I
  immer noch still II
  schon immer always III U2, 34
in to; in; at I; into II
  in der Schule at school I
  in ganz all over II
  in Ordnung fine I
Indianer Native American III U4, 75
Indianerin Native American III U4, 75
indianisch Native American III U4, 75
Industrie industry III U1, 28
Information(en) information II
Ingenieur engineer II
Ingenieurin engineer II
inlineskaten to skate II
  inlineskaten gehen to go skating II
Insel island III U3, 68
interessant interesting I
sich **interessieren** für to be interested in III U4, 76
interessiert sein an to be interested in III U4, 76
Internetseite website III U2, 34
Internettagebuch blog I
die **Iren** the Irish III U3, 53
irgendeine any I
irgendetwas anything III U3, 58
irgendjemand anybody III U3, 58
irgendwelche any I
Irisch Irish III U3, 52
irisch Irish III U3, 52

J

ja yes I
Jacke coat I
Jahr year I
Jahreszeit season II
Jahrgangsstufe year I; grade *(AE)* II
Jahrhundert century III U2, 42
Jahrmarkt fair II
Januar January I
jede every I; each III U3, 54
jeder everyone II; anybody III U3, 58
jemals ever III U2, 38
jemand somebody I; anybody; someone III U3, 58
jene that I; those II
jetzt now I
jeweils each III U3, 54
Job job I
Jugend- youth I; teen II
Jugendliche teen II
Jugendlicher teen II
Juli July I
jung young II
Junge boy I
Juni June I

K

Käfig cage II
Kalender planner II
kalt cold I
Kälte cold II
Kampf battle III U2, 42
kämpfen to fight II
Kanal canal III U1, 28
Kaninchen rabbit I
Kanone cannon III U1, 21
Kanonenkugel cannon ball III U1, 21
Kanufahren canoeing I
Kapitän captain II
Kapitänin captain II
Karneval carnival I
Karte map II; card III U3, 62
Käse cheese I
Katholik Catholic III U3, 68
Katholikin Catholic III U3, 68
katholisch Catholic III U3, 68
Katze cat I
kaufen to buy I
kein no I; not ... any III U3, 58
keine no I; not ... any III U3, 58
kennen to know I
kennenlernen to meet I
Kette chain III U2, 49

L

M

Mann man I
Mannschaft team I
Mannschaftsführer captain II
Mannschaftsführerin captain II
Markt market I
März March I
Match match I
Mathe Maths I
Matsch mud I
Mauer wall II
Maus mouse I
Medaille medal II
soziale **Medien** social media III U4, 76
Meer sea I
am Meer at the seaside I
Meerschweinchen guinea pig II
Megafon megaphone III U4, 80
mehr more II
nicht mehr not … any more III U3, 58
die **Mehrheit** most III U2, 51
Meile mile III U2, 32
mein my I
meine mine III U1, 16
meinen to mean III U3, 62
einer **Meinung** sein (mit) to agree (with) II
am **meisten** most III U2, 51
die **meisten** most III U2, 51
eine **Menge** a lot of I
Mensa cafeteria I
Mensch person II
Menschen people *(pl only)* I
sich **merken** to remember III U4, 76
merkwürdig funny I
Messe fair II
Meter metre II
mich me I; myself III U2, 34
Miete rent III U1, 20
mieten to rent III U1, 28
Milch milk III U1, 12
mild mild II
Million million I
eine halbe Million half a million III U1, 12
Minute minute I
mir me I
mit with I; on II
mit (dem Zug) by (train) I
mitbringen to bring II
mitmachen (bei) to take part (in) II
mitnehmen to take I
mitspielen to act III U1, 16
Mittagessen lunch; dinner I
Mittagspause lunchtime I
Mittagszeit lunchtime I
Mitte centre III U1, 12; center *(AE)* III U4, 75; middle III U3, 70
mitten in in the middle of II
Mittwoch Wednesday I
Mode fashion III U1, 26
modern modern I
mögen to like; to want (to) I
gern mögen to love I
nicht mögen to hate I
ich möchte nicht … I wouldn't like (to) … I
ich möchte … I'd like (to) … (= I would like to) I
Möchtest du …? Would you like (to) …? I
möglich possible III U2, 49
Möglichkeit chance III U3, 58
im **Moment** at the moment II
momentan at the moment II
Monat month II
Montag Monday I
Morgen morning I
heute Morgen this morning II
morgen tomorrow II
motivieren to motivate III U4, 85
müde tired I
Muffin muffin II
Müll rubbish I
Mund mouth II
Museum museum II
Musical musical III U1, 26
Musik music I
Musikgruppe band II
Musiktheaterstück musical III U1, 26
Muslim Muslim I
Muslimin Muslim I
müssen to have to; must II; to need to III U2, 34
mutig brave III U2, 43
Mutter mother I
Mutti mum I
Mütze hat II

N

Na ja, … Well, … II
nach to; after I
nach *(bei Uhrzeitangaben)* past II
nach Hause home I
nach unten down III U2, 32
Nachbar neighbour I
Nachbarin neighbour I
nachdenken über to think about III U2, 34
Nachmittag afternoon I
nachmittags *(Uhrzeit)* p.m. III U1, 16
Nachricht message II
Nachricht(en) news II
nachschauen to look I
nächste next I
als Nächstes next II
Nacht night I
Nacken neck II
nah near II
in der **Nähe** von near I
Name name I
Nase nose II
die Nase voll haben (von) to be fed up (with) III U3, 58
nass wet I
national national III U4, 74
National- national III U4, 74
Nationalpark national park III U4, 74
natürlich of course II
Naturwissenschaft science III U1, 11
neben next to I; by III U1, 21
nebenher at the same time II
nehmen to take I; to use III U2, 49
nehmen to catch III U1, 16
nein no I
nennen to call III U3, 56
nenne mich call me I
nett nice I
Netz web III U2, 42
neu new I
neueste latest III U4, 76
Neuigkeit(en) news II
neun nine I
neunzehn nineteen I
neunzig ninety I
nicht not I
nicht können can't I
nicht mögen to hate I
nicht mehr not … any more III U3, 58
nichts nothing II; not … anything III U3, 58
nie never II

sich **niederlassen** to settle III U4, 75
niemals never II
niemand no one I; nobody II
noch still II; even III U3, 62
immer noch still II
noch ein another III U2, 40
noch einmal again I
noch nicht not … yet III U2, 34
Nord- north III U1, 12
Norden north III U1, 12
Nordwesten northwest III U1, 12
im Nordwesten von in the northwest of III U1, 12
normalerweise usually II
Note grade *(AE)* II
November November I
null zero I
Null *(bei Uhrzeiten und Telefonnummern)* oh III U1, 16
Nummer number I
nun now I
nur only I; just III U2, 38
nutzen to use III U2, 49
nützlich useful III U4, 78

O

oben up II
oberer Teil top II
oberes Ende top II
oberhalb above II
Obst fruit I
oder or I
öffentliche Verkehrsmittel public transport III U3, 54
öffnen to open I
oft often II
ohne without II
okay OK (okay) I
Oktober October I
Öl oil II
Oma grandma I
Onkel uncle I
online online II
online stellen to post III U4, 76
Online- online II
Orange orange I
orange orange I
Orchester orchestra III U3, 52
in **Ordnung** fine I
in Ordnung bringen to tidy II
organisieren to organize I
Ort place I
örtlich local II
Ost- east III U1, 12
Osten east III U1, 12
oval oval III U4, 84

P

ein **paar** some I
packen to pack III U2, 34
paddeln to paddle III U4, 80
Papa dad I
Papier paper III U3, 62
Park park I
Partner partner I
Partnerin partner I
Partnerstadt twin town III U2, 50
Party party I
eine Party feiern to have a party I
passieren to happen II
Das ist passiert. That's what happened. II
Pause break I
Pausenhof playground I
Person person II
Pferd horse I
Pflanze plant III U4, 74
Pflaume plum I
Pfund *(brit. Währungseinheit)* pound (£) I
Picknick picnic I
Pier pier II
pink pink I
Pizza pizza I
Plakat notice III U3, 54
Plan map II; plan III ZI 9
Planer planner II
Platz place I
plaudern to chat II
plötzlich suddenly I
Polizeibeamter police officer I
Polizeibeamtin police officer I
Pommes frites chips *(pl)* I
Pop *(Musik)* pop II
Pop- popular III U1, 27
positiv positive III U3, 58
posten to post III U4, 76
Poster poster II
Postkarte postcard I
Präsentation presentation III U2, 50
Präsident president III U4, 81
Präsidentin president III U4, 81
Preis price I; prize II
prellen to bounce III U4, 85
pro Stück each III U3, 54
probieren to try III U3, 58
Problem problem I; trouble III U3, 68
Profil profile III U4, 92
Programm programme III U1, 28
auf dem Programm stehen to be on III U2, 38
Projekt project II
Prospekt brochure III U1, 29
Protestant Protestant III U3, 68
Protestantin Protestant III U3, 68
protestantisch Protestant III U3, 68
protestieren to protest III U4, 90
Prozent percent (%) III U4, 85
prüfen to test II
Pullover pullover I
Puma mountain lion II
Punkt point III U4, 85
putzen to clean II

R

Rad wheel II
Radiergummi rubber I
Radio radio III U1, 27
Raft raft III U4, 80
raften gehen to go rafting III U4, 75
Rafting rafting III U4, 74
Rakete rocket III U1, 11
Rap rap I
Rat advice III U3, 58
raten to guess I
Ratschlag advice III U3, 58
Raum room I
Raumfahrt space III U4, 75
Du hast **recht**. You're right. I
Recht right III U4, 90
rechte right II
rechts right; on the right II
Rechtschreibung spelling I
reden (mit) to talk (to) I
Referat presentation III U2, 50
Regal shelf II
Regalbrett shelf II
Regenbogen rainbow III U3, 62
regnen to rain I
regnerisch rainy II
Reis rice II
gebratener Reis mit Hühnerfleisch chicken fried rice II

Reise trip I; tour III U1, 28; journey III U3, 54
reisen to travel II
Reiten horse riding I
reiten to ride I
Religion religion III U3, 68
Rennen race II
rennen to run II
Reservat reservation III U4, 76
reservieren to book III U2, 34
Reservierung reservation III U4, 76
Rest rest II
Restaurant restaurant II
retten to save II
richtig right I
richtigstellen to correct II
riesengroß huge III U4, 74
Riesenrad big wheel II
riesig huge III U4, 74
Ritt ride II
Roboter robot III U1, 11
Rock skirt III U2, 33
Rolle part II
Rollstuhl wheelchair I
rosa pink I
rot red I
Hin- und **Rückfahrkarte** return ticket III U3, 54
rufen to shout I; to call III U3, 56
Rugby rugby III U2, 34
ruhig quiet II

S

Sache thing I
Sack bag I
Sackhüpfen sack race II
Saft juice I
sagen to say; to tell I
Saison season II
Salat salad I
Geld **sammeln** to raise money II
Sammlung collection III U1, 28
Samstag Saturday I
samstags on Saturdays I
Sandwich sandwich I
Sänger singer I
Sängerin singer I
sauber clean III U1, 12
  sauber machen to clean II
Säulenhalle gallery III U1, 26
Saxofon saxophone I
Schachtel box I
Schade! That's too bad. II
Schaf sheep I
Frieden **schaffen** to make peace III U2, 43
Schal scarf II
Schatzsuche treasure hunt II
Schau mal. Look. I
schauen to look I
  Lass mich mal schauen. Let me see. I
Schauspielen acting III U1, 26
Schauspieler actor III U1, 20
Schauspielerei drama III U1, 16; acting III U1, 26
Schauspielerin actor III U1, 20
schenken to give I
schicken to send I
schieben to push I
Schiff ship I
Schild sign III U3, 69
Schimpanse chimpanzee II
Schlacht battle III U2, 42
schlafen to sleep II
Schlafzimmer bedroom II
schlagen to hit III U4, 84
Schläger bat III U4, 84
Schlagzeile headline III U3, 62
Schlamm mud I
schlecht bad I
schlechter worse II
schlechteste worst II
schließen to close I
  Freundschaft(en) schließen to make friends II
schließlich finally III U3, 62
schlimm bad II
schlimmer worse II
schlimmste worst II
Schlittschuh laufen to skate II
Schlittschuhlaufen gehen to go skating II
Schloss castle III U2, 32
Schlumpf smurf I
Schluss end II
  zum Schluss finally III U3, 62
Schlüssel key III U3, 54
Schminken face painting II
schmutzig dirty I
Schnee snow II
schneereich snowy II
schnell fast II
Schnitzeljagd treasure hunt II
Schokolade chocolate I
schön fine; nice I; beautiful III U4, 76
schon already; yet III U2, 34
  schon einmal before III U1, 12; ever III U2, 38
  schon immer always III U2, 34
  Schon gut. Never mind. II
Schotte Scot III U2, 32
Schottenrock kilt III U2, 33
Schottin Scot III U2, 32
schottisch Scottish III U2, 33
schrecklich awful I
Schreibtisch desk II
schreien to shout I
Schritt step II
Schuh shoe I
Schul-AG club I
Schulausflug school trip II
Schule school I
  in der Schule at school I
Schüler student I
Schülerin student I
Schulfach subject I
Schulhof playground I
Schulstunde lesson I
Schwanz tail I
schwarz black I
schwenken to swing III U2, 49
schwer hard; serious II; difficult III U2, 34; heavy III U2, 48
Schwester sister I
schwierig hard II; difficult III U2, 34; heavy III U2, 48
Schwierigkeiten trouble III U3, 68
Schwimmbad swimming pool I
schwimmen to swim I
  schwimmen gehen to go swimming I
schwingen to swing III U2, 49
Science-Fiction science fiction I
sechs six I
sechzehn sixteen I
sechzig sixty I
secondhand second-hand I
See lake III U4, 92
sehen to spy; to see; to look I
  Wir sehen uns. See you. II
Sehenswürdigkeit sight II
sehr very I

Seilrutsche zip line III U2, 32
sein to be; his; its I
einer Meinung sein (mit) to agree (with) II
weit weg sein to be a long way away II
seine his III U1, 19
seit since III U3, 69
seitdem since III U3, 69
Seite side II
selbst myself III U2, 34; themselves III U4, 76; yourself III U4, 92
sie selbst themselves III U4, 76
selbstverständlich of course II
selten rarely III U2, 48
Seminar workshop III U3, 54
senden to send I
Sendung programme III U1, 28
September September I
setzen to put I
sich setzen to sit (down) I
Shirt shirt I
Shorts shorts *(pl)* II
Show show I
sich each other III U3, 62; themselves III U4, 76
sicher sure II; safe III U2, 34
sie it; she I; her II
Sie you I
sie *(Pl.)* they; them I
sieben seven I
siebzehn seventeen I
siebzig seventy I
siedeln to settle III U4, 75
siegen to win I
Sieger winner I
Siegerin winner I
singen to sing I
Skateboard skateboard I
Skater skater I
Skaterin skater I
Ski fahren to ski III U2, 37
Ski- skiing III U2, 32
Skifahren skiing III U2, 32
SMS message II
Snowboard snowboard I
so so II
so … wie as … as III U2, 49
soeben just III U2, 38
sogar even III U3, 62
sollte should III U3, 58
Sommer summer II
Sonne sun II
sonnig sunny II
Sonntag Sunday I
sich Sorgen machen to worry I
Mach dir keine Sorgen. Don't worry. I
sorgfältig careful III U2, 34
Sorte kind II; type III U3, 69
Souvenir souvenir II
sowohl … als auch … … as well as … II
soziale Medien social media III U4, 76
spannend exciting I
sparen to save II
Spaß fun I
Spaß machen to be fun II
spaßig fun III U2, 38
(zu) spät late II
zu spät kommen to be late II
später later I
Bis später. See you later. III U2, 38
Spaziergang walk I
Speck bacon I
speziell special I
Spiel game; match I
spielen to play I; to act III U1, 16
Spieler player II
Spielerin player II
Spielfeld playing field III U4, 84
Spielplatz playground I
Spinne spider III U2, 42
Spitze top II
Sport sport III U1, 28
Sportarten sports *(pl only)* I
Sportfest sports day II
Sportgeschäft sports shop II
Sportplatz playing field II
Sportunterricht PE (Physical Education) I
Sportzentrum sports centre I
sprechen to say; to speak I
sprechen (mit) to talk (to) I
springen to jump III U4, 85
spülen to wash II
die Spülmaschine ausräumen to empty the dishwasher II
die Spülmaschine einräumen to load the dishwasher II
Spur clue I
Squaredance *(amerikanischer Volkstanz)* square dance II
Staat state III U4, 74
Stadion stadium I
Stadt city; town I
Stadtmitte city centre II
Stadtzentrum city centre II
Stamm tribe III U4, 76
Stand stall I
Star star I
stark strong III U2, 34; heavy III U2, 48
starten to start I
staubsaugen to hoover II
Steckbrief profile III U4, 92
stecken to put II
stecken bleiben to be stuck I
stehen to stand II
auf dem Programm stehen to be on III U2, 38
steigen to climb II
Stein stone III U2, 49; rock III U4, 80
Steinstoßen stone put III U2, 49
Stell dir vor! Guess what? II
Stelle place I
stellen to put I
online stellen to post III U4, 76
Stellt euch vor! Guess what? II
sterben to die III U3, 69
Stift pen I
Stiftung charity II
still quiet II
Stimmt etwas nicht? Is something wrong? II
Stockwerk floor II
Strand beach I
Straße street; road I
Straßenbahn tram I
Streich trick II
streichen to paint II
Streit argument II
(sich) streiten to fight II
Stromschnelle rapid III U4, 80
Strömung current III U4, 80
ein Stück … a piece of II
pro Stück each III U3, 54
Studio studio III U1, 29
Stufe step II
Stuhl chair I
Stunde hour II
Stundenplan timetable I
Sturm storm I

von etw. **stürzen** to fall off II
Süd- south III U1, 11
Süden south III U1, 11
super cool I
Supermarkt supermarket I
surfen gehen to go surfing III U1, 10
Süßigkeit sweet I

T

Tablet tablet III U4, 76
Tafel blackboard I
Tag day I
  ein ausgefüllter Tag a busy day II
  eines Tages one day I
Tagebuch diary I
Tal valley III U4, 74
Talent talent I
Talentwettbewerb talent show I
Tandem tandem II
  Tandem fahren to go tandem bike riding II
Tante aunt I
Tanz dancing III U2, 48
Tanzen dancing III U2, 48
tanzen to dance I
Tänzer dancer I
Tänzerin dancer I
tapfer brave III U2, 43
Tasche bag I
Taschenlampe torch I
Taschenrechner calculator I
eine **Tasse** ... a cup of II
Tatsache fact II
tausend a/one thousand II
Team team I
Technik DT (Design Technology) I; technology III U1, 28
Techniker engineer II
Technikerin engineer II
Techno *(Musik)* techno III U1, 27
Technologie technology III U1, 28
Teddybär teddy I
Tee tea I
Teenager teen II
Teil part II
  oberer Teil top II
teilen to share III U4, 76
teilnehmen (an) to take part (in) II
Telefon phone I
Telefonanruf phone call I
telefonieren to phone II
Telefonzelle telephone box II
Tennis tennis I
Teppich carpet II
Terrorismus terrorism III U3, 69
testen to test II
teuer expensive I
Theater theatre III U1, 11
Theater- drama III U1, 16
Theaterstück play III U1, 11
Ticket ticket II
tief deep III U4, 80
Tier animal I
Tierheim animal rescue shelter I
Tisch table I; desk II
Tochter daughter I
toll great I; amazing II
Tomate tomato I
Tombola raffle II
Topf pot III U3, 62
Tour tour III U1, 28; trip III U4, 74
Tourist tourist II
Touristin tourist II
Tradition tradition III U2, 33
tragen to wear I; to carry III U1, 20
Training practice I
Transport transport II
Traum dream I
traurig sad I; unhappy II
Treff club I
treffen to meet I; to hit III U4, 84
  (sich) treffen to meet II
treiben to drive III U1, 11
Trick trick I
Trickfilm animation III U1, 27
trinken to have I; to drink II
Trip trip III U4, 74
trocken dry II
Trompete trumpet II
Tschüss. Bye. I; See you. II
T-Shirt T-shirt II
Tuch scarf II
tun to do; to make I
  etw. tun werden to be going to do sth III U2, 34
  Tut mir leid. Sorry. I
Tunnel tunnel III ZI 8
Tür door II
Türklingel doorbell I
Turm tower II
Turnschuh trainer II
Tüte bag I
Typ type III U3, 69

U

U-Bahn underground I
über about I; above; across II; over III U2, 38
überall all over; everywhere II
überallhin everywhere II
sich **übergeben** to be sick I
überhaupt ever III U2, 38
überlegen to guess I
  sich überlegen to think about III U2, 34
übernachten to stay I
überprüfen to check II
überrascht surprised II
Überraschung surprise III U3, 63
Überschrift headline III U3, 62
übrig left III U2, 38
Übung exercise; practice I
Übungsheft exercise book I
Uhr clock II
Uhr *(Zeitangabe bei vollen Stunden)* o'clock I
Uhrzeit time I
um at I; around III U4, 74
  um zu to II
  um ... herum around II
(sich) **umdrehen** to turn over III U4, 80
Umgebung environment II
umkippen to turn over III U4, 80
umsteigen to change III U3, 54
Umwelt environment II
umziehen to move II
Umzug procession II
Unabhängigkeit independence III U4, 90
und and I
  Und ...? What about ...? II
Unfall accident I
ungefähr about II
ungefährlich safe III U2, 34
unglaublich amazing II
unglücklich unhappy II
unheimlich scary I
Uniform uniform I
Universität university III U2, 50
Unordnung mess I
uns us II
unser our I

V

W

Wie alt bist du? How old are you? I
Wie geht es dir? How are you? I
Wie heißt du? What's your name? I
Wie ist das Wetter? What's the weather like? II
Wie spät ist es? What time is it? I
Wie viel (kostet/kosten) ...? How much (is/are) ...? I
Wie viel Uhr ist es? What time is it? I
so ... wie as ... as III U2, 49
wieder again I
Auf **Wiedersehen**. Goodbye. I
willkommen (bei/in) welcome (to) I
Wind wind I
windig windy II
Winter winter I
wir we I; us II
wirklich really I
wissen to know I
Ich weiß (es) nicht! I don't know. I
Wissenschaft science III U1, 11
Witterung weather II
witzig sein to be fun II
wo where I
Woche week I
Wochenende weekend I
woher where I
Woher kommst du? Where are you from? I
wohin where I
wohltätige Zwecke charity II
Wohltätigkeits- charity II
Wohltätigkeitsorganisation charity II
wohnen to live I
Wohnung flat I
Wohnzimmer living room II
Wolf wolf II
Wolke cloud II
wolkig cloudy II
Wolle wool I
wollen to want (to) I
Workshop workshop III U3, 54
Wort word II
wunderschön beautiful III U4, 76
ich **würde** I'd (= I would) I
ich würde gerne ... I'd like (to) ... (= I would like to) I
ich würde nicht gerne ... I wouldn't like (to) ... I
Würdest du gern ...? Would you like (to) ...? I
wütend angry II

Z

Zahl number I
Zahn tooth II
Zauberer wizard II
Zauberkünstler magician II
Zauberkünstlerin magician II
zaubern to do magic II
zehn ten I
Zeichen sign III U3, 69
zeigen to show II
Zeile line III U2, 38
Zeit time I
Zeitalter age III ZI 9
Zeitung newspaper III U4, 76
Zeitungsstand newspaper kiosk II
Zelt tent II
zelten gehen to go camping III U3, 71
Zeltplatz campsite III U3, 70
Zentrum centre III U1, 12; center *(AE)* III U4, 75
Ziege goat III U1, 12
ziehen to pull I
ziemlich quite II
Zimmer room I
zornig angry II
zu to; at; too I
zu Fuß on foot I
zu Hause back home III U3, 62
zuerst first II
Zug train I
Zuhause home I
zuhören to listen (to) I
zum 200. Mal for the 200th time III U4, 80
zum Beispiel for example III U2, 49
zum Schluss finally III U3, 62
zumachen to close I
zurück back II
zusammen together I; everyone II
zuschauen to watch II
zusehen to watch II
zustimmen to agree (with) II
zuvor before III U1, 12
zwanzig twenty I
wohltätige **Zwecke** charity II
zwei two I
zweite second II
aus zweiter Hand second-hand I
zwischen between III U2, 42
zwölf twelve I

Instructions

Arbeitsanweisungen mit Operatoren

Act the dialogue with your partner.	**Spiele** den Dialog mit deinem Partner / deiner Partnerin.
Answer the questions.	**Beantworte** die Fragen.
Ask questions.	**Stelle Fragen.**
Ask your partner.	**Frage** deinen Partner / deine Partnerin.
Ask for feedback.	**Bitte um** Rückmeldung.
Choose one of the tasks • the right answers.	**Wähle** eine der Aufgaben • die richtigen Antworten **aus**.
Collect ideas.	**Sammle** Ideen.
Complete the sentences • dialogue • story.	**Vervollständige** die Sätze • den Dialog • die Geschichte.
Correct the (wrong) sentences.	**Verbessere** die (falschen) Sätze.
Describe the picture.	**Beschreibe** das Bild.
Discuss in groups.	**Besprecht** euch in Gruppen.
Find the right order • the words • the answers.	**Finde** die richtige Reihenfolge • die Wörter • die Antworten.
Find out what the words mean.	**Finde heraus**, was die Wörter bedeuten.
Give feedback.	**Gib** Rückmeldung.
Interview your partner.	**Interviewe** deinen Partner / deine Partnerin.
Listen, **read** and **say**.	**Höre zu**, **lies mit** und **sprich nach**.
Listen to the dialogue • interview.	**Höre** dir den Dialog • das Interview **an**.
Look at the photos • the pictures • the map.	**Schaue** dir die Fotos • die Bilder • die Karte **an**.
Make sentences • questions • statements.	**Bilde** Sätze • Fragen • Aussagen.
Make notes.	**Mache** dir Notizen.
Make a dialogue with your partner.	**Erstelle** einen Dialog mit deinem Partner / deiner Partnerin.
Make a list • a poster • a table.	**Erstelle** eine Liste • ein Poster • eine Tabelle.
Match the headlines • the sentences.	**Ordne** die Überschriften • die Sätze **zu**.
Match the sentences with the pictures.	**Ordne** die Sätze den Bildern **zu**.
Present your poster to your class.	**Stelle dein / Stellt euer** Poster der Klasse **vor**.
Put in the right word • the right form • the right verbs.	**Setze** das richtige Wort • die richtige Form • die richtigen Verben **ein**.
Put the sentences **in the right order**.	**Bringe** die Sätze **in die richtige Reihenfolge**.
Put the words into groups.	**Sortiere** die Wörter in Gruppen.
Read the story • the dialogue • the text.	**Lies** die Geschichte • den Dialog • den Text.
Report to the class.	**Berichte** der Klasse.
Are the sentences **right or wrong**?	Sind die Sätze **richtig oder falsch**?
Show your brochure to your group.	**Zeige** deiner Gruppe deine Broschüre.
Talk about the photos • the film • the story.	**Sprich über** die Fotos • den Film • die Geschichte.
Talk to your partner.	**Sprich mit** deinem Partner / deiner Partnerin.
Tell your partner **about** what you do at home.	**Erzähle** deinem Partner / deiner Partnerin, was du zu Hause machst.
Watch the film.	**Schaue** den Film **an**.
Write a diary entry • an e-mail • a text.	**Schreibe** einen Tagebucheintrag • eine E-Mail • einen Text.

Classroom phrases

Before or after the lesson

Good morning, Mr/Mrs/Miss	Guten Morgen, Herr/Frau ....
I'm sorry I'm late.	Tut mir leid, dass ich mich verspätet habe.
I'm sorry I don't have my exercise book / my homework with me.	Tut mir leid, ich habe mein Heft / meine Hausaufgaben nicht dabei.
What's for homework?	Was haben wir als Hausaufgabe auf?

Asking for help

What page are we on?	Auf welcher Seite sind wir?
Can you help me, please?	Können Sie / Kannst du mir bitte helfen?
What does ... mean?	Was heißt ...?
Can you say that again, please?	Können Sie / Kannst du das bitte wiederholen?
Can you write that on the board?	Können Sie das an die Tafel schreiben?
Mr/Mrs/Ms ..., I don't feel well.	Herr/Frau ..., mir geht es nicht gut.

Asking for information

What page is it on, please?	Auf welcher Seite ist das?
What's the German/English word for ...?	Was ist das deutsche/englische Wort für ...?
How do you spell ...?	Wie schreibt man ...?
What does that mean?	Was heißt/bedeutet das?
Sorry, I don't understand / I don't know.	Tut mir leid, ich verstehe das nicht / ich weiß es nicht.

Working together

Can we work in pairs/groups?	Können wir zu zweit / in Gruppen arbeiten?
Do you want to work with me/us?	Willst du / Wollt ihr mit mir/uns arbeiten?
Let's make/draw a	Lass(t) uns ein ... machen/zeichnen.
Whose turn is it?	Wer ist dran?
It's my/your turn.	Ich bin dran. / Du bist dran.

Your teacher can say ...

Listen, please.	Hört bitte zu.
Open your books at page	Öffnet eure Bücher auf Seite ....
Turn to page	Schlagt Seite ... auf.
Look at line	Schaue in Zeile ....
Take out your pens.	Holt eure Stifte raus.
Do exercise	Macht Aufgabe ....
Look at the board.	Schaut an die Tafel.
Who can do number ...?	Wer kann Nummer ... machen?
Put your hands up, please.	Meldet euch, bitte.
Try again.	Versuche es noch einmal.
Sit down, please, and be quiet.	Setz dich bitte und sei ruhig. / Setzt euch bitte und seid ruhig.
Talk to your partner.	Sprecht mit eurem Partner / eurer Partnerin.
Please speak up.	Bitte sprich lauter.

Lösungen

Zoom in – The British Isles, p. 8

1 Do the British Isles quiz with a partner.

1. England, Wales, Scotland, Northern Ireland and the Republic of Ireland
2. England
3. The Republic of Ireland
4. Scotland
5. Northern Ireland
6. London
7. The Republic of Ireland
8. England

Unit 4, p. 79

63/7 8 (WRITING) Make a quiz.

a) 1. the coldest (Alaska)
2. most popular (American Football)
3. the smallest (Rhode Island)
4. the biggest (New York)
5. most famous (Pocahontas)

Bildquellennachweis

Vorsatz hinten.1 TRANSDEV Ireland, Dublin; **Cover.1** Alamy stock photo (Top-Pics TBK), Abingdon, Oxon; **Cover.2** Getty Images (Photolibrary), München; **9.1** iStockphoto (TimZillion), Calgary, Alberta; **9.2** iStockphoto (Khrizmo), Calgary, Alberta; **9.3** iStockphoto (ifourth), Calgary, Alberta; **9.4** plainpicture GmbH & Co. KG (Design Pics/The Irish Image Collection), Hamburg; **9.5** Alamy stock photo (Lola Akinmade Akerstrom/National Geographic Creative), Abingdon, Oxon; **9.6** Thinkstock (Jessica Hunnicutt), München; **9.7** iStockphoto (Guillermo Perales Gonzalez), Calgary, Alberta; **9.8** Thinkstock (Comstock Images), München; **9.9** Thinkstock (Brian Doty), München; **9.10** iStockphoto (jcarter), Calgary, Alberta; **10.1** Thinkstock (Jupiterimages), München; **10.2** Alamy stock photo (Kevin Britland), Abingdon, Oxon; **11.1** ddp images GmbH (CAMERA PRESS/ED/BS), Hamburg; **11.2** ddp images GmbH (abaca press), Hamburg; **11.3** iStockphoto (Nick Daly), Calgary, Alberta; **12.1** Fotolia.com, New York; **12.2** Alamy stock photo (Fredrick Kippe), Abingdon, Oxon; **13.1** Thinkstock (Purestock), München; **13.2** shutterstock (Denis Radovanovic), New York, NY; **13.3** dreamstime.com (Debu55y), Brentwood, TN; **15.1** Getty Images (Photodisc), München; **15.2** Klett-Archiv (Thomas Weccard), Stuttgart; **16.1** Alamy stock photo (Barry Diomede), Abingdon, Oxon; **19.1** Klett-Archiv (Thomas Weccard), Stuttgart; **23.1** Ernst Klett Verlag, Stuttgart/in Kooperation mit der Filmakademie Baden-Württemberg; **23.2** Ernst Klett Verlag, Stuttgart/ in Kooperation mit der Filmakademie Baden-Württemberg; **23.3** Ernst Klett Verlag, Stuttgart/in Kooperation mit der Filmakademie Baden-Württemberg; **23.4** Ernst Klett Verlag, Stuttgart/in Kooperation mit der Filmakademie Baden-Württemberg; **23.5** Ernst Klett Verlag, Stuttgart/in Kooperation mit der Filmakademie Baden-Württemberg; **25.1** shutterstock (Dean Mitchell), New York, NY; **25.2** Charlotte Eisenblätter, Stuttgart; **25.3** iStockphoto (Nickos), Calgary, Alberta; **25.4** Klett-Archiv (Peter Nierhoff), Stuttgart; **26.1** Avenue Images GmbH (Corbis RF), Hamburg; **26.2** Alamy stock photo (Alex Segre), Abingdon, Oxon; **26.3** Getty Images (Anadolu Agency), München; **26.4** ddp images GmbH (CAMERA PRESS/B. Hester), Hamburg; **27.1** Imago (EntertainmentPictures), Berlin; **27.2** Getty Images (2014 Joseph Okpako/ Redferns), München; **28.1** shutterstock (jeafish Ping), New York, NY; **28.2** shutterstock (Marco Crupi), New York, NY; **28.3** shutterstock (Shahid Khan), New York, NY; **28.4** shutterstock (TasfotoNL), New York, NY; **32.1** Mauritius Images (Alamy), Mittenwald; **32.2** Alamy stock photo (Ian Dagnall), Abingdon, Oxon; **32.3** Dream Maker Software, Colorado; **33.1** Alamy stock photo (Colin McPherson), Abingdon, Oxon; **33.2** Alamy stock photo (Gordon Photography), Abingdon, Oxon; **33.3** Alamy stock photo (Paul Thompson Photography), Abingdon, Oxon; **34.1** Thinkstock (monkeybusinessimages), München; **34.2** shutterstock (MJTH), New York, NY; **37.1** shutterstock (Yaping), New York, NY; **37.2** shutterstock (Matt Ledwinka), New York, NY; **37.3** iStockphoto (shank_ali), Calgary, Alberta; **37.4** shutterstock (Racheal Grazias), New York,

NY; **37.5** shutterstock (Evgenyrychko), New York, NY; **37.6** shutterstock (Guoqiang Xue), New York, NY; **37.7** Thinkstock/iStock/Wojciech Gajda, Getty Images RF/PhotoDisc, shutterstock/Worytko Pawel; **38.1** iStockphoto (kenhurst), Calgary, Alberta; **38.2** Alamy stock photo (Stephen Finn), Abingdon, Oxon; **39.1** iStockphoto (James Pauls), Calgary, Alberta; **39.2** shutterstock (Mark Nazh), New York, NY; **40.1** iStockphoto (leisadavis), Calgary, Alberta; **40.2** iStockphoto (SolStock), Calgary, Alberta; **40.3** shutterstock (Celso Diniz), New York, NY; **40.4** shutterstock (Maxx-Studio), New York, NY; **40.5** shutterstock (YanLev), New York, NY; **40.6** iStockphoto (Allan Tooley), Calgary, Alberta; **44.1** shutterstock (Evgeny Bakharev), New York, NY; **44.2** shutterstock (Christian Bertrand), New York, NY; **44.3** Adobe Stock (ifh85), Dublin; **45.1** February Films, London; **46.1** Alamy stock photo (Astrakan Images), Abingdon, Oxon; **47.1** Alamy stock photo (Hero Images Inc.), Abingdon, Oxon; **48.1** Avenue Images GmbH (Corbis RF), Hamburg; **48.2** Alamy stock photo (Sinibomb Images), Abingdon, Oxon; **48.3** Alamy stock photo (Itsik Marom), Abingdon, Oxon; **49.1** Getty Images (The Image Bank), München; **49.2** Alamy stock photo (imageBROKER/Thomas Sbampato), Abingdon, Oxon; **49.3** iStockphoto (doubtfulneddy), Calgary, Alberta; **50.1** Alamy stock photo (Stephen McDonald), Abingdon, Oxon; **50.2** iStockphoto (Martin McCarthy), Calgary, Alberta; **50.3** iStockphoto (Fintastique), Calgary, Alberta; **52.1** Alamy stock photo (Gareth McCormack), Abingdon, Oxon; **52.2** Alamy stock photo (MIKEL BILBAO GOROSTIAGA- TRAVELS), Abingdon, Oxon; **53.1** plainpicture GmbH & Co. KG (Westend61/Boy), Hamburg; **53.2** Alamy Stock Photo (Peter Cavanagh), Abingdon, Oxon; **53.3** Alamy stock photo (Michael Cullen), Abingdon, Oxon; **54.1** Adobe Stock (shootingankauf), Dublin; **54.2** ShutterStock.com RF (Kolonko), New York, NY; **55.1** iStockphoto (Leonid Andronov), Calgary, Alberta; **58.1** iStockphoto (Martinan), Calgary, Alberta; **58.2** Adobe Stock (Samuel B.), Dublin; **59.1** iStockphoto (PeopleImages), Calgary, Alberta; **62.1** ShutterStock.com RF (astudio), New York, NY; **63.1** Alamy stock photo (reallifephotos), Abingdon, Oxon; **64.1** Picture-Alliance (Jens Kalaene/dpa), Frankfurt; **65.1** February Films, London; **65.2** February Films, London; **65.3** February Films, London; **66.1** shutterstock (Jacob Lund), New York, NY; **66.2** shutterstock (Jacob Lund), New York, NY; **66.3** shutterstock (Jacob Lund), New York, NY; **66.4** shutterstock (Jacob Lund), New York, NY; **66.5** shutterstock (Jacob Lund), New York, NY; **66.6** shutterstock (Jacob Lund), New York, NY; **67.1** shutterstock (Jacob Lund), New York, NY; **68.1** Avenue Images GmbH (Corbis RF), Hamburg; **68.2** Getty Images (Stockbyte), München; **69.1** Getty Images (Christopher Pillitz), München; **69.2** Getty Images (Perspectives), München; **74.1** Getty Images (Matteo Colombo/Moment), München; **74.2** shutterstock (PnPy), New York, NY; **75.1** shutterstock (Philip Arno Photography), New York, NY; **75.2** Mauritius Images (imageBROKER / J & C Sohns), Mittenwald; **75.3** Getty Images (Getty Images Sport), München; **76.1** Alamy stock photo (Hero Images Inc), Abingdon, Oxon; **76.2** Thinkstock (iStockphoto), München; **76.3** Thinkstock (iStockphoto), München; **76.4** Thinkstock (iStockphoto), München; **78.1** shutterstock (goodluz), New York, NY; **79.1** shutterstock (Doug Meek), New York, NY; **79.2** iStockphoto (GCShutter), Calgary, Alberta; **80.1** shutterstock (Ammit Jack), New York, NY; **80.2** Thinkstock (iStockphoto), München; **81.1** Fotolia.com (naughtynut), New York; **84.1** Thinkstock (Mike Watson Images), München; **84.2** shutterstock (Joseph Sohm), New York, NY; **85.1** shutterstock (Jamie Lamor Thompson), New York, NY; **85.2** Getty Images (Allen Einstein/NBAE), München; **86.1** iStockphoto (DeshaCAM), Calgary, Alberta; **87.1** scoop films (Katharina Hermann), Berlin; **87.2** scoop films (Katharina Hermann), Berlin; **87.3** scoop films (Katharina Hermann), Berlin; **89.1** Klett-Archiv (Thomas Weccard), Stuttgart; **90.1** Getty Images RF (The Image Bank), München; **90.2** Getty Images (Popperfoto), München; **90.3** Getty Images (M_a_y_a), München; **90.4** Alamy stock photo (Richard Levine), Abingdon, Oxon; **91.1** Getty Images (De Agostini Picture Library), München; **91.2** iStockphoto (fstop123), Calgary, Alberta; **92.1** shutterstock (Antonio Guillem), New York, NY; **97.1** shutterstock (Yaping), New York, NY; **97.2** shutterstock (Matt Ledwinka), New York, NY; **97.3** iStockphoto (shank_ali), Calgary, Alberta; **97.4** shutterstock (Racheal Grazias), New York, NY; **97.5** shutterstock (Evgenyrychko), New York, NY; **97.6** shutterstock (Guoqiang Xue), New York, NY; **98.1** iStockphoto (leisadavis), Calgary, Alberta; **98.2** iStockphoto (SolStock), Calgary, Alberta; **98.3** shutterstock (Celso Diniz), New York, NY; **98.4** shutterstock (Maxx-Studio), New York, NY; **98.5** shutterstock (YanLev), New York, NY; **98.6** iStockphoto (Allan Tooley), Calgary, Alberta; **99.1** iStockphoto (Leonid Andronov), Calgary, Alberta; **100.1** iStockphoto (Martinan), Calgary, Alberta; **100.2** Adobe Stock (Samuel B.), Dublin; **102.1** Alamy stock photo (Hero Images Inc), Abingdon, Oxon; **128.1** shutterstock (Pajor Pawel), New York, NY; **128.2** iStockphoto (bluejayphoto), Calgary, Alberta; **128.3** iStockphoto (Meinzahn), Calgary, Alberta; **128.4** picturemaxx.net (RF), München; **128.5** Thinkstock (Medioimages/ Photodisc), München; **128.6** Getty Images RF (Photodisc), München; **128.7** Thinkstock (iStockphoto), München; **130.1** iStockphoto (stockcam), Calgary, Alberta; **130.2** shutterstock (anweber), New York, NY; **130.3** Fotolia.com (axeldrosta), New York; **130.4** iStockphoto (Marcel Pfost), Calgary, Alberta; **130.5** Fotolia.com (Pavel Losevsky), New York; **130.6** Fotolia.com (thorabeti), New York; **130.7** iStockphoto (Dominic Burke RF), Calgary, Alberta; **130.8** Fotolia.com (blondsteve), New York; **130.9** Fotolia.com (naughtynut), New York; **131.1** Thinkstock (iStock/Michael Braun), München; **131.2** Thinkstock (Comstock), München; **131.3** Fotolia.com (Steve Lovegrove), New York; **131.4** Thinkstock (Lifesize), München; **131.5** Thinkstock (istockphoto), München; **131.6** Fotolia.com (Ints), New York; **131.7** Thinkstock (iStockphoto), München; **131.8** shutterstock (RF / McNally), New York, NY; **131.9** shutterstock (FlashStudio), New York, NY; **131.10** shutterstock (bodrumsurf), New York, NY; **131.11** Corbis RF (RF), Berlin; **131.12** Thinkstock (Comstock), München; **131.13** shutterstock (gorillaimages), New York, NY; **131.14** Thinkstock (mavrek), München; **131.15** iStockphoto (Liz Leyden), Calgary, Alberta; **131.16** shutterstock (PrinceOfLove), New York, NY; **131.17** Getty Images Plus (E+ / Vertigo3d), München; **131.18** shutterstock (Stefan Schurr), New York, NY; **131.19** dreamstime.com (Denyskuvaiev), Brentwood, TN; **131.20** iStockphoto (technotr), Calgary, Alberta; **131.21** Getty Images RF (PhotoDisc), München; **131.22** Avenue Images GmbH (Ingram Publishing), Hamburg; **131.23** iStockphoto (Webphotographeer), Calgary, Alberta; **131.24** Thinkstock (iStockphoto), München; **131.25** creativ collection Verlag GmbH, Freiburg; **131.26** Avenue Images GmbH (image source), Hamburg; **131.27** Ingram Publishing, Tattenhall Chester; **131.28** Thinkstock (iStock/Ljupco), München; **131.29** Fotolia.com (mustgo), New York; **131.30** shutterstock (Cathleen A Clapper), New York, NY; **131.31** Thinkstock (Jupiterimages), München; **133.1** Weccard, Thomas, Ludwigsburg; **134.1** iStockphoto (Lorraine Boogich), Calgary, Alberta; **134.2** Fotolia.com (Thaut Images), New York; **134.3** Fotolia.com (ang17a), New York; **134.4** shutterstock (Scott Sanders), New York, NY; **134.5** Corbis RF, Berlin; **134.6** shutterstock (William Attard McCarthy), New York, NY; **134.7** Fotolia.com (thorabeti), New York; **134.8** shutterstock (Hadrian), New York, NY; **138.1** Fotolia.com (Markus Mainka), New York; **138.2** Thinkstock (Jupiterimages), München; **138.3** shutterstock (nullplus), New York, NY; **138.4** shutterstock (Alexey Fursov), New York, NY; **138.5** Thinkstock (Comstock), München; **138.6** Fotolia.com (Steve Lovegrove), New York; **138.7** Thinkstock (Lifesize), München; **138.8** Thinkstock (istockphoto), München; **138.9** shutterstock (Fotokostic), New York, NY; **138.10** iStockphoto (Christopher Futcher), Calgary, Alberta; **138.11** Corbis RF (RF), Berlin; **138.12** Fotolia.com (Boris Ryaposov), New York; **138.13** shutterstock (Impact Photography), New York, NY; **138.14** Adobe Stock (lunamarina), Dublin; **138.15** iStockphoto (Alex Bramwell), Calgary, Alberta; **138.16** iStockphoto (David Mathies), Calgary, Alberta; **138.17** Fotolia.com (Achim Thomae), New York; **138.18** iStockphoto (kodachrome25), Calgary, Alberta; **138.19** Fotolia.com (Sharpshot), New York; **138.20** shutterstock (Poznukhov Yuriy), New York, NY; **138.21** Fotolia.com (Anja Ergler), New York

Sollte es in einem Einzelfall nicht gelungen sein, den korrekten Rechteinhaber ausfindig zu machen, so werden berechtigte Ansprüche selbstverständlich im Rahmen der üblichen Regelungen abgegolten.

Dublin tram map

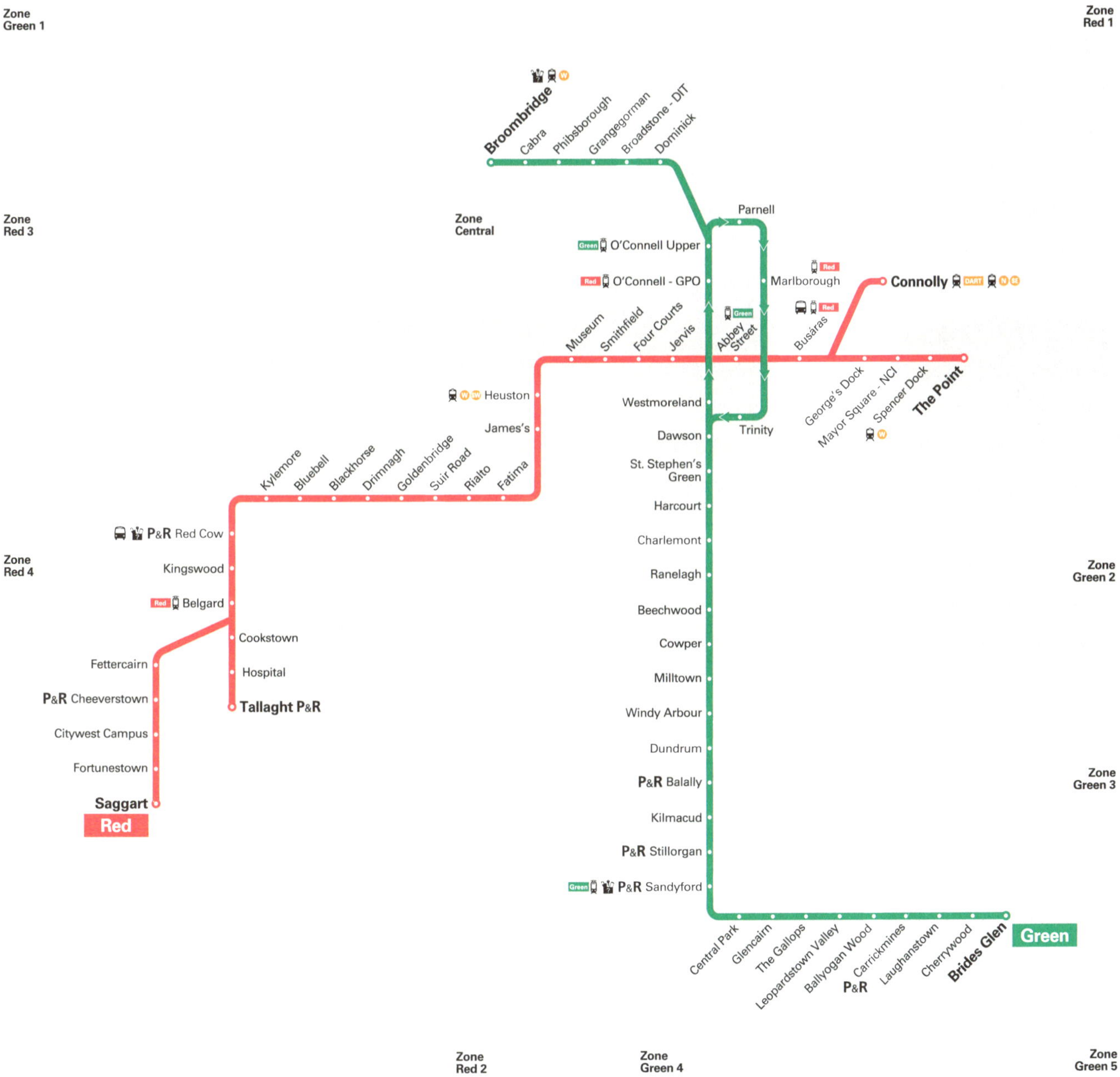

ALASKA
Denali
CANADA
Anchorage
CANADA
Seattle
Portland
WASHINGTON
OREGON
MONTANA
NORTH DAKOTA
Rocky Mountains
IDAHO
WYOMING
SOUTH DAKOTA
Minne
M
NEVADA
NEBRASKA
San Francisco
UTAH
Denver
CALIFORNIA
COLORADO
KANSAS
Las Vegas
HOLLYWOOD
OKLAHOMA
Los Angeles
ARIZONA
Pacific Ocean
Phoenix
San Diego
NEW MEXICO
Da
TEXAS
Hous
HAWAII
MEXICO